Microsoft®
Access 2000
Step by Step

Catapult **Microsoft** Press

PUBLISHED BY
Microsoft Press
A Division of Microsoft Corporation
One Microsoft Way
Redmond, Washington 98052-6399

Copyright © 1999 by Catapult, Inc.

Library of Congress Cataloging-in-Publication Data
    Microsoft Access 2000 Step by Step / Catapult, Inc.
       p.   cm.
    Includes index.
    ISBN 1-57231-976-3
    1. Microsoft Access.   2. Database management. I. Catapult, Inc.
QA76.9.D3M5569 1999
005.75'65--dc21   98-48188
                                            CIP

Printed and bound in the United States of America.

9 10 11 12 13   QWT   6 5 4 3 2 1

Distributed in Canada by Penguin Books Canada Limited.

A CIP catalogue record for this book is available from the British Library.

Microsoft Press books are available through booksellers and distributors worldwide. For further information about
international editions, contact your local Microsoft Corporation office or contact Microsoft Press International directly
at fax (425) 936-7329. Visit our Web site at www.microsoft.com/mspress. Send comments to *mspinput@microsoft.com*.

For Catapult, Inc.
Director of Publications: Bryn Cope
Project Editor: Cynthia Slotvig-Carey
Production Manager: Carolyn Thornley
Production/Layout: Chris Burns, Editor;
   Marie Hammer; Kim McGhee
Manuscript Editor: Pm Weizenbaum
Writers: Dafydd Neal Dyar; Mary Fujimaki
Copy Editors: Debbie Wall; Tresy Kilbourne
Technical Editors: Christina Johnson;
   Jason Whitmarsh; Avon Murphy

For Microsoft Press
Acquisitions Editor: Susanne Forderer
Project Editor: Jenny Moss Benson

Contents

Understanding Hyperlinks, Hypertext, and HTML 262 • Connecting
Through Cyberspace 263 • Adding Hyperlinks to Your Database 264
• Publishing a Database Object as a Web Page 269 • Understanding
Data Access Pages 274 • One Step Further: Adding a Microsoft
Office Web Component 277 • Lesson 13 Quick Reference 281

Installing Windows, Windows NT, or Product Components A-1
• Using the Default Windows Settings A-2

Database Design Process B-1 • Expanding an Existing Database B-2

What Are Expressions? C-1 • Rules for Entering Expressions C-2
• Creating Expressions with the Expression Builder C-3 • Using
Expressions in Forms and Reports C-5 • Using Expressions as
Validation Rules C-7 • Using Expressions in Queries and Filters C-7

*Quick*Look Guide

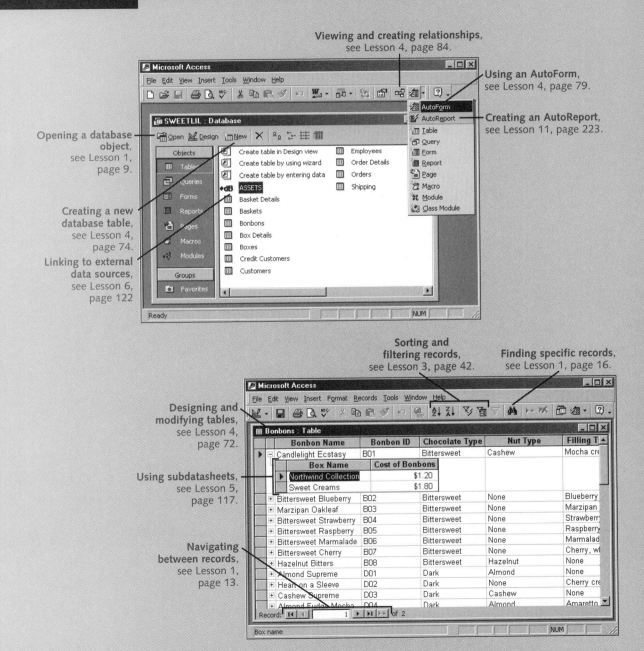

Viewing and creating relationships, see Lesson 4, page 84.

Using an AutoForm, see Lesson 4, page 79.

Creating an AutoReport, see Lesson 11, page 223.

Opening a database object, see Lesson 1, page 9.

Creating a new database table, see Lesson 4, page 74.

Linking to external data sources, see Lesson 6, page 122

Sorting and filtering records, see Lesson 3, page 42.

Finding specific records, see Lesson 1, page 16.

Designing and modifying tables, see Lesson 4, page 72.

Using subdatasheets, see Lesson 5, page 117.

Navigating between records, see Lesson 1, page 13.

Adding data validation,
see Lesson 5, page 97.

Adding and deleting records,
see Lesson 1, page 23.

Switching views,
see Lesson 2,
page 30.

Adding
calculated
controls,
see Lesson 9,
page 187.

Entering and
updating records,
see Lesson 1,
page 13.

Adding validation
message text,
see Lesson 5,
page 98.

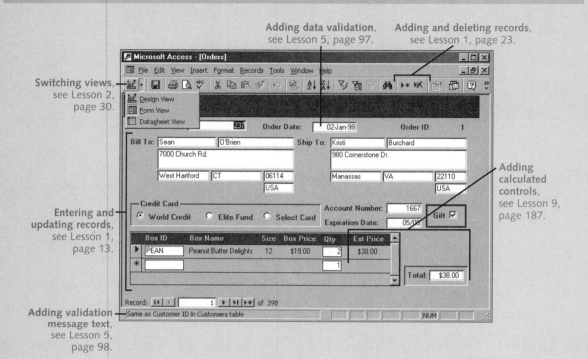

Calculating totals in a query,
see Lesson 8, page 164.

Creating queries,
see Lesson 7,
page 141.

Modifying
queries,
see Lesson 8,
page 162.

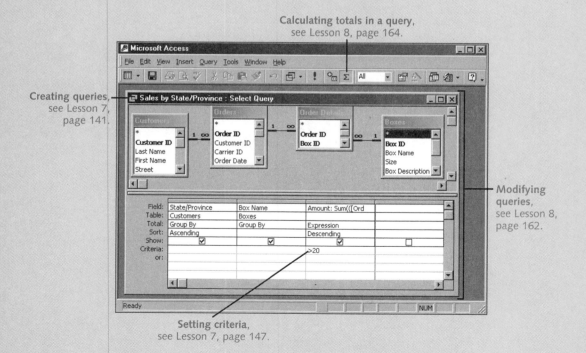

Setting criteria,
see Lesson 7, page 147.

Printing and previewing reports,
see Lesson 3, page 50.

Using Access 2000 on the World Wide Web,
see Lesson 13, page 261.

Adding hyperlinks to database objects,
see Lesson 13, page 264.

Creating subforms,
see Lesson 9, page 182.

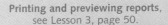
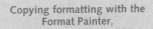
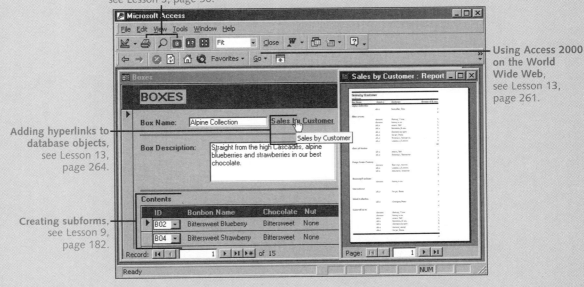

Copying formatting with the Format Painter,
see Lesson 10, page 209.

Formatting controls,
see Lesson 10, page 208.

Adding pictures to forms,
see Lesson 10, page 213.

Aligning controls,
see Lesson 10, page 210.

Adding controls,
see Lesson 5, page 100.

Setting and changing field properties,
see Lesson 4, page 82.

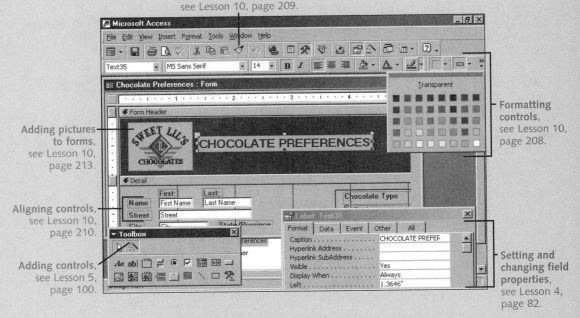

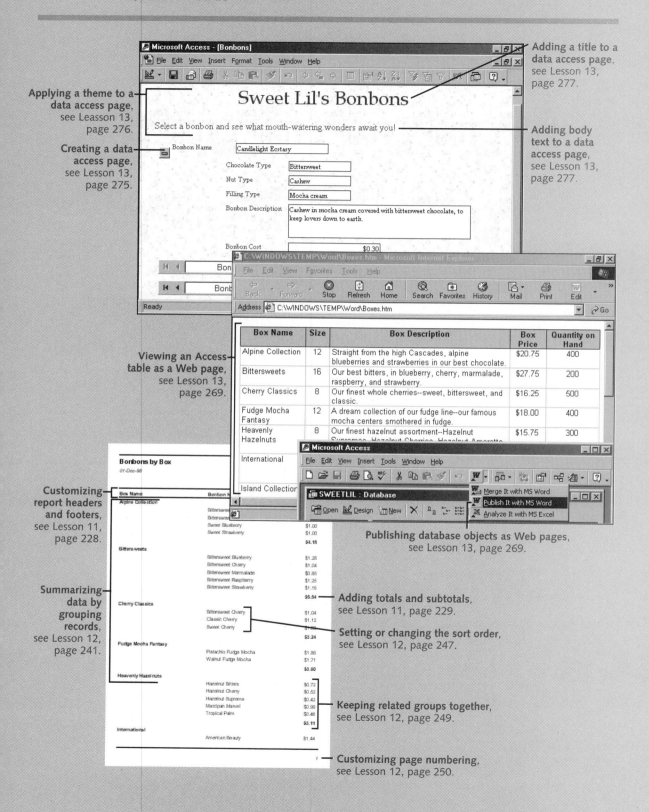

Applying a theme to a data access page, see Leasson 13, page 276.

Creating a data access page, see Lesson 13, page 275.

Adding a title to a data access page, see Lesson 13, page 277.

Adding body text to a data access page, see Lesson 13, page 277.

Viewing an Access table as a Web page, see Lesson 13, page 269.

Customizing report headers and footers, see Lesson 11, page 228.

Summarizing data by grouping records, see Lesson 12, page 241.

Publishing database objects as Web pages, see Lesson 13, page 269.

Adding totals and subtotals, see Lesson 11, page 229.

Setting or changing the sort order, see Lesson 12, page 247.

Keeping related groups together, see Lesson 12, page 249.

Customizing page numbering, see Lesson 12, page 250.

Finding Your Best Starting Point

Microsoft Access 2000 is a powerful database management system that you can use to efficiently desing and manage databases. With *Microsoft Access 2000 Step by Step*, you'll quickly and easily learn how to use Access 2000 to get your work done.

important

This book is designed for use with Microsoft Access 2000 for the Windows operating system. To find out which version of Access you're running, you can check the product package or you can start the program, click the Help menu, and then click About Microsoft Access. If your software is not compatible with this book, a Step by Step book matching your software is probably available. Please visit our World Wide Web site at *http://mspress.microsoft.com* or call 1-800-MSPRESS (1-800-677-7377) for more information.

Finding the Best Starting Point for You

This book is designed for beginning users of a database management system, as well as for readers who have had experience with these types of programs and are switching to Access or upgrading to Microsoft Access 2000. Use the following table to find your best starting point in this book.

If you are	Follow these steps
New to computers to graphical (as opposed to text-only) computer programs to Windows	**1** Install the practice files as described in "Using the Microsoft Access 2000 Step by Step CD-ROM." **2** Become acquainted with the Windows operating system and how to use the online Help system by working through Appendix A, "If You Are New to Windows or Access 2000," located on the Microsoft Access 2000 Step by Step CD-ROM. **3** Learn basic skills for using Microsoft Access 2000 by working through Lesson 1. Gain further basic skills by working through Lessons 2 through 4. Lessons 5 through 13 can be completed in any order.

If you are	Follow these steps
Switching from a different database program	**1** Install the practice files as described in "Using the Microsoft Access 2000 Step by Step CD-ROM." **2** Learn basic skills for using Microsoft Access 2000 by working through Lesson 1. Then work through Lessons 2 through 4. Lessons 5 through 13 can be completed in any order.

If you are	Follow these steps
Upgrading from Microsoft Access 97	**1** Learn about the new features of Access 2000 that are covered in this book by reading the following section, "New Features in Microsoft Access 2000." **2** Install the practice files as described in "Using the Microsoft Access 2000 Step by Step CD-ROM." **3** Complete the lessons that cover the topics you need. You can use the table of contents and the *Quick*Look Guide to locate information about general topics. You can use the index to find information about a specific topic or feature.

If you are	Follow these steps
Referencing this book after working through the lessons	**1** Use the index to locate information about specific topics, and use the table of contents and the *Quick*Look Guide to locate information about general topics.
	2 Read the Quick Reference at the end of each lesson for a brief review of the major tasks in the lesson. The Quick Reference topics are listed in the same order as they are presented in the lesson.

New Features in Microsoft Access 2000

The following table lists the major new features of Microsoft Access 2000 that are covered in this book and the lesson in which you can learn how to use each feature. You can also use the index to find specific information about a feature or a task that you want to perform.

To learn how to	See
Find answers to your questions about Microsoft Access 2000 with the Office Assistant.	Lesson 1
Insert any related table or query as a subdatasheet to any datasheet.	Lesson 5
Import, export, or link data from HTML lists and tables in a Web page, and export tables and lists for use in Active Server Pages	Lesson 6
Import, export, or link data from files in HTX and IDC formats	Lesson 6
Convert tables into Microsoft Excel 2000 spreadsheets directly using the drag-and-drop feature	Lesson 6
Save copies or an Access 2000 database in Access 97 format	Lesson 6
Create *data access pages* (interactive Web pages that are updated whenever their data sources change)	Lesson 13
Add hyperlinks to e-mail addresses, database objects, Web pages and other Office 2000 documents	Lesson 13
Integrate Office chart, pivot table, and spreadsheet functions in a Web page	Lesson 13

Corrections, Comments, and Help

Every effort has been made to ensure the accuracy of this book and the contents of the Microsoft Access 2000 Step by Step CD-ROM. Microsoft Press provides corrections and additional content for its books through the World Wide Web at:

http://mspress.microsoft.com/support

If you have comments, questions, or ideas regarding this book or the CD-ROM, please send them to us.

Send e-mail to:

mspinput@microsoft.com

Or send postal mail to:

Microsoft Press
Attn: Step by Step Editor
One Microsoft Way
Redmond, WA 98052-6399

Please note that support for the Access 2000 software product itself is not offered through the above addresses. For help using Access 2000, you can call Access 2000 Technical Support at (425) 635-7070 on weekdays between 6 A.M. and 6 P.M. Pacific Time.

Visit Our World Wide Web Site

We invite you to visit the Microsoft Press World Wide Web site. You can visit us at the following location:

http://mspress.microsoft.com

You'll find descriptions of all of our books, information about ordering titles, notices of special features and events, additional content for Microsoft Press books, and much more.

You can also find out the latest in software developments and news from Microsoft Corporation by visiting the following World Wide Web site:

http://www.microsoft.com/

We look forward to your visit on the Web!

Using the Microsoft Access 2000 Step by Step CD–ROM

The Microsoft Access 2000 Step by Step CD–ROM inside the back cover of this book contains the practice files that you'll use as you perform the exercises in the book and audiovisual files that demonstrate nine of the exercises. By using the practice files, you won't waste time creating the sample databases used in the lessons—instead, you can concentrate on learning how to use Microsoft Access 2000. With the files and the step-by-step instructions in the lessons, you'll also learn by doing, which is an easy and effective way to acquire and remember new skills.

important

Before you break the seal on the Microsoft Access 2000 Step by Step CD–ROM package, be sure that this book matches your version of the software. This book is designed for use with Microsoft Access 2000 for the Windows 95, Windows 98, and Windows NT operating systems. To find out which version of Access 2000 you are running, you can check the product package or you can start the software, click the Help menu, and then click About Microsoft Access 2000. If your program is not compatible with this book, a Step by Step book matching your software is probably available. Please visit our World Wide Web site at *http://mspress.microsoft.com* or call 1-800-MSPRESS for more information.

Installing the Practice Files

Follow these steps to install the practice files on your computer's hard disk so that you can use them with the exercises in this book.

1 If your computer isn't on, turn it on now.

2 If you're using Windows NT, press Ctrl+Alt+Del to display a dialog box asking for your user name and password. If you are using Windows 95 or Windows 98, you will see this dialog box if your computer is connected to a network.

Close

3 If necessary, type your username and password in the appropriate boxes, and click OK. If you see the Welcome dialog box, click the Close button.

4 Remove the CD-ROM from the package inside the back cover of this book and insert it in the CD-ROM drive of your computer.

5 In My Computer, double-click your CD-ROM drive.

6 Double-click Setup.exe, and then follow the instructions on the screen.

The setup program window appears with recommended options preselected for you. For best results in using the practice files with this book, accept these preselected settings.

7 When the files have been installed, remove the CD-ROM from your CD-ROM drive and replace it in the package inside the back cover of the book.

A folder called Access 2000 SBS Practice has been created on your hard disk, and the practice files have been placed in that folder.

If your computer is set up to connect to the Internet, you can double-click the Microsoft Press Welcome shortcut to visit the Microsoft Press Web site. You can also connect to this Web site directly at *http://mspress.microsoft.com*

Using the Practice Files

Practice files are needed for the lessons in this book. The lesson will explain when and how to use the practice files and will include instructions on how to open the file. The lessons are built around scenarios that simulate a real work environment, so you can easily apply the skills you learn to your own work. For the scenarios in this book, imagine that you're a partner at Impact Public Relations, a small public relations firm. Impact represents Sweet Lil's Chocolates, Inc., a rapidly growing gourmet chocolate company. Sweet Lil's has recently begun using Access 2000 to improve its information management and to help take its business worldwide. You'll be assisting with these goals.

The screen illustrations in this book might look different from what you see on your computer, depending on how your computer is set up. To help make your screen match the illustrations in this book, please follow the instructions in Appendix A, "Matching the Exercises."

Here's a list of the files included on the practice CD–ROM:

Filename	Description
SWEETLIL.MDB	The Sweet Lil's database
ASSETS.DBF	Sweet Lil's fixed-assets register table is dBASE IV format
PAYROLL.XLS	Sweet Lil's payroll table in Microsoft Excel 2000 format
SWEETLIL.BMP	Sweet Lil's logo in Microsoft Paint bitmap format
Multimedia	
ValidationCheck	Add a data validation check
ReferentialIntegrity	Set a field property to establish referential integrity
FieldProperty	Set a field property to keep primary keys consistent
CreateQuery	Create a query
FormHeader	Add a label control to a form header
FormFormatting	Apply a standardized format
FormatPicture	Add a Sweetlil.bmp picture to the Presenting Bonbons form
AddCalculation	Add a calculation to the report footer
WebPage	Connect a form to a report

Using the Multimedia Files

Throughout this book, you will see icons for multimedia files for particular exercises. Use the following steps to run the multimedia files.

1 Insert the Microsoft Access 2000 Step by Step CD-ROM in your CD-ROM drive.

2 On the Windows taskbar, click Start then click Run.

3 In the Run dialog window, type D:\Multimedia (where D is your CD-ROM drive) and press Enter.

The contents of the CD-ROM are displayed.

④ Double-click the audiovisual file you need.

Microsoft Camcorder runs the video of the exercise. After the video is finished, Camcorder closes and you return to Windows Explorer.

⑤ Close the window, and return to the exercise in the book.

Uninstalling the Practice Files

Use the following steps when you want to delete the practice files added to your hard disk by the Step by Step setup program.

① On the Windows taskbar, click Start, point to Settings, and then click Control Panel.

② Double-click the Add/Remove Programs icon.

③ Select Microsoft Access 2000 Step by Step from the list, and then click Add/Remove.

A confirmation message appears.

④ Click Yes.

The practice files are uninstalled.

⑤ Click OK to close the Add/Remove Programs Properties dialog box.

⑥ Close the Control Panel window.

Need Help with the Practice Files?

Every effort has been made to ensure the accuracy of this book and the contents of the Microsoft Access 2000 Step by Step CD–ROM. If you do run into a problem, Microsoft Press provides corrections for its books through the World Wide Web at:

http://mspress.microsoft.com/support/

We invite you to visit our main Web page at:

http://mspress.microsoft.com

You'll find descriptions of all of our books, information about ordering titles, notices of special features and events, additional content for Microsoft Press books, and much more.

Conventions and Features in This Book

You can save time when you use this book by understanding, before you start the lessons, how instructions, keys to press, and so on are shown in the book. Please take a moment to read the following list, which also points out helpful features of the book that you might want to use.

Conventions

- Hands-on exercises for you to follow are given in numbered lists of steps (1, 2, and so on). A round bullet (●) indicates an exercise that has only one step.
- Text that you are to type appears in **bold**.
- A plus sign (+) between two key names means that you must press those keys at the same. For example, "Press Alt+Tab" means that you hold down the Alt key while you press Tab.
- The following icons are used to identify certain types of exercise features:

Icon	Alerts you to
	Skills that are demonstrated in files available on the Microsoft Access 2000 Step by Step CD–ROM.
	New features in Microsoft Access 2000 or Office 2000.

Other Features of This Book

■ You can get a quick reminder of how to perform the tasks you learned by reading the Quick Reference at the end of a lesson.

■ You can practice the major skills presented in the lessons by working through the Review & Practice sections at the end of each part.

■ You can see an audiovisual demonstration of some of the exercises in the book by following the instructions in "Using the Multimedia Files" in the "Using the Microsoft Access 2000 Step by Step CD-ROM" section of this book.

PART 1

Entering and Viewing Data in Microsoft Access 2000

1

Using Forms

In this lesson you will learn how to:

✔ *Open a database.*

✔ *Enter and update data using a form.*

✔ *Navigate between records in a form.*

✔ *Use the Microsoft Access editing tools.*

✔ *Find and remove data in a form.*

✔ *Replace data that meets certain criteria.*

ESTIMATED TIME
40 min.

The key to juggling many items, whether they are bowling pins, carpooling schedules, or other complex data, is to organize the items so that you can find them quickly and easily. Your chosen method may be as simple as a wallet calendar or as complex as an enterprise-wide computer system, but the principle is the same: assemble the information you need in one place, and keep it handy.

The information that you store for future reference is called *data*, and one place in which you can store the data is a *database*. In Microsoft Access, data can be dates, sums of money, graphical images, words, entire files, and almost anything else that can be stored on a computer disk. For example, among the data that you'll work with in these lessons are bonbon pictures, recipes, and chocolate sales information.

In an Access database, data is entered and manipulated in a *form* and stored in a *table*. Forms resemble familiar paper forms; an interactive text box, often referred to as a *field*, takes the place of each printed box on the paper form. All the fields on a form make up a *record*. This lesson focuses on the basics of forms in Access and on entering data into forms.

The Office Assistant

Have you met your new assistant yet? As you begin working with Microsoft Office 2000 programs, the animated *Office Assistant,* Clippit, jumps in to offer helpful messages as you work. You can type any question to your Office Assistant in the Assistant balloon, and then click Search. Clippit will guide you through Access Help. Clippit also remembers your last question and search results so that you can quickly find additional Help topics related to your question.

Clippit is ready with Help topics and tips on your tasks as you work, telling you what you need to know, just when you need to know it. Clippit displays a light bulb to indicate that it has a tip about the action that you're currently performing. Click the light bulb to see the tip.

The Assistant appears whenever you:

- Click the Office Assistant button on any Access toolbar.
- Choose Microsoft Access Help on the Help menu, or press F1.
- Click certain commands or try new tasks.

You can close any Office Assistant tip or message by pressing the Esc key.

Office Assistant

important

For simplicity and clarity, the Office Assistant won't appear in any other illustrations in this book. If you want to match the illustrations, right-click the Office Assistant, and then click Hide. If you want to leave the Office Assistant displayed but find it getting in your way, simply drag it to another area of the screen.

Imagine that you're a partner at Impact Public Relations, a small public relations firm that specializes in designing multimedia campaigns for midsize companies. Impact represents Sweet Lil's Chocolates, Inc., a rapidly growing gourmet chocolate company. Sweet Lil's recently decided to start using Access 2000 to improve its information management and to help take its business worldwide. You'll be designing its international campaign.

The marketing department at Sweet Lil's has accepted your proposal for a worldwide campaign using Access 2000 to handle the resulting data needs. You'll be assisting the Sweet Lil's staff in implementing the systems you've proposed.

As the first phase of the marketing campaign, Impact has just completed a survey of people in selected locations around the world concerning their chocolate preferences. To verify that the new data entry system is functioning properly, you open the Sweet Lil's database and spot-check the new Chocolate Preferences form by adding and updating a few entries yourself.

Opening a Database

If you're just starting to use Access 2000 with this lesson, follow these steps for starting Access and opening a database.

important

If you haven't installed this book's practice files yet, do so now. See the "Using the Practice Files" section earlier in the book for more information.

Start Microsoft Access 2000

1   On the taskbar, click the Start button.

2   Point to Programs, and then click Microsoft Access.
The Microsoft Access dialog box appears.

From here,
you can either
open an
existing
database or
create a new
database.

Open a database

In this exercise, you open the Sweet Lil's database.

1 In the Microsoft Access dialog box, be sure that the Open An Existing File
option is selected, and click OK.

The Open dialog box appears.

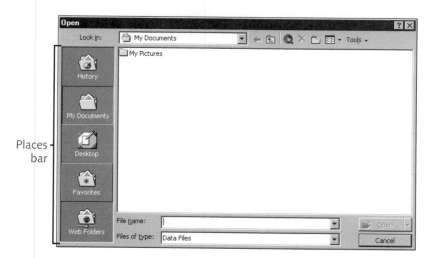

You can use the Database window to open and work with any object in the database.

2 In the Look In drop-down list, select your hard disk. Double-click the Access 2000 SBS Practice folder.

3 Double-click the filename Sweetlil.mdb.

The Database window for the Sweet Lil's database opens. On the left side of the Database window is the Objects bar, which you can use to view the tables, queries, forms, reports, pages, macros, and modules of the open database.

Objects bar

tip

Once you've opened a database, you can take advantage of two shortcuts. The next time you start Access 2000, you'll see that same database filename listed in the Microsoft Access dialog box. You can then open the database quickly: just double-click the database filename to open the database from the Microsoft Access dialog box.

Short and Expanded Menus

If this is your first time using Access 2000, you'll notice that when you select a menu, it displays a short list of commands. The commands that appear on the *short menu* the first time you use Access 2000 are the default commands for that menu.

After selecting a menu, if you rest your pointer on the menu for a moment, the menu expands to display the full selection of commands available for that menu. This is called an *expanded menu*. Another quick way to view the full selection of commands is to move your mouse pointer down the menu and click the arrows at the bottom.

Each time you select a command from the expanded portion of the menu, that command automatically gets moved to the short menu of default commands. In this way, over time the short menus become tailored to your particular usage patterns.

To have the expanded menu appear at all times, right-click the toolbar, click Customize, and then clear the Menus Show Most Recently Used Commands First check box.

Understanding Forms

Access 2000 stores data in tables, but the most common way to work with data is with a form. Like a paper form, the Access 2000 form contains text boxes, the fields into which you type the appropriate information.

To learn more about designing and creating a database, see Appendix B, "Designing a Database" on the Microsoft Access 2000 Step by Step CD-ROM.

Every element in an Access 2000 database is a graphical object. Graphical objects that accept, display, or locate data are called *controls*. Any field that contains or accepts data on a form is actually a control. In addition to text boxes, which are your windows into the database, a form has other controls, such as option buttons and command buttons, for working with the database.

As your business needs change, so do your information needs—and so must any database that you use to track your information. You'll want to add records to your database, as well as locate records that need to be changed or deleted. Using forms is the best way to perform all these actions.

Entering and Updating Data

Now that you've opened the Sweet Lil's database, you can open the Chocolate Preferences form and begin checking the data entry system.

Open a form

1 In the Database window, click Forms on the Objects bar to open the forms list.

A list of forms is displayed in the Database window.

2 Double-click Chocolate Preferences.

The Chocolate Preferences form opens.

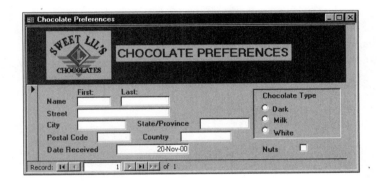

Enter data using a form

You use the blank Chocolate Preferences form you just opened to enter the information for a respondent from Canada.

If you make a mistake, just press Backspace to erase, and then retype.

1 Type **Amanda** in the First Name field of the Chocolate Preferences form.

As you begin typing, a small triangle symbol in the left margin of the form changes to a pencil, indicating that information is being changed.

2 Press the Tab key to move the insertion point to the Last Name field.

3 Type **Hart** in the Last Name field.

*You can press
F2 to place the
insertion point
at the end of
the field.*

 Type the following address information, pressing Tab to move from field
to field.

Street:	**10 MacLeod**
City:	**Melfort**
State/Province:	**Saskatchewan**
Postal Code:	**S0E 1A0**
Country:	**Canada**

When you press Tab after entering Canada in the Country field, the insertion point disappears, and a dotted line appears around the Dark option in
the Chocolate Type option group.

tip

Some fields are automatically filled with predetermined data. In the Chocolate
Preferences form, for example, the Date Received field is filled with the current
date. Access skips over these fields automatically as you move from field to field.

Selecting Dialog Box Options

In the Chocolate Preferences form, Chocolate Type is an *option group*, a set of
mutually exclusive option button controls. The Nuts field contains a *check box*,
which requires a yes-or-no response.

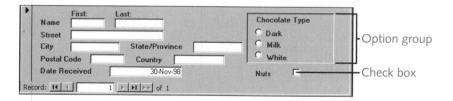

Select an option button

*You can also
press the
Down arrow
key or the
Up arrow key
to select Milk.*

Amanda Hart enjoys milk chocolate, so you select the Milk option button
for her.

● Select the Milk option button.

A dot appears in the Milk option button, indicating that the option is selected.

Select a check box

You can also press the Spacebar to select or clear a check box.

In this form, a check mark in the check box means yes (nuts are fine); an empty box means no (I don't like nuts in my chocolates). Amanda Hart likes nuts in her milk chocolate, so you select the Nuts check box for her.

● Select the Nuts check box.

   A check mark appears in the Nuts check box.

Modify records in a form

Each set of fields on a form represents a separate record. When you get to the end of the form, which in this case is the Nuts check box, pressing Tab again takes you to the next record.

important

Whenever you move the insertion point out of a record, Access 2000 automatically saves any changes you made to the record. This differs from how you save documents in Microsoft Word, for example; in a database form or table, you don't need to save new data manually as you work.

1 In the form, while still in the Nuts check box, press Tab.

   The insertion point appears in the First Name field of the next form.

2 Type **Rita** in the First Name field.

It's a good idea to proofread your entries after adding information.

3 Enter the following information, pressing Tab to move from field to field.

Last Name:	**Corquette**
Street:	**300 Locust Avenue**
City:	**Thousand Oaks**
State/Province:	**CA**
Postal Code:	**91320**
Country:	**USA**
Chocolate Type:	**Dark**
Nuts:	**No**

Update an existing record

Looking over your data entries, you notice that you didn't type the word *Drive* in Amanda Hart's street address. You'll try returning to the previous record and updating it now.

Previous Record

1 Click the Previous Record button on the navigation bar.

2 In the Street field of Amanda Hart's record, click after the *d* in *MacLeod* to return to the end of that field.

The insertion point appears where you click.

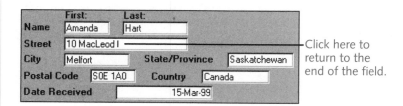

Click here to return to the end of the field.

3 Press the Spacebar to insert a space after MacLeod, and then type **Drive**

As you begin typing, the triangle symbol in the margin changes to a pencil to indicated edit made.

4 Click the Next Record button on the navigation bar.
The change is saved. The pencil symbol disappears.

New Record

Close a form

You've successfully opened the Chocolate Preferences form and used it to enter and update records in the database. All that remains to do is to close the form.

Close

Click the Close button to close the Chocolate Preferences form.

Click here to close the form.

important

Be sure that you click the Close button on the form window only. Do not click the Close button on the Database window or the Microsoft Access window, or you will close the database prematurely. As soon as you close the form, the record you're working in is saved.

Navigating Between Records

Wherever a Microsoft Access 2000 window shows a series of data, a *navigation bar* appears on the bottom edge of the form. You've just seen an example of a navigation bar in the Chocolate Preferences form. The navigation bar shows which record is currently being displayed; it also includes navigation buttons that allow you to move quickly among the records. You can move forward or backward one record at a time, to the beginning or end of the records, or to a particular record. You can also add a new record from the navigation bar.

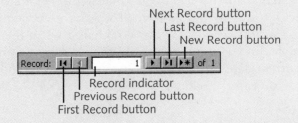

The First Record button takes you immediately to the first record. The Previous Record button moves you back one record at a time. The record indicator displays the number of the current record and allows you to enter a record number and move to that record immediately. The Next Record button moves you forward one record at a time. The Last Record button takes you immediately to the last record. The New Record button generates a new, blank record.

On the keyboard, press Ctrl+Home for the first record, the Page Up and Page Down keys for the previous and next records, and Ctrl+End for the last record.

Entering Data Efficiently and Correctly

You'll learn more about how to create forms for automatic data entry in Lesson 5, "Keeping Database Information Reliable."

Forms can help make data entry faster and more accurate by letting you choose values from a list and by letting you know when you've entered incorrect values into a field.

The Bonbons form presents two different kinds of lists from which you can select a value. Chocolate Type is a *list box* control, which displays only predetermined values that are always visible. A related control is the *combo box*, in which the predetermined values are not fully visible. A combo box has a *drop-down arrow* on the right side to open and close the list. Filling Type and Nut Type are both combo boxes.

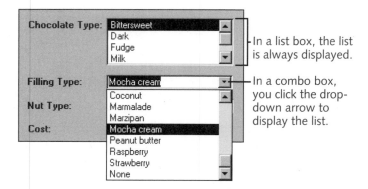

In a list box, the list is always displayed.

In a combo box, you click the drop-down arrow to display the list.

To ensure accurate data entry, Access 2000 can also display a message when you enter incorrect information into a form. The value you enter in a field is checked against a *validation rule* that was established when the form was created. For example, in the Orders form, you cannot enter an order date that is later than the current date. If the value you enter breaks a validation rule, a message appears. You can't exit the field until you correct or delete the invalid data.

Because sales of Candlelight Ecstasy bonbons dropped last year, Sweet Lil's has altered that recipe, changing the Candlelight Ecstasy filling from raspberry to marzipan. The marketing department has asked you to demonstrate how to reflect this change in the database.

Select a value from a combo box

1. In the Database window, double-click the Bonbons form in the forms list.

   The Bonbons form opens to the first record, which is for the Candlelight Ecstasy bonbon.

2. In the Filling Type combo box, click the drop-down arrow to display the list.

   This list shows all the fillings that Sweet Lil's uses in its bonbons.

You can type just marz instead; because Marzipan is the only value that starts with those four letters, it is selected.

3. In the Filling Type combo box, type **Marzipan** or select the word from the list.

Enter a new price in a field

Marzipan is a more expensive filling than Mocha cream, so the marketing department asks you to change the price from $0.30 to $1.35.

1. Press Tab twice to move to the Cost field, and then type **1.35**

   The entry $0.30 is replaced.

2 Press Tab.

A message tells you that the value you entered is too high.

3 Click OK.

You check with the marketing department; there's been a mistake. The cost should be $0.35.

4 Delete 1.35 by pressing the Backspace key, and then type **.35**

5 Press Tab.

Access accepts this price, adds a dollar sign, and moves the insertion point to the Bonbon ID field.

6 Close the Bonbon form.

Efficient Editing Tools

Access includes many convenient editing features to help you keep your database accurate and up-to-date.

You can get an introduction to editing features by scanning and using the Edit menu. Next to each command name, you'll see the corresponding toolbar button face (left side) and keyboard shortcut (right side). These visual cues are an excellent tool for learning to associate the buttons and key combinations with the commands you use most often.

Most people find that using a toolbar button is faster than clicking a menu command. If you'd rather use the keyboard, the keyboard shortcuts can be even faster. Find the method that works best for you.

Another helpful editing tool is the *Microsoft Office Clipboard* toolbar, which appears the first time you cut or copy more than one item. This toolbar allows you to collect and paste up to 12 different items or objects at a time. ScreenTips display the first few words of each item to identify what's on the Clipboard. Close the Clipboard toolbar to cut or copy a single item at a time.

When you quit Access 2000, you may get a message noting a large amount of information on the Clipboard and asking whether you want to share it with other programs. Unless you plan to paste it elsewhere, click No.

Finding Records

Information doesn't do you any good unless you can lay your hands on it quickly and easily. Of the many features that Access 2000 provides, the most important is finding the needle you want amid the haystack of information that you've gathered. Often you know what you're searching for; sometimes you need to do a little detective work. Either way, Access 2000 can help you.

Find the record you want

Sweet Lil's is starting to receive calls from customers who've recently completed the Chocolate Preferences marketing questionnaire and want to confirm that their information has been received. You decide to test the questionnaire data entry system yourself by taking the next call, from a customer named Claudia Hemshire. In this exercise, you look up Claudia Hemshire in the Customers table using the View Customers form.

1   In the Database window, double-click the View Customers form in the forms list.

    The View Customers form opens.

2   On the View Customers form, click in the Last Name field.

3   On the Form View toolbar, click the Find button.

    The Find And Replace dialog box appears, with the Find tab active. The contents of the Find What box, the Look In list, and the Match list reflect the last search you performed.

Find

For a case-sensitive search (to find Polish *but ignore* polish*), click More, and then select the Match Case check box.*

If the Find And Replace dialog box is hiding the View Customers form, drag the dialog box off to the side.

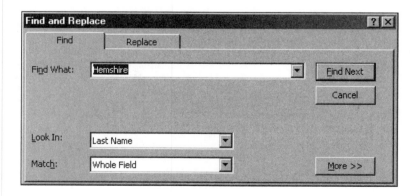

④ In the Find What box, type **Hemshire**

⑤ In the Look In list, select Last Name.

⑥ In the Match list, select Whole Field.

⑦ Click Find Next.

The record for a Claudia Hemshire appears in the View Customers form. This appears to be the record you want, but first you must be sure there aren't any other customers with the same name.

⑧ Click Find Next again.

A message appears, confirming that there are no other matches.

You can click Cancel or the Close button.

⑨ Click OK, and then close the Find And Replace dialog box.

Wildcard Characters

There will be times when you don't know quite which records you need. For example, you might find that some database entries were misspelled or otherwise entered incorrectly, so searching for the correct spelling fails to find these entries. To find and replace erroneous data, you'll have to be able to search for a mixture of known and unknown text.

Wildcard characters are special symbols that represent unknown characters in a word or term. The question mark (?) represents any single unknown character, and the asterisk (*) represents one or more unknown or unspecified characters within a word or term. For example, a search for *?ouse* would match *douse, house, louse, mouse, rouse,* and *souse*; the character in the first position can be anything, but the second character must be an *o,* the third a *u,* the fourth an *s,* and the fifth an *e.*

The asterisk wildcard character is especially useful, as it allows you to find almost anything for which you can approximate a match. For example, if you're trying to find someone whose name is unknown other than it sounds like *Newman,* you could search for *N*man** and find the records for *Newman, Newmann, Neuman,* and *Neumann.*

Find a record when you're missing details

Occasionally the Sweet Lil's shipping department can't make out the address on a shipping label. Fred Mallon, the shipping coordinator, just asked you to help out with a tough case—all that's left on the label he's holding is a partial street name, *rose*. In this exercise, you teach him to use wildcard characters to find the customer information he needs to fulfill this order.

1 On the View Customers form, click anywhere in the Street field.

2 On the Form View toolbar, click the Find button.

The Find And Replace dialog box appears. The contents of the Find What box, the Look In list, and the Match list reflect the last search you performed.

Find

3 In the Find What box, type **rose**

The previous entry is replaced.

4 In the Match list, click Any Part Of Field.

Because *rose* is only part of the street name, you want to search for it no matter where it occurs in the field.

You don't have to go back to the first record of the database; Find searches the entire table from any record.

5 In the Find And Replace dialog box, click Find Next.

A record appears with the word *Parkrose* in the address. You note the customer's name, address, and phone number.

6 Click Find Next again.

Another record appears, this time with *Montrose* in the address. Again you note the customer's name and phone number.

7 Click Find Next one more time.

A message appears, confirming that there are no other matches.

8 Click OK, and then close the Find And Replace dialog box.

9 Close the View Customers form.

You have found two possible candidates. The shipping coordinator now has all the information he needs to contact the two customers, determine which one placed the order, and recreate the illegible label.

Adding and Removing Record Text

The marketing department at Sweet Lil's often needs to alter bonbon descriptions in response to changes in customer preferences or the availability of ingredients. Mary Culvert, Sweet Lil's marketing vice president, has asked you to make these changes.

In the following exercises, you'll add new record text, modify existing records, undo changes you've made, and delete records.

Using the Form View Toolbar

The toolbars that appear beneath the Access 2000 menu bar are dynamic, changing as you move from the Database window to another window. When the Database window is active, Access 2000 displays the Database toolbar, with toolbar buttons that are specific to database administration. When you open a form, the Form View toolbar replaces the Database toolbar.

Some toolbar buttons become available only when certain database objects are being viewed. For example, the OfficeLinks and New Object toolbar buttons are available when you're viewing the tables and queries lists in the Database window, but they're not when you're viewing the Forms list. And some toolbar buttons are available only in a particular context; for example, the Paste button is unavailable until you've used Copy or Cut.

The Form View toolbar has buttons that are specific to forms, along with general purpose buttons for text editing. The toolbar buttons that you will use to train the marketing department are Save, Cut, Copy, Paste, Undo, Find, New Record, and Delete Record.

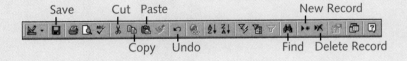

Adding Text in a Form

Mary Culvert first asks you to promote sales of all bonbons with hazelnuts, the most expensive nut ingredient, by adding a bit more local color to the descriptions of those bonbons. In this exercise, you make this change by adding the phrase *Pacific Northwest* in front of the bonbon descriptions that include the word *hazelnut*.

Add text to a field

Find

1 In the Database window, double-click the Bonbons form in the forms list.

The Bonbons form opens.

2 Click in the Nut Type field.

3 On the Form View toolbar, click the Find button.

The Find And Replace dialog box appears. The contents of the Find What box, the Look In list, and the Match list reflect the last search you performed.

4 In the Find What box, type **hazelnut**

5 In the Look In list, verify Nut Type is selected.

6 In the Match list, select Whole Field.

7 Click Find Next.

The first record to highlight Hazelnut in the Nut Type field is record 8: Hazelnut Bitters.

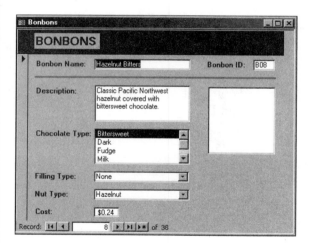

8 Close the Find And Replace dialog box.

9 In the Description field for the Hazelnut Bitters bonbons, click just to the left of the word *hazelnut*.

The insertion point appears where you click.

10 Type **Pacific Northwest** and then press the Spacebar to insert a space before the word *hazelnut*.

Copy text from one field to another

Rather than retyping the phrase *Pacific Northwest* again and again, in this exercise you copy it to the Description fields of the remaining hazelnut bonbon records.

① In the Description field for the Hazelnut Bitters bonbons, select the phrase *Pacific Northwest* including the trailing space.

② On the Form View toolbar, click the Copy button.

A copy of the selected text is placed on the Clipboard.

Copy

③ Click the Nut Type field.

④ On the Form View toolbar, click the Find button.

The Find And Replace dialog box appears, with the correct settings from the previous procedure.

⑤ In the Find And Replace dialog box, click Find Next.

The next record to indicate Hazelnut should be record 13: Hazelnut Supreme.

Paste

⑥ In the Description field for the Hazelnut Supreme bonbons, click just to the left of the word *hazelnut*. On the Form View toolbar, click the Paste button.

The insertion point appears just in front of *hazelnut,* and the phrase *Pacific Northwest* is copied from the Clipboard to the field.

⑦ Repeat steps 5 and 6 to update the other hazelnut bonbon records.

⑧ Click Find Next one more time.

A message appears, confirming that there are no other matches.

⑨ Click OK, and then close the Find And Replace dialog box.

Cut

tip

Moving text is similar to copying it; on the Form View toolbar, just click the Cut button instead of the Copy button.

Add another record using the toolbar

Because a number of respondents to the questionnaire indicated a preference for dark chocolate with nuts, Mary asks that you add another bonbon style. In this exercise, you enter a record for a new Chocolate Kiwi bonbon.

New Record

1 On the Form View toolbar, click the New Record button.

A new, blank record appears in the Bonbons form.

2 Enter the following information.

Bonbon Name:	**Chocolate Kiwi**
Description:	**Brazil nut surrounded by dark chocolate, cross-sectioned like a kiwi fruit.**

3 Select the appropriate values—Dark, None, and Brazil—in the Chocolate Type, Filling Type, and Nut Type fields, respectively.

4 In the Cost field, type **.29**

5 In the Bonbon ID field, type **D12**

Undoing Changes in a Record

The Undo button on the Form View toolbar is handy for going back to the previous stage of the current field or record. The ScreenTip and menu command for the Undo button change to reflect the current reversible action. For example, the Undo button ScreenTip and menu command display *Undo Typing* if your last change was typing a word, and *Undo Delete* if you just deleted a word. Once the record has been saved, however, you can no longer undo any of the changes.

Undo your most recent action

Previous Record

1 On the navigation bar, click the Previous Record button until you reach the record for the Calla Lily bonbon.

2 In the Description box for the Calla Lily bonbon, position the insertion point after the word *sculpted* and use the Backspace key to delete the word.

3 Position the insertion point between the word *lily* and the period at the end of the description. Press the Spacebar and type **pad**

Undo

You can also press Ctrl+Z to undo your most recent action.

4 On the Form View toolbar, rest the mouse over the Undo button.

The ScreenTip displays *Undo Typing* to describe your most recent change.

5 On the Form View toolbar, click the Undo button.

The word *pad,* your most recent change, is deleted.

Undo all edits in the current field or record

You realize that the original text in that field was better after all, so you try Undo again.

The action of the Undo feature itself has altered, because you undid your most recent change in the previous exercise. Rather than restore the original text one change at a time, Undo now undoes all edits that you made in the current field.

1 On the Form View toolbar, rest the mouse over the Undo button.

The ScreenTip displays *Undo Current Field/Record* because you undid your most recent change in the previous exercise.

2 On the Form View toolbar, click the Undo button.

All your previous edits are discarded. The Undo button is then disabled, and the ScreenTip changes to *Can't Undo* when you rest the mouse over it.

Delete an entire record in a form

Because no customer who responded to the questionnaire indicated a preference for white chocolate with nuts, in this exercise you delete the record for the Broken Heart bonbon.

1 Click in the Bonbon Name field.

2 On the Form View toolbar, click the Find button.

The Find And Replace dialog box appears.

Find

3 In the Find What box, type **Broken Heart**

4 In the Look In list, verify Bonbon Name is selected.

5 In the Match list, verify Whole Field is selected.

6 Click Find Next.

The Broken Heart record appears.

7 On the Form View toolbar, click the Delete Record button.

A message appears, asking you to confirm the deletion.

Delete Record

8 Click Yes.

The record is now deleted. The record indicator on the navigation bar reflects the change to the number of records in the database.

9 Close the Find And Replace dialog box.

10 Close the Bonbons form.

important

Do not confuse Delete with Delete Record. Delete is a key on the keyboard and removes only selected text or objects. Delete Record is a button on the Form View toolbar and removes an entire record. Both are listed as commands on the Edit menu, but they do not look the same. Delete has a keyboard shortcut just to its right, and Delete Record has the same face as the toolbar button just to its left.

One Step Further ## Replacing Data

You'll encounter many situations in which you'll want to find information in the database and then replace it with more current information. The Replace feature quickly replaces any information that meets your criteria. For example, if you know that a customer address or an internal company term has changed, you can combine finding and replacing that data in a single step.

Replace data that meets known criteria

As part of its move to worldwide sales, Sweet Lil's has merged its marketing and sales departments. All employees of both departments are now members of the marketing department. To update the database to reflect this change, you must replace every occurrence of *Sales* in the Department Name field of the Employees database table with *Marketing*. In this exercise, you do so using the Employees form.

Find

You can also click Replace on the Edit menu, or press Ctrl+H.

1. In the Database window, double-click Employees in the forms list.

   The Employees form opens.

2. On the Employees form, click in the Department Name field.

3. On the Form View toolbar, click the Find button.

   The Find And Replace dialog box appears.

4. In the Find And Replace dialog box, click the Replace tab.

   The Replace tab is identical to the Find tab, but with the addition of a Replace With box (currently empty), a Replace button, and a Replace All button.

5. In the Find What box, type **Sales**

6. In the Replace With box, type **Marketing**

7. In the Match list, verify Whole Field is selected.

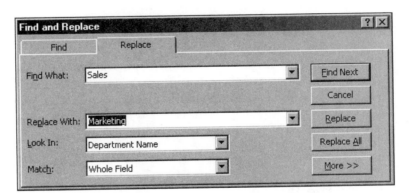

8. Click Replace All.

   A message appears, warning you that you won't be able to undo this Replace operation.

9. Click Yes.

   All occurrences of *Sales* are changed to *Marketing* in the Department Name field throughout the Employees table.

10. Close the Find And Replace dialog box.

11. Close the Employees form.

Using Forms

How the Year 2000 Affects Computers

Much has been said about "the year 2000 problem" and its effect on computers worldwide. But what exactly does this mean for computers in general, and how is Access 2000 affected?

There are two main issues concerning the year 2000 and your computer.

The first issue relates to how computers store dates and make calculations using dates. The most common method used to store dates in software is to save just the last two digits of the year, based on the assumption that the first two digits are *19*. As a result, computers read the date *2000* as *00*; lacking the first two digits, they incorrectly use the year 1900.

A second problem relates to leap year. Many computer systems and programs do not recognize the year 2000 as a leap year. This causes all dates after February 29, 2000, to be off by one day.

Access 2000 has been carefully tested against the Microsoft Year 2000 Compliance Standard and has been rated in its top category: Compliant. That means Access 2000 will recognize the year 2000 on January 1, 2000, will correctly display leap day, February 29, 2000, and will continue to display the correct date on March 1, 2000. It also means that any date calculations using the year 2000 (and beyond) will be correct.

Finish the lesson

1. To continue to the next lesson, on the File menu, click Close.
2. If you are finished using Access 2000 for now, on the File menu, click Exit.

Lesson 1 Quick Reference

To	Do this
Open a database	In the Microsoft Access dialog box, double-click the database name.
Open a form	In the Database window, click Forms on the Objects bar, and then double-click the form name.
Update an existing record	Click within the field at the place you want to insert text, and then begin typing.

Lesson 1 Quick Reference

To	Do this	Button
Move among records	On the navigation bar, click the navigation buttons.	
Move directly to a specific record	Type the record number in the record indicator on the navigation bar, and then press Enter.	
Find a record	Click in the field containing text you want to find. Click the Find button on the Form View toolbar. Enter the text you want to find, and then click Find Next.	
Add another record	Click the New Record button on the Form View toolbar.	
Copy text to another record	Select the text to copy, and use the Copy and Paste buttons on the Form View toolbar.	
Save your work	Data is saved automatically when you move to to another record or window, close a form, or exit the program.	
Undo your most recent action	Click the Undo button on the Form View toolbar.	
Undo all edits in the current field or record	Click the Undo Current Field/Record button on the Form View toolbar.	
Delete an entire record	Click anywhere in the record you want to delete. Click the Delete Record button on the Form View toolbar or Navigation bar.	
Replace text in records	Click the Find button on the Form View toolbar. Click the Replace tab, enter the text you want to find and the text you want to replace it with, and then click Find Next.	

Using Forms

2

Using Tables and Subforms

**ESTIMATED
TIME
25 min.**

In this lesson you will learn how to:

✓ *Open a database table.*

✓ *Present a datasheet effectively.*

✓ *Update multiple records using a table.*

✓ *View multiple tables with a subform.*

✓ *Freeze and hide columns in a datasheet.*

Behind every good form there stands a good table. This paraphrased adage is probably not applicable in all situations, but it is true of any well-constructed database. A table is where your data is stored, and a form is the most common vehicle for viewing and changing that data. The View Customers form that you used in Lesson 1, for example, is a convenient way of viewing and manipulating data in the *underlying* Customers table, the table that the View Customers form is based on. There are situations, however, where working with data directly in a table is the better option.

A typical Microsoft Access 2000 database contains a number of tables. The rows and columns of each table house the data for one topic; the Bonbons table, for example, contains the specifics about each bonbon in the Sweet Lil's product line. Each row of the table is a separate record, and each column of the table is a field in the records. In each record of the Bonbons table, there are eight fields: Bonbon Name, Bonbon ID, Bonbon Description, Chocolate Type, Filling Type, Nut Type, Bonbon Cost, and Picture.

To generate interest in Sweet Lil's new Bonbon Baskets line, Impact Public Relations has set up a promotional campaign in which sample baskets of bonbons are mailed to Sweet Lil's customers four times during the next calendar year.

In this lesson, you make use of tables, forms, and subforms to present information about the different sample baskets to the marketing department at Sweet Lil's. In the process, you open an existing database table and arrange the table to make it easier to use. You also use a main form and subform to examine records from multiple tables at one time.

Start Microsoft Access 2000 and reopen the database

●　If Access 2000 isn't started yet, start it. Open the Sweet Lil's database. If the Microsoft Access window doesn't fill your screen, maximize the window.

　　If you need help opening the database, see Lesson 1, "Using Forms."

Viewing Data

In Access 2000, data in a table, form, report, or query can be presented in several ways, called *views*.

For a table or a form, *Datasheet view* displays all the data in a tabular format, each row a record and each column a field. When you open a table, it always appears first in Datasheet view, because Datasheet view is the *default view* of a table. Both tables and forms in Datasheet view are usually called datasheets.

If a form has already been created based on a table, *Form view* for either the table or the form displays the table data within the associated form. Form view presents only the fields required for a given task, arranged to show each individual record to its best advantage. (When you open a form, it always appears first in Form view, which is the default view of a form.)

For details on a form's Design view, see Lesson 10, "Presenting a Form More Effectively."

In *Table Design view* the table is displayed as a list of fields and their associated properties, which can be changed as well as viewed. *Form Design view* lets you create a new form or revise the structure of an existing one. Design view is never a default view. Instead, you must switch to Design view from another view.

(continued)

View

continued

To switch between Design view and the default view, just click the View toolbar button. When you change views, the View toolbar button face switches to show the alternate view. With the View button you can also switch almost as easily to another view: click the drop-down arrow next to the View button, and then click the view you want from the list.

Form view is generally the easiest and safest view to use, because it has the most safeguards and fewest complications. There are times, however, when you need to see multiple records at the same time or view a table for which no form has been developed. Datasheet view lets you see the database as a table and work directly with the data it contains.

Viewing a Datasheet

Most of the tables in the Sweet Lil's database can be viewed through forms. For example, you never actually need to show the Sweet Lil's marketing department the entire Bonbons table when you demonstrate how to alter bonbon descriptions; instead, you work in the Bonbons form, modifying fields that show information about individual records in the underlying Bonbons table.

A database table works much like a spreadsheet, so a table viewed in this row-and-column format is often referred to as a *datasheet*—a database spreadsheet. The datasheet displays every record and every field in a table. In large tables, some columns might contain a lot of text, and there are probably many fields, so you might not be able to view all the table data at once. There are therefore several strategies available for making large datasheets easier to work with.

In these exercises, you open the Bonbons table to become more familiar with the Sweet Lil's product line. You rearrange the fields for optimum viewing of fields, using the record and field selectors.

Open a table

1 In the Database window, click Tables on the Objects bar to open the tables list.

A list of tables is displayed in the Database window.

Click Tables to open the tables list.

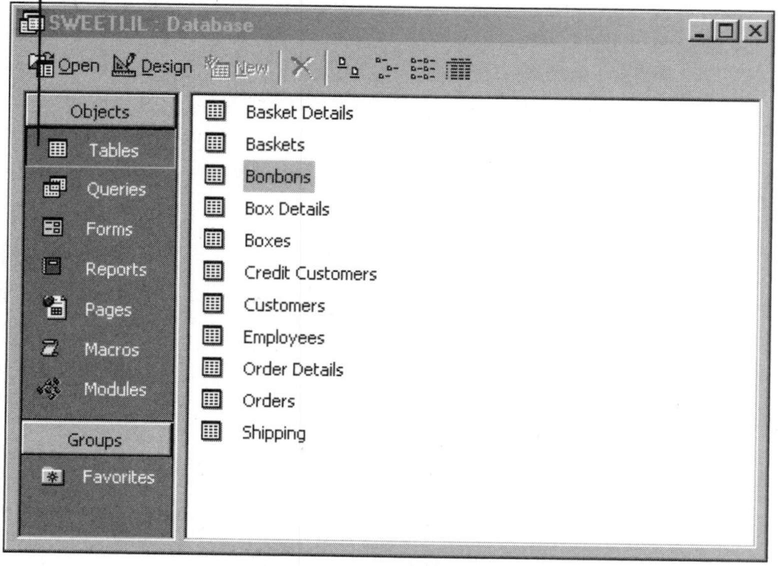

② In the tables list, double-click Bonbons.
The Bonbons table opens in Datasheet view.

When you first open a table, it is displayed with each row as a record and each column as a field. A triangular pointer appears to the left of the first record, indicating that it is the current record. The first field of the first record is selected, indicating that it is the current field.

Selecting Records Within a Table

The triangular pointer that indicates the current record is the *record indicator*. It appears in a column of gray boxes that runs along the left side, called *record selectors*. A similar set of *field selectors* runs across the top row of the table. The field selectors include the field name.

(continued)

continued

Field selector

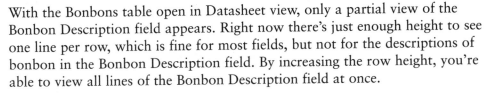

Record selector

Record indicator

The record indicator shows where you are in the table. You can click a record selector to select an entire row of fields, which is by definition a single record. You can click a field selector to select an entire column. You can also select several field or record selectors at once to make a change to multiple columns or rows. Only adjacent fields or rows can be selected.

Change the row height of a table

Field text wraps when a row is tall enough to fit more than one line of text.

With the Bonbons table open in Datasheet view, only a partial view of the Bonbon Description field appears. Right now there's just enough height to see one line per row, which is fine for most fields, but not for the descriptions of bonbon in the Bonbon Description field. By increasing the row height, you're able to view all lines of the Bonbon Description field at once.

Maximize

1 Verify that the Microsoft Access window and the Bonbons datasheet are maximized.

The datasheet for the Bonbons table expands to fill the Microsoft Access window.

2 Position the mouse pointer on the border between any two record selectors.

The mouse pointer becomes a double-headed arrow.

		Bonbon ID	Bonbon Name	Chocolate Type	Nut Type
▶	⊞	**B01**	Candlelight Ecstasy	Dark	Cashew
	⊞	B02	Bittersweet Blueberry	Bittersweet	None
	⊞	B03	Marzipan Oakleaf	Bittersweet	None
	⊞	B04	Bittersweet Strawberry	Bittersweet	None
	⊞	B05	Bittersweet Raspberry	Bittersweet	None

Position the mouse pointer here.

A single row can't be sized differently from the other rows.

3 Drag the border down to make the row immediately above it grow taller.

All rows are resized.

4 Scroll to the right, adjust the row height approximately one inch (1") until you can read the entire text of the Bonbon Description field.

Change the column width of a table

Now you go on to make the Nut Type and Bonbon ID columns narrower so that you can see additional table fields.

1 Position the mouse pointer on the border between the field selectors for the Nut Type and Filling Type fields.

The mouse pointer becomes a double-headed arrow.

Position the mouse pointer here.

To view additional fields without resizing, use the horizontal scroll bar to scroll to the right.

Nut Type	Filling Type
Almond	Amaretto
Hazelnut	None
None	Cherry, whole

You can resize columns independently of one another.

2 Double-click the border between the Nut Type and Filling Type field selectors.

The Nut Type column is resized to match the width of the widest entry in the field, including the complete field name at the top of the column.

Save

3 Drag the right border of the Bonbon ID column to the left until it's just slightly larger than the three-character Bonbon ID entries.

4 On the Datasheet View toolbar, click the Save button.

The Bonbons table will now retain its current layout in Datasheet view.

5 Close the Bonbons table.

Records are automatically saved as you move from record to record, but you must manually save your changes to the layout of a table or form so that it appears this way every time you use it.

Updating Data Using a Table

For a review of Access editing tools, see Lesson 1, "Using Forms."

Many of the editing tools that you use in Form view are also available in Datasheet view, including Find, Cut, Copy, Paste, New Record, and Delete Record.

It's often helpful to view multiple records using Datasheet view. Updating records directly in a table should be done with caution, however. Fewer data validation tools are available in Datasheet view, so you increase the chance of introducing errors into your data. And if you do spot an error, the Undo command can undo only the changes you've made since your most recent save.

It's best to use Form view to perform update operations.

Viewing Multiple Tables with a Subform

For details on how to create a subform, see Lesson 9, "Merging Data onto One Form."

Think of a *subform* as a form within a form. A subform lets you work with records from several separate tables within a single form. The fields of the main form reflect data from one table, while the data in the subform reflects the other table—or tables. This makes the data both easier to use and more reliable, because information from the various tables is kept separate, while the relationship is maintained.

Now that you've reviewed descriptions of the bonbons, it's time to look over information about the various baskets that have been set up for the promotional mailing. To do so, you use the Baskets form, which includes a subform called Basket Details.

The Baskets tables, viewed using the Baskets form, stores information about the various basket types in which bonbons are packaged. The Basket Details subform displays selected fields from the Basket Details and Bonbons tables. With this structure, the form displays information about the basket itself (name, ID number, and a general description of its contents) in the main form and information about the basket's contents (what types of bonbons it contains and details about each bonbon type) in the subform. The subform provides a direct connection between one set of records, defining baskets, and another, defining basket contents. Using the form and subform together, you can add and delete bonbon types to define the contents of a new basket, until you've assembled a basket that holds the exact mix that you want.

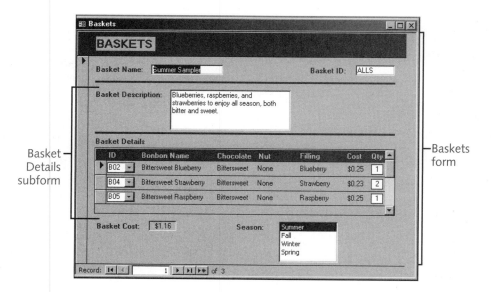

Basket Details subform

Baskets form

In these exercises, you use the Baskets form and its Basket Details subform to create a new basket for the winter promotional mailing.

Add a record in a main form

1 In the Database window, click Forms on the Objects bar to display the forms list.

2 In the forms list, double-click Baskets.

The Baskets form opens, displaying the first record of the Baskets table in the main form and its associated Basket Details subform below.

3 On the Form View toolbar, click the New Record button.

New Record

A new, blank record appears, with the insertion point in the Basket Name field.

4 Type the following information into the appropriate fields of the main form.

Basket Name: **By The Fire**

Basket ID: **WINT**

Basket Description: **Nuts and berries coated with chocolate and fudge for those long winter evenings.**

5 Press the Tab key to move to the subform.

The insertion point appears in the ID field of the Basket Details subform.

Add records in a subform

In this exercise, you define the contents of the By The Fire basket, selecting the ideal combination of bonbon types for this basket. Each bonbon you select will be saved as a separate record in the Basket Details table. The records will be linked, however, to the record for the By The Fire basket in the Baskets table.

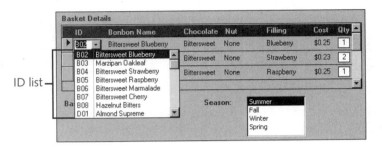

1. In the ID field of the Basket Details subform, click the drop-down arrow of the first ID cell, and then select B02 Bittersweet Blueberry.

   B02 appears in the field, and the Bonbon Name, Chocolate, Nut, Filling, and Cost fields are filled in with corresponding values. A new, blank record appears below the first record.

2. Press Tab to move to the Qty field.

3. In the Qty field, type **1** and press Tab.

   Access 2000 saves the first record in the subform.

4. Type the following records into the subform.

ID	Bonbon Name	Qty
B05	**Bittersweet Raspberry**	**1**
D03	**Cashew Supreme**	**1**
F01	**Walnut Fudge Mocha**	**2**

   The Basket Cost field on the main form changes as each new record is added to the subform. The main form automatically calculates the cost of the basket based on its contents, as defined in the subform.

5. Scroll back through the subform to check your work. Be sure that each record is correct before you continue.

Pressing Ctrl+Tab and Ctrl+Shift+Tab moves the insertion point from the subform to the next and previous fields, respectively, in the main form.

6 In the last record in the subform, press Ctrl+Tab.

The insertion point moves from the subform to the Season field in the main form.

Complete the main form

To complete the By The Fire basket, all you need to do is select the season during which it will be mailed.

1 In the Season field, select Winter and press Tab.

Access saves the completed record and opens a new, blank record.

3 Press Shift+Tab to return to the previous main form and subform.

Access returns to the record you just entered and discards the blank record.

3 Close the Baskets form.

One Step Further   Refining Datasheet Views

Datasheet view can be difficult to use when there are a large number of fields. You often get lost in the Bonbons datasheet, even after resizing the fields and columns, due to the size and complexity of the table. Two strategies for refining the Datasheet view come in handy now: freezing the most useful column and hiding an unnecessary column.

Freeze a datasheet column

The Bonbon Name field provides a reference point for the table, identifying which row of data belongs to which bonbon. You freeze the entire Bonbon Name column so that it remains visible on the left, no matter how many fields you scroll through on the right.

1 Click Tables on the Objects bar, and open the Bonbons table in Datasheet view.

2 Click the Bonbon Name field in any row.

To unfreeze columns at any time, click Unfreeze All Columns on the Format menu.

③ On the Format menu, click Freeze Columns.

A bold vertical line appears along the right border of the Bonbon Name column. The column is now frozen and can't be scrolled.

You drag the horizontal scroll box back and forth a few times to test this. Sure enough, the Bonbon Name column remains frozen on the left as all the other columns are scrolled freely back and forth.

Hide a datasheet column

The Picture field is a good choice for a column to hide. Its bonbon graphics aren't currently visible because the table is too large to fit on the screen without scrolling, so the Picture field isn't useful to you at the moment. In this exercise, you hide the Picture field to make the datasheet less cluttered.

Drag from here...
...to here.

	Bonbon Name	Bonbon Cost	Picture
⊞	Candlelight Ecstasy	$0.30	Bitmap Image
⊞	Bittersweet Blueberry	$0.25	Bitmap Image
▶ ⊞	Marzipan Oakleaf	$0.40	Bitmap Image
⊞	Bittersweet Strawberry	$0.23	Bitmap Image
⊞	Bittersweet Raspberry	$0.25	Bitmap Image
⊞	Bittersweet Marmalade	$0.17	Bitmap Image
⊞	Bittersweet Cherry	$0.26	Bitmap Image
⊞	Hazelnut Bitters	$0.24	Bitmap Image

To reveal any hidden columns, click Unhide Columns on the Format menu, and then select the appropriate check boxes.

① Drag the right border of the Picture field selector to the left until it covers its own left border.

The Picture column is hidden.

Save

② On the Datasheet View toolbar, click the Save button.

The Bonbons table will now retain its current layout in Datasheet view.

③ Close the Bonbons table.

Finish the lesson

1. To continue to the next lesson, on the File menu, click Close.
2. If you're finished using Access 2000 for now, on the File menu, click Exit.

Lesson 2 Quick Reference

To	Do this	Button
Open a table	In the Database window, click Tables on the Objects bar, and then double-click the table name.	
Resize all datasheet rows	Drag the border between record selectors.	
Resize a datasheet column	Drag the right border of the field selector for the column you want to resize.	
Switch views	Click the View drop-down arrow on the Datasheet, Form, or Design View toolbar, and then select the view you want.	
Add a new record in a main form	Click the New Record button on the Form View toolbar.	▶✳
Add a new record in a subform	In the subform, click the first drop-down arrow, and select an item.	
Move from a form to a subform	Click the field to which you want to move.	
Freeze a column	Click anywhere in the column, and then click Freeze Columns on the Format menu.	
Hide a column	Drag the right border of the field selector over the left border of the field selector.	
Unhide a hidden column	On the Format menu, click Unhide Columns, and then select the hidden field in the Unhide Columns dialog box.	

3

Using Filters and Reports

In this lesson you will learn how to:

ESTIMATED
TIME
40 min.

✔ *Sort records.*

✔ *Extract specific information by using a filter.*

✔ *Report only the information you need.*

✔ *Preview report details.*

✔ *Print all or part of a report.*

✔ *Create mailing labels.*

The sheer volume of information in a database can be overwhelming. In most cases, you're not interested in the bulk of the information, just the information you need at the moment. You want to focus on the information you're after, without wading through distracting data, and share that information quickly and easily with others or preserve it for future reference. You can do that by using the Microsoft Access 2000 sorting, filtering, and reporting tools.

The sales department at Sweet Lil's has collected a year's worth of records about the orders they've filled. Now the department needs to make sense of that data and put it to good use. In this lesson, you help rearrange and refine the data to extract needed information and demonstrate how to open, preview, and print reports, including mailing labels.

Viewing Only the Information You Need

Access allows you to change your view of the data in a database without affecting the actual physical arrangement of the database itself, so you can organize the data to make it more meaningful. The two most useful techniques for organizing data are sorting and filtering.

Sorting is simply rearranging the records into a specific order based on the contents of a given field or fields. You can sort records alphabetically, by number, by date, or by a specified characteristic, such as being male or female. Records can be sorted in ascending (A–Z and 0–9) or descending (Z–A and 9–0) order.

Filtering is screening out all records that do not match a given set of criteria defined in a *filter*. A filter makes it possible to view a particular group of records exclusively. For example, you could apply a filter to view only those orders that were placed on a certain date.

Sorting and filtering can be done in either Form view or Datasheet view. Neither sorting nor filtering changes the actual data; each process simply adjusts your view of the data. When you sort a form, the sort order is saved automatically so that when you reopen the form, the records are displayed in the order in which you last sorted them. When you sort a table, Access gives you the option of saving the sort order. Filters, however, are *not* saved along with the form or table and must be reapplied each time you want to see the filtered view.

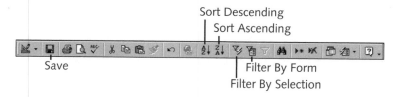

Sorting Records

To make sense of Sweet Lil's candy orders, it's not enough simply to list them in the order in which they were placed. You also need to group the records together in various ways to see how they're related. For example, grouping the records in the Orders table by customer name might help you determine who the "best" customers are and how much repeat business they're doing.

There's no one ideal arrangement or order for records in a database, because people consult a database in response to a wide range of needs. Rowen Gilbert, vice-president of planning for the sales department, typically needs to know how orders are distributed geographically, so the best arrangement for him is usually by region. Liz Yarrow, an administrative assistant for the operations department, always needs to find the most recent orders as quickly as possible, so the best arrangement for her is by order number, in reverse chronological order. Robin Saito, a shipping clerk, needs all orders listed by their unique ID numbers.

To sort by multiple fields, select the fields you want to sort by prior to clicking a Sort button.

To see the records grouped together in different ways, you can sort them by different fields using the Sort Ascending and Sort Descending buttons. In this exercise, you show Rowen, Liz, and Robin how to sort the Orders records to suit their different needs. Sorting is so quick and easy in Access that you can help all three get their answers at once.

Start Microsoft Access 2000 and reopen the database

● If Access isn't started yet, start it. Open the Sweet Lil's database. If the Microsoft Access window doesn't fill your screen, maximize the window.

If you need help opening the database, see Lesson 1, "Using Forms."

Switching Between Views

Access allows you to switch quickly and easily between available views. In a form, you have the option of switching between Form, Datasheet, and Design view, and in a table, you can switch between Datasheet and Design view. You have three view options in Form view because a table exists independent of any forms that might be created from it, but a form is dependent on an underlying table.

To switch between views, click the drop-down arrow next to the View button on the toolbar, and then click the view you want from the list. When you select the view you want, the View button face changes to show the view that will be displayed if you click the button. The toolbar button always toggles between Design view and the default view of the object with which you're working, such as a table, a query, a form, a report, or a page.

In general, it's best to stay in Form view for most of your work, switching to Datasheet view (and thus the underlying table) only when necessary and switching back to Form view immediately thereafter. You must open a table directly if you intend to change its design, however, because each database object has its own distinct Design view.

Sort records on a specific field

1 In the Database window, click Forms on the Objects bar to display the forms list.

2 In the forms list, double-click Orders.

The Orders form opens in Form view. Notice the OrderID number for record 1.

View

3 On the Form View toolbar, click the View drop-down arrow, and then click Datasheet View.

The Orders form reappears in Datasheet view. The arrangement of the records is more apparent in Datasheet view.

4 On the Orders datasheet, scroll to the right until you can see the Ship StateOrProvince field, and then click the Ship StateOrProvince field selector.

When the mouse pointer passes over the field selector, the pointer becomes a downward-pointing arrow. Now when you click the field selector, the entire column is selected.

Sort Ascending

5 On the Datasheet View toolbar, click the Sort Ascending button.

All the records are rearranged so that the states and provinces are listed in ascending alphabetical (A–Z) order. Rowen can now see how the orders are distributed by state.

6 On the Datasheet View toolbar, click the View drop-down arrow, and then click Form View.

The displayed record changes to order ID 228.

7 Click order ID number 228.

Now that Rowen has the information he needs, you can help Liz sort the records by order ID number.

Sort Descending

8 On the Form View toolbar, click the Sort Descending button.

The record changes from order ID number 228 to order ID number 413. The records are now sorted in descending numerical order by order ID number. Order ID 413 is now the first record in the table.

You can sort records in either Form view or Datasheet view, but the results are more apparent in Datasheet view.

9 On the Form View toolbar, click the View drop-down arrow, and then click Datasheet View.

Liz can now see the records in reverse chronological order, with the most recent order first.

10 In the Orders datasheet, select the Order ID field.

Robin also needs to see the records sorted by order ID, but in chronological order.

View

⓫ On the Datasheet View toolbar, click the Sort Ascending button.

All the records are grouped by order ID, in ascending numerical order. Robin can now see the original sequence in which the orders were placed.

Refining Your View of the Data

Sorting is very useful for quick reference, but it has its limitations. Sorting records displays a table in a more helpful arrangement, but you still have to view all the records in the table. No matter how you sort the records, you can't screen out records in which you have no interest. To do that, you must use a filter.

This morning, Rowen Gilbert arrives at your desk with an urgent request: he needs you to find out how many orders have been shipped to Canada. You show him how easy it is to set up a filter for just this kind of question.

Filtering a Form by Selection

Filter By Selection works much like a sort, except that it matches against the *contents* of the field and allows only matching records to pass through. The Filter By Selection feature allows you to filter selectively by a single criterion per field, that criterion being the contents of the field at the time you select it. The field and contents you select serve as an *example* of the information you want to see.

Filter by selection

You can also filter by multiple fields by selecting the fields you want prior to clicking the Filter By Selection button.

In this exercise, you use Filter By Selection to display just the Canadian orders for Rowen.

❶ Be sure the Orders form is open in Datasheet view.

❷ In the Orders datasheet, scroll right until you can see the ShipCountry column, and then click any ShipCountry field containing the word *Canada*.

This sets, by example, the criterion for the filter: a ShipCountry field with the word *Canada* in it.

Filter By Selection

❸ On the Datasheet View toolbar, click the Filter By Selection button.

The filter displays only the records with the word *Canada* in the ShipCountry field. The word *(Filtered)* appears on the navigation bar, indicating that this is a filtered view. The Apply Filter toolbar button becomes the Remove Filter toolbar button.

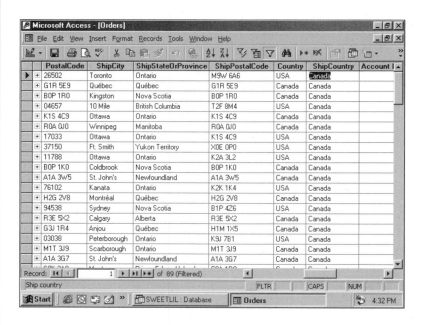

Filtering by Form

The Filter By Form feature allows you to filter selectively by more than one criterion per field. Like Filter By Selection, it sets criteria by example. But where Filter By Selection simply applies the current contents of a particular field, Filter By Form allows you to select any one of the possible items in a particular field.

Filter by form

Sweet Lil's accepts three major credit cards: World Credit, Elite Fund, and Select Card. Rowen now asks you to find out how many of those Canadian orders were paid for with an Elite Fund credit card. In this exercise, you use the Filter By Form feature to further filter the results, displaying only the Canadian orders that were placed using the Elite Fund credit card.

Filter By Form

1 On the Datasheet View toolbar, click the Filter By Form button.

The view collapses to a single row of fields. A drop-down arrow appears by the ShipCountry field and the word *Canada* is selected in the ShipCountry list. The Filter/Sort toolbar replaces the Datasheet View toolbar.

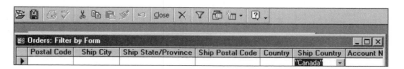

2 Scroll to the right until you see the Credit Card field.

❸ On the Orders Filter By Form grid, click the Credit Card field, click the drop-down arrow, and then select 2.

Because the Credit Card field is an option group on the Orders form, the credit card type is stored as a number. The Elite Fund credit card is the second choice in the option group, so it has been assigned the number 2.

❹ On the Filter/Sort toolbar, click the Apply/Remove Filter button.

The filter displays only the records with *Canada* in the Ship Country field and in the Credit Card field. The Datasheet View toolbar replaces the Filter/Sort toolbar, with the Apply Filter button becoming the Remove Filter button.

❺ On the Datasheet View toolbar, click the Apply/Remove Filter button.

The normal Datasheet view reappears, with all records displayed.

❻ Close the Orders form. If asked to save changes, click No.

*Apply/Remove
Filter*

Preserving Your View in a Report

After you've gotten the desired view of your data, you might want to share that view with others at Sweet Lil's or Impact Public Relations. You can do this by using a *report*. A report is similar to a form in that they both extract specific information from the database and organize it in a meaningful fashion. Forms, however, are used primarily for data manipulation, whereas reports are used for data presentation. Reports can be printed on paper, saved in your local directory, sent via e-mail, posted to a shared folder for use by a workgroup, published to an intranet to reach an entire corporation, or published on the Internet to reach as wide an audience as possible.

Sweet Lil's newest marketing agent, Nora Bromsler, has taken the lead in mastering Access. To assist the marketing department, she has created the Sales By Box report, which displays sales records for any range of dates in calendar year 1998.

*You set
criteria by
example for
a filter, but
you enter
parameter
values
manually to
set criteria
for a report.*

Sales By Box is an interactive report: it prompts the user for a start and end date for the period to be covered in the report. These dates are the *parameter values* or report criteria. The Sales By Box report then extracts and presents only the records that meet those criteria. The range of dates can vary from a single day to the entire year.

Sweet Lil's marketing vice president, Mary Culvert, needs to review sales for the first two weeks of June 1998, the beginning of the traditional summer season. In the following exercises, you help Mary open, preview, and print the information she needs using the Sales By Box report.

Open a report

When the Sales By Box report is opened, Access requests the start and end dates for the period to be covered. Entering the report criteria is thus a part of opening the report.

1 In the Database window, click Reports on the Objects bar to display the reports list.

2 In the reports list, double-click Sales By Box.

The message *Enter Parameter Value* appears, prompting for the start date of the period Mary wants the report to cover.

Access 2000 accepts date entries in a number of formats, but you must clearly distinguish the month, day, and year.

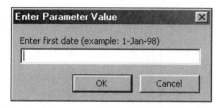

3 In the Enter Parameter Value text box, type **1-Jun-98** and press Enter.

The Enter Parameter Value message prompts for the end date of the period Mary wants covered.

4 Type **June 15, 1998** and press Enter.

Mary's report opens in Print Preview view. The Print Preview toolbar replaces the Database toolbar.

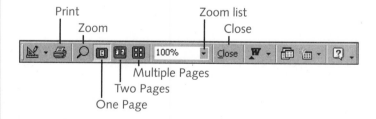

Microsoft Windows Regional Settings

Microsoft Windows 95, Windows 98, and Window NT use regional settings to determine how to interpret numeric dates. For example, the numeric date *1/2/98* is interpreted as month-day-year (January 2, 1998) if the regional settings are for United States English, and as day-month-year (1 February 1998) if the regional settings are for British English.

Access recognizes a number of ways to enter dates, but you must clearly distinguish the month from the day. When you enter the month alphabetically, either abbreviated (Jan) or in full (January), Access recognizes and accepts it regardless of the month and day order. When you enter a date numerically, however, Access looks to your regional settings to determine the month and day order.

For example, Access recognizes both *13/1/98* and *1/13/98* as January 13, 1998—there are only 12 months in a year, so the date isn't ambiguous. But both *12/1/98* and *1/12/98* can be interpreted as either January 12, 1998 or December 1, 1998, depending on your regional settings.

Some regional settings put the year first, so other dates are also ambiguous in an international environment. For example, *3/2/1* can be January 2, 2003, or February 1, 2003, or February 3, 2001, or March 2, 2001.

Previewing a Report

The Print Preview view includes a navigation bar similar to that of a form or datasheet.

A report is automatically saved and opened in Print Preview view the moment it is created. The view of the information contained in a report serves as a snapshot of that view, which you can view or print. Reports were originally designed with printing in mind, however, so the layout you see is dependent on the default printer settings of your computer.

When you open a report, it appears at full magnification so you can clearly read the information it contains. The mouse pointer becomes a magnifying glass with a minus sign (-) when it passes over any part of the report page. The degree of magnification is displayed in the Zoom box on the Print Preview toolbar.

Preview a report

To help Mary Culvert learn more about reports, you want to show her the many ways to view both the contents and the layout of a report in the Print Preview view.

1 Click anywhere in the fully magnified report page.

The view zooms out to show you the entire page, and the minus sign (-) on the mouse pointer becomes a plus sign (+).

2 Click anywhere in the zoomed-out report page.

You can use the Multiple Pages button to view the layout of up to six pages at a time.

The view zooms in to 100 percent magnification centered on the point you clicked, and the mouse pointer plus sign becomes a minus sign. On the Print Preview toolbar, the Zoom box now displays *100%*.

3 Use the vertical scroll bar to move up and down the page, and use the horizontal scroll bar to move from side to side to view the page.

4 On the Print Preview toolbar, click the Two Pages button.

Two Pages

The view zooms out to show two pages, side by side. On the Print Preview toolbar, the Zoom box now displays *Fit* again.

5 On the Print Preview toolbar, click the One Page button.

One Page

All but the first page disappears.

Print a report

A printer must be selected before you can print a report.

By just viewing the report in Print Preview view, Mary learned everything she needed to know, but she also wants a printed copy for an upcoming meeting. She notices that the default quarter-inch left margin is too narrow and would like to widen it to a full inch. Mary asks you to adjust the page setup, print a single "proof page" for her approval, and then print the entire report in time for her meeting.

1 On the File menu, click Print.

The Print dialog box appears.

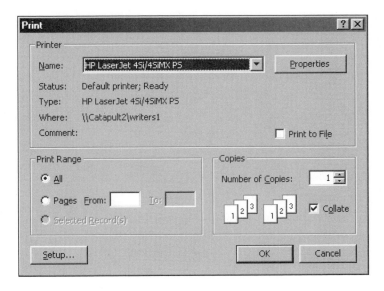

② In the Print dialog box, click Setup.

The Page Setup dialog box appears, with the Margins tab active.

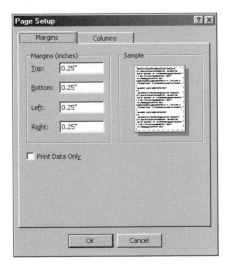

When you make a change to the page setup, the change is saved and becomes the new default setting.

③ Double-click in the Left Margin box, and then type **1**

The left margin changes from the default 0.25 inches to one inch. In the Sample preview picture, the left margin of the report shifts to the right.

④   Click OK.

The Page Setup dialog box closes. The left margin of the report is now set to one inch. All future Sales By Box reports will also have one-inch left margins, until the page setup is changed again.

⑤   In the Print Range area of the Print dialog box, select Pages.

When you select the Pages option, the insertion point appears in the From box. You want to print page 1 of the report as a proof page for Mary.

⑥   In the From box, type **1**

When you type in the From box, the To box becomes available.

⑦   In the To box, type **1** and press Enter.

Only the first page (range 1 to 1) of the Sales By Box report is printed. This proof page confirms that the report will indeed be printed as expected, and Mary approves final printing of the entire report.

Print

⑧   On the Print Preview toolbar, click the Print button.

Access prints the entire Sales By Box report exactly as you see it in Print Preview view. This is the most convenient way to print a report once the page layout has been checked.

Close

⑨   On the Print Preview toolbar, click the Close button.

The Sales By Box report closes, and the Database window reappears.

tip

When you double-click a report in the Database window reports list, Access 2000 opens it in Print Preview view. To print a report without opening it first, just click the report in the Database window, and then click the Print button on the Database window toolbar. To specify how many copies to print and whether to collate the copies, click Print on the File menu.

Creating Mailing Labels

At Impact's suggestion, Sweet Lil's plans to promote its newest bonbon, Chocolate Kiwi, by mailing a free sample to all of its customers. Henry Czynski, the senior shipping clerk, needs to create a set of mailing labels of a suitable size and layout to fit on a single-serving candy box; the labels must be sorted by postal code so that all the boxes addressed to the same area can be shipped out together.

In Access 2000, a set of mailing labels is simply a specialized report whose layout matches that of your label stock. This mailing label report extracts the names and mailing addresses from the database, sorts them into a specified order, and arranges them in whatever label format you choose. The Label Wizard steps you through the process of creating a mailing label report.

Your mailing label report contains the design of the mailing labels—text appearance, layout, and sorting order—but not the actual names and addresses to be printed on the candy box labels. These remain stored in the Customers table of the database, which is updated as needed in the normal course of Sweet Lil's business. Each time the mailing label report is used, Access extracts the current information from the database. The design is saved and reused, but the data will always be current.

In these exercises, you show Henry how to use the Label Wizard to design and print the single-serving candy box labels that he needs, sorted by postal code. He loads the label stock into the printer and sits down to watch you create his labels.

Start the Label Wizard

1   In the Database window, be sure the reports list is displayed.

2   On the Database window toolbar, click the New button.

The New Report dialog box appears.

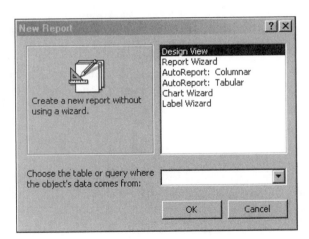

3   In the list at the top of the New Report dialog box, select Label Wizard.

You can press C to jump to tables beginning with C.

④ In the drop-down list at the bottom of the New Report dialog box, select Customers.

The Customers table contains all of Sweet Lil's customer information, including names and addresses.

⑤ Click OK.

The first page of the Label Wizard appears.

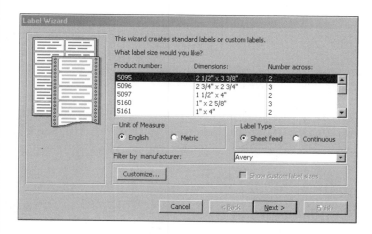

Select a standard mailing label

If none of the listed labels meets your needs, you can define a custom label in the dimensions that match your label stock.

Access comes with an extensive library of standard label formats, listed by manufacturer and dimensions in either English (inch) or metric (millimeter) measurements, for both sheet feed and continuous feed printing.

Henry Czynski tells you that the Avery 5160 1-inch by 2⅝-inch sheet-feed label, with three columns of labels per sheet, is the most suitable label stock for the Sweet Lil's single-serving candy box.

❶ On the first page of the Label Wizard, select 5160 in the Product Number column.

English is already selected as the unit of measurement, Sheet Feed as the label type, and Avery as the manufacturer. Whenever your stock differs from this in the future, you'll select the appropriate values before you select the label size.

2 Click Next.

The second page of the Label Wizard appears.

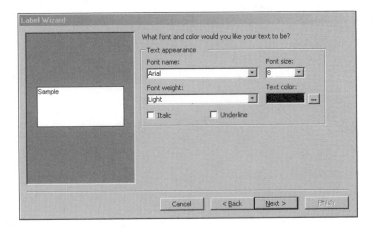

Refining the Look of Labels

For your labels, you can select any font available on your computer and any color available on your default printer. The font selection may vary, depending on the capabilities of the default printer; for example, some printers provide a wider range of point sizes or formatting options, such as bold or italic, for the same font than other printers do.

Define the text appearance of labels

To make the mailing labels look as distinctive and friendly as possible, befitting Sweet Lil's image, Henry suggests using an italic, 9-point Century Gothic Light font.

1 On the second page of the Label Wizard, select Century Gothic Light in the Font Name list.

The font of the word *Sample* in the sample box changes to Century Gothic Light.

important

Century Gothic Light is a standard font in Microsoft Windows 98. If you don't find it in your font list, substitute a font that is available on your computer.

② In the Font Size list, select 9.

The font size of the word *Sample* in the sample box changes to 9 points.

③ Select the Italic check box.

The font style of the word *Sample* in the sample changes to italic text.

④ Click Next.

The third page of the Label Wizard appears.

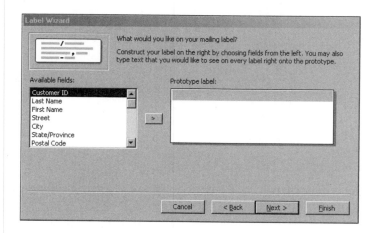

Define the layout of labels

You can select any field from the Customers table and place it on the Label Wizard's prototype label in the order that you want the corresponding information to be printed. Henry confirms that the Sweet Lil's shipping department uses a four-line layout consisting of the customer's full name, followed by a standard two-line address, and the country name. You reproduce that layout here. A shaded bar shows you the line of print you'll be filling in on the label.

tip

The Sweet Lil's layout requires only four lines of text, but the Avery 5160 label holds five lines of 9-point text. This gives you a margin of error, should one of the four lines exceed the length of the smaller-than-usual label format when filled in with the corresponding information.

You can also select the field name and then click Add.

❶ On the third page of the Label Wizard, double-click FirstName in the Available Fields list.

The FirstName field is added to the first line of the prototype label, and the insertion point appears at the end of the field.

❷ Press the Spacebar.

A blank space appears after the FirstName field on the prototype label.

If you make a mistake, select the line on the prototype label and press Backspace to remove your typing.

❸ In the Available Fields list, double-click LastName.

The LastName field is added after the FirstName field on the first line of the prototype label, with a space between the two fields.

❹ At the end of the first line of the prototype label, press Enter.

The insertion point and shaded bar move to the second line of the prototype label.

❺ On the second line, add the Street field, and then press Enter.

❻ On the third line, add the City, State, and Postal Code fields. Type a comma and space between the City and StateOrProvince fields and a space between the StateOrProvince and PostalCode fields, and then press Enter.

❼ On the fourth line, add the Country field.

❽ Click Next.

The fourth page of the Label Wizard appears.

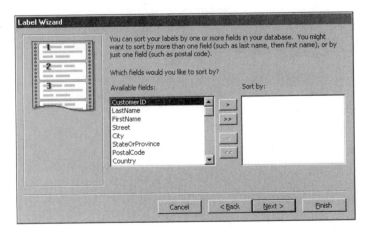

Sorting Labels by Fields

You can sort by any field in the Customers table. You can even sort by multiple fields. For example, you could sort by last name and then first name to get all the labels in alphabetic order by last name and all the labels with the same last name in alphabetic order by first name.

Sort mailing labels

To group together all the boxes addressed to the same area, as Henry requested, you sort the labels by their postal code.

1 On the fourth page of the Label Wizard, double-click PostalCode in the Available Fields list.

The PostalCode field is added to the Sort By list.

2 Click Next.

The final page of the Label Wizard appears. Access 2000 suggests a name, *Labels Customers,* for the mailing labels report and gives you the option of previewing the mailing labels or modifying the label design.

Create a label report and print labels

Now that he's helped to create a label design, you show Henry that he can save the design and print the labels at any time.

1 On the final page of the Label Wizard, be sure the See The Labels As They Will Look Printed option is selected and click Finish.

The mailing label report is saved as Labels Customers and is displayed in Print Preview view.

2 On the Print Preview toolbar, click the Print button.

Access prints the Labels Customers report directly onto the label stock Henry has loaded into the printer.

3 On the Report window, click the Close button to close the report.

Print

Close

One Step Further

Creating More Complex Filters

Six months ago, Impact Public Relations launched a Sweet Lil's marketing campaign in Canada. Now it's time to evaluate how successful it's been, before deciding whether to expand the campaign into the United States. To do this, you can use filters to set criteria for just the Canadian orders that have been placed since the marketing campaign began.

Create a complex filter using Advanced Filter/Sort

The Canadian campaign began on November 15, 1998. To see only the records relevant to the campaign, you must create a filter that shows only Canadian customers added on or after November 15, 1998.

1. In the Database window, click Forms on the Objects bar to display the forms list.

2. In the forms list, double-click Customer Review.

   The Customer Review form opens in Form view.

3. On the Form View toolbar, click the Filter By Form button.

   The Filter By Form dialog box appears, with the Look For tab active. The Filter/Sort toolbar replaces the Database toolbar.

Filter By Form

Filter By Form works differently in Form view than in Datasheet view.

4. Click the Country field, click the drop-down arrow, and then select Canada.

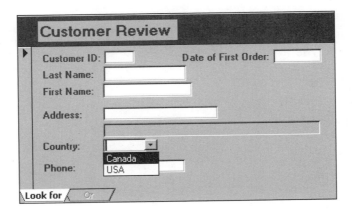

Canada appears as a criterion in the Filter By Form dialog box. You could run a simple filter now by clicking the Apply Filter button on the Filter/Sort toolbar, but you first must add another criterion and set a sort order to get the specific information that you need for your evaluation of Canadian sales data.

5 On the Filter menu, click Advanced Filter/Sort.

The Filter window opens, displaying the filter criteria you set in the Filter By Form dialog box. Now you can add a filter for the order date and sort the filtered records into reverse chronological order.

6 Move to the first empty Field box in the Filter criteria grid. Click the Field drop-down arrow, and then select DateOfFirstOrder.

7 Click in the Sort box below DateOfFirstOrder, click the Sort drop-down arrow, and then select Descending.

An expression is a formula that calculates a value. You'll learn more about expressions in Appendix C, "Using Expressions" on the Microsoft Access 2000 Step by Step CD-ROM.

8 In the Criteria box below the Sort box, type the expression **>=15-Nov-98** and then press Enter.

This expression means *on or after November 15, 1998.* After you enter the expression, Microsoft Access converts it to *>=#11/15/98#* to indicate that it's a date/time value.

9 On the Filter/Sort toolbar, click the Apply/Remove Filter button.

In the filtered view you see only the new orders placed in Canada during the campaign.

10 Close the Customer Review form.

Apply/Remove Filter

Advanced filter criteria are saved for future reference. These criteria will be displayed the next time you use Advanced Filter/Sort. You can accept them or delete them and apply other criteria at that time.

Based on the disappointingly low number of orders in response to the Canadian campaign, you decide not to expand the campaign into the United States.

Finish the lesson

1 To continue to the next lesson, on the File menu, click Close.

2 If you're finished using Access 2000 for now, on the File menu, click Exit.

Lesson 3 Quick Reference

To	Do this	Button
Sort records	Select a field, and then click the appropriate Sort button.	
Set criteria for a filter	Select an example of the criteria on the form or datasheet.	
Set criteria for an advanced filter	In the Filter criteria grid, select a field and enter an expression.	
Apply a filter by selection	Set one criterion per field in the form or datasheet, and then click the Filter By Selection button on the Datasheet View toolbar.	
Apply a filter by form	Set one criterion per field in the form or datasheet, and then click the Filter By Form button on the Datashet View toolbar. Select one item in a field or fields, and then click the Apply Filter button on the Filter/Sort toolbar.	
Remove a filter by form after applying it	Click Remove Filter on the Datasheet View toolbar or Form View toolbar.	
Open a report	Click Reports on the Objects bar of the Database window, and then double-click the report you want.	
Zoom in or out on a report	Click anywhere in the Print Preview view of the report.	
View two pages	Click the Two Pages button on the Print Preview toolbar.	
Print an entire report	Click the Print button on the Print Preview toolbar.	
Print specific report pages	On the File menu, click Print, and then enter the page numbers you want to print.	
Create mailing labels	Click Reports on the Objects bar of the Database window. Click the New button on the Database window toolbar, select Label Wizard, and follow the instructions.	

Review & Practice

**ESTIMATED
TIME
20 min.**

You will review and practice how to:

✔ *Open a database and a form.*

✔ *View and edit data in a form.*

✔ *Find records.*

✔ *Filter records.*

✔ *Sort records.*

✔ *Create a report.*

Before you move on to Part 2, which covers creating and expanding databases, you can practice the skills you learned in Part 1 by working through this Review & Practice section.

Scenario

Charlie Beatty, an administrative assistant in the Sweet Lil's operations department, created the Orders form and subform to enter data into the Orders and Order Details tables. To verify that the Orders form and subform work as intended, you open the form and use it to enter and delete a test record and edit an existing record known to be incorrect. You invite Sweet Lil's shipping clerks to observe as you perform routine tasks such as browsing, entering, and editing data; finding, sorting, and filtering records; and creating a mailing label report.

Step 1:   Open a Database and Browse Through the Data

You must complete the exercises in steps 1 through 6 sequentially.

To verify that the Orders form and subform work as intended, you open the form and browse through the data using the form. The shipping clerks express some confusion over the concept of views, so you demonstrate the differences by switching to Datasheet view and resizing a column to "best fit" the data it contains.

1. Start Microsoft Access, and open the Sweet Lil's database.
2. In the Database window, open the Orders form, and then use the navigation buttons to browse through the records, look at the last record, and return to the first record.
3. Switch to Datasheet view.
4. Change the width of the Street column so you can view the entire field.
5. Switch to Form view.

For more information about	See
Opening a database	Lesson 1
Opening a form	Lesson 1
Using the navigation buttons	Lesson 1
Resizing columns and rows	Lesson 2
Switching between views	Lesson 3

Step 2:   Enter and Edit Data in a Form

The two best tests of a data entry form are to enter a new record and to use the form to edit an existing record. Here the test record is an order for the three boxes that contain fudge bonbons, billed and shipped to the first customer in the database. The record to be edited is the one for order 404. You enter the test record in Form view and then delete it in Datasheet view. You then return to Form view to edit the incorrect order record.

❶ With the Orders form open in Form view, create a new record, and then enter the following information.

Customer ID:	**1**
Date:	[*today's date*]
Order ID:	**414**
Ship To:	[*copy the Bill To information*]
Credit Card:	**World Credit**
Account Number:	**2979**
Expiration Date:	**01-May-00**
Gift:	**No**

Box ID: **NORT**	Quantity: **1**
Box ID: **FUDG**	Quantity: **2**
Box ID: **SWE2**	Quantity: **1**

❷ Switch to Datasheet view, and delete the newly created record for Order ID 414.

❸ Switch to Form view.

❹ Go to the record for Order ID 404, and increase to 2 the number of Cherry Classics boxes.

For more information about	See
Entering data into a form	Lesson 1
Moving from field to field in a form	Lesson 1
Deleting an entire record	Lesson 1
Adding records to a form or subform	Lesson 2
Moving between a main form and subform	Lesson 2

Step 3:   Find Records

You've verified that the Orders form and subform work correctly, but there are a number of routine clerical tasks worth demonstrating for the clerks. The most important of these is finding a specific record. You show the clerks how to find all the orders placed by customers whose last name is Smith.

❶ In the Bill To area of the Orders form, click in the Last Name field.

❷ Find the seven orders placed by customers named Smith: three by Rose, two by Hillary, and one each by Rebecca and Stacey.

❸ Close the Find And Replace dialog box.

For more information about	See
Finding records	Lesson 1

Step 4:   Sort Records

Sorting is one of the most frequently used methods of arranging records. You help out the Sweet Lil's operations department by sorting the order records into reverse chronological order by order date, and then into ascending numerical order by order ID.

1. Click the Order Date field.
2. Sort the records in descending order.
3. Click the Order ID field.
4. Sort the records in ascending order.

For more information about	See
Sorting records	Lesson 3

Step 5:   Apply Filters

One of the clerks expresses a common concern: there's so much data that it's hard to find the necessary records. Upon further questioning, it becomes evident that the clerks need to view only the most recent order records. They note that the majority of their calls come from customers wanting to know if something they ordered for themselves has been shipped yet. You address both concerns by applying filters to view only the records for orders placed after December 1, 1998, and for which the person placing the order is also the person receiving the order.

1. On the Orders form, click the Order Date field.
2. Apply Filter By Form using **>=12/1/98** in the Order Date field as the filter criterion.
3. Type **=[ShipLastName]** in the Last Name field of Bill To.
4. Remove the filter, and then close the Orders form.

For more information about	See
Applying Filter By Form	Lesson 3
Applying Advanced Filter/Sort	Lesson 3

Step 6:   **Create a Mailing Label Report**

The shipping clerks at Sweet Lil's spend much of each day fulfilling orders and mailing candy boxes to their recipients. You show the shipping team how to create a set of mailing labels for all current orders, arranged in the sequence in which the orders were placed.

1   In the Database window, click Reports on the Objects bar, and then click New.

2   Use the Label Wizard to create a mailing label report based on the Orders table, using Avery 5160 labels and Arial 8–point normal weight in the following layout:

{ShipFirstName} {ShipLastName}
{ShipStreet}
{ShipCity} {ShipStateOrProvince} {ShipPostalCode}
{ShipCountry}

3   Sort the report by order ID and name it Shipping Labels.

4   Print a proof page, and then close the mailing label report.

For more information about	See
Using the Label Wizard	Lesson 3

Finish the Review & Practice

1   To continue to the next lesson, on the File menu, click Close.

2   If you're finished using Access 2000 for now, on the File menu, click Exit.

PART 2

Creating and Expanding Databases

4

Managing Database Change

**ESTIMATED
TIME
45 min.**

In this lesson you will learn how to:

- ✔ *Determine when a new table is needed.*
- ✔ *Create a table with the Table Wizard.*
- ✔ *Design and modify a table.*
- ✔ *Define the fields in a table.*
- ✔ *Change field properties.*
- ✔ *Create database relationships.*
- ✔ *Combine data from several related tables.*

The only thing that remains constant is change. Over time, your needs and interests shift as you grow and develop. Information that was once of great importance may become unnecessary or even distracting, while information that was once of no use or interest may suddenly become vital. As the amount of information in your life or business increases, you may need to reorganize or redistribute it in order to keep track of it all. You may find that you must purchase a new bookcase, new file folders, or even an entire set of new file cabinets to cover a new area of interest.

The same is true of your database. When you begin one, the data can be managed almost at a glance, but as the data grows, you must change views or apply filters to make sense of it. When something changes significantly, you may have to modify a portion of the database to track that change. For example, you might have an address table that lists names, street addresses, phone numbers, and fax numbers. It will prove inadequate after you start making contacts through the Web unless you can add new fields for e-mail addresses and Web sites.

Sweet Lil's has grown to the point that it's having trouble meeting customer needs. The management has identified the problem but needs you to implement the solution. In this lesson, you'll create a new database table, define its fields, add and modify fields to meet changing needs, and create new relationships within a database.

Start Microsoft Access 2000 and reopen the database

●   If Access 2000 isn't started yet, start it. Open the Sweet Lil's database. If the Microsoft Access window doesn't fill your screen, maximize the window.

     If you need help opening the database, see Lesson 1, "Using Forms."

Modifying Database Tables

For more information about database creation and design, see Appendix B, "Matching the Exercises" on the Microsoft Access 2000 Step by Step CD-ROM.

When your database doesn't include information that you need to track, it's time to expand it. This may be as simple as adding a new field or even just a single new record to an existing table. It might, however, involve creating an entirely new table.

Often you'll add a new table to an existing database in response to some new or unforeseen need. In most cases, the nature of the need dictates the organization of the new information.

For example, the Sweet Lil's database is currently organized into 11 tables, each of which covers a different topic or entity within the database—baskets, basket details, bonbons, boxes, box details, customers, credit customers, employees, orders, order details, and shipping. Each record in each table describes an individual unit or unique item of that entity, such as a particular customer or a certain type of bonbon. Each field in each record describes a different characteristic or attribute of that item—the name of a particular customer or the filling in a certain type of bonbon.

Whenever you create a table, ideally you should already have the entity it represents clearly in mind, along with a concise definition of all the fields needed for each record. Each record should contain all the information needed to describe the item it represents. You will be designing a better table by defining the fields needed, determining the type of data you want to store, and thinking about special restrictions or field properties.

Sweet Lil's is growing rapidly, but so are customer demands. Customers expect gift orders to be delivered within two or three days. To meet these demands, Sweet Lil's must speed up delivery.

The shipping coordinator, Fred Mallon, determined that the main bottleneck in delivery was the reliance on a single shipping company. He has made arrangements with two more companies, both offering air delivery service, to eliminate the bottleneck and expedite deliveries. Fred has been using a Shipping table to store each company's shipping costs to various regions, but there's currently no address information on the companies themselves. Adding that information to the existing Shipping table would be inefficient, because one carrier can have many different shipping charges depending on where the item is shipped, so the same address information would have to be entered many times. This indicates that the information Fred needs is not directly relevant to the Shipping table—what he needs is a new table.

Fred requires the new table for tracking information on the three shipping companies Sweet Lil's now uses. This new Carriers table should be linked to the existing Shipping table so that cost information is available if needed, without compromising the existing table.

In the following exercises, you'll show Fred how to create the new Carriers table using the Table Wizard and working in Design view. You will also show him how to create a relationship between the Carriers and Shipping tables.

Using the Table Wizard

Access 2000 can help you create a new table. Using the Table Wizard is a quick way to add a new table to an existing database. You can select the fields that reflect the attributes of each item in the new table. If you don't think of all the fields you need while working in the Table Wizard field list, you can add them later in Design view.

Standard Field Naming Convention

Although Access 2000 allows spaces and punctuation in field names, there's a standardized naming convention to which your field names must conform if you plan to use your data in other database programs. Since you can't be sure when you might need to share data, you should use only letters and numbers, without spaces or punctuation, in field names.

For database programs (like Access) that allow mixed uppercase and lowercase letters, multiple-word field names use capitalization to distinguish words in a field name. For example, First Name would be FirstName, with the two words in the field name distinguished by capitalization. For database programs that use only uppercase letters, multiple-word field names use the underscore (_) character to separate words in a field name. For example, First Name would be FIRST_NAME, with the two words in the field name separated by an underscore instead of a space.

The name that appears on the form label or datasheet column heading does not need to be the same as the field name. Each field has a Caption property, which determines the name that's displayed as a label or column heading. For example, a CustID field with a Caption property set to Customer ID will display Customer ID on forms and datasheets, but it will still use CustID as the actual field name for queries and relationships.

Create a table using the Table Wizard

In this exercise, you show Fred how to use the Table Wizard to add a Carriers table to the Sweet Lil's database. Fred has prepared for creating the new table by listing the relevant attributes that describe a shipping company's address: the company's name, a street address, a city, a state or province, and a postal code. With this clear definition in hand, you are now ready to create the new Carriers table for Fred.

1 In the Database window, click Tables on the Objects bar to display the tables list.

2 In the tables list, double-click Create Table By Using Wizard.

The first page of the Table Wizard appears.

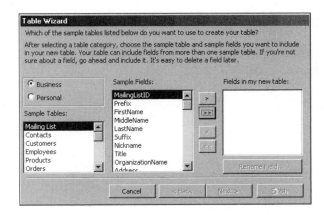

3 On the first page of the Table Wizard, be sure the Business option is selected, and in the Sample Tables list, select Suppliers.

4 In the Sample Fields list, double-click the fields that most closely match Fred's list.

Fred's List	Sample Field
Carrier Name	SupplierName
Street Address	Address
City Address	City
State Address	StateOrProvince
Postal Code	PostalCode

As you select each field, it appears in the Fields In My New Table list.

5 In the Fields In My New Table list, select SupplierName, and then click Rename Field.

The Rename Field dialog box appears.

6 In the Rename Field dialog box, type **CarrierName**, then press Enter..

The Rename Field dialog box closes.

7 Repeat steps 5 and 6, changing the StateOrProvince field name to **State**, and then click Next.

The second page of the Table Wizard appears, with Suppliers selected in the What Do You Want To Name Your Table? box.

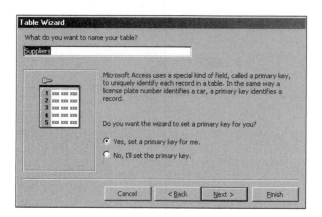

8 In the What Do You Want To Name Your Table? box, type **Carriers**

9 Be sure the Yes, Set A Primary Key For Me option is selected, and then click Next.

The third page of the Table Wizard dialog box appears. You tell Fred that at this point the Carriers table doesn't require any relationship with any other table.

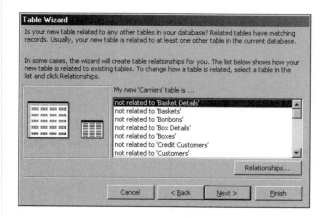

⑩ Click Next again, and when the last page of the Table Wizard appears, click Finish.

The Carriers table opens in Datasheet view. The new table contains all the fields you selected, plus an automatically numbered CarriersID field, which is set as the primary key. Every record will now have a unique identification number, represented by the contents of the CarriersID field.

CarriersID	CarrierName	Address	City	State	Postal Code
(AutoNumber)					

Record: ◄◄ ◄ 1 ► ►► ►* of 1

⑪ Close the Carriers table.

The Primary Key

A *primary key* is a field or group of fields that uniquely identifies each record in a table. No two records in a given table can have the same value in their primary key field. An employee identification number is often used as a primary key in accounting systems because every employee must have an one, and every one is unique.

Primary key fields serve a number of purposes. Because the primary key field uniquely identifies each record in the table, the primary key is used to create a *relationship* between tables, allowing all the records in one table to be matched to the records in another. In the absence of a specific sort order, records in a table are sorted by the primary key field.

A primary key can consist of one or more fields. Multiple-field primary keys are used when the value in the field chosen as the primary key can't be unique. For example, the Shipping table lists each carrier more than once because each carrier has a different charge for each area, so the carrier doesn't uniquely identify a record. But, because there's only one delivery route from a given carrier to a given area, the combination of carrier and area does uniquely identify a record.

Access 2000 has an *AutoNumber* feature that assigns a unique number to each record as it's created. AutoNumber fields are thus well suited for use as primary keys. It's usually easiest and safest to let Access 2000 use the AutoNumber field as the primary key.

Managing Database Change 4

Changing a Table in Design View

With Access, you have a number of ways to create new tables—letting the Table Wizard guide you, using Design view, and even typing directly into a blank datasheet. No matter which approach you take, at some point you will probably need to change a table design. The best place to make these changes is in Design view.

Now that you have finished creating the Carriers table using the Table Wizard, Fred has asked you to show him how to add a field that will indicate whether the shipping company provides air delivery service. In the following exercises, you show Fred how to add the AirDelivery field in Design view.

Add a field in Design view

1   In the Database window, verify that Tables on the Objects bar is selected.

2   In the tables list, verify Carriers is selected, and then click the Design button on the Database window toolbar.

The Carriers table opens in Design view, with the names and data types of the Carriers table fields listed in the grid in the upper portion of the window. The properties of the selected field are shown in the Field Properties in the lower portion of the window. The Table Design toolbar replaces the Database toolbar.

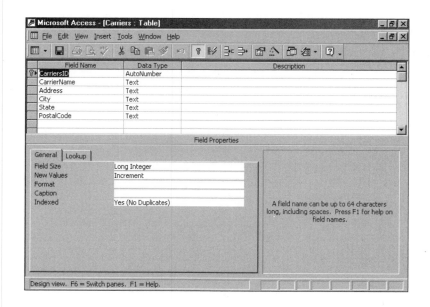

3 In the grid, scroll down to the first empty row and click the Field Name cell of the first empty row.

The triangular record indicator appears in the record selector.

4 Type **AirDelivery** and then press Tab.

When you press Tab, the selected word *Text* and a drop-down arrow appear in the Data Type cell of that row. Information about that field also appears in the property sheet.

5 In the Data Type cell of the AirDelivery row, click the drop-down arrow, and then select Yes/No.

The data type changes to Yes/No. The change is reflected in the property sheet.

6 On the Table Design toolbar, click the Save button.

The changes are saved, but you want to show them to Fred.

7 On the Table Design toolbar, click the View button to switch to Datasheet view.

The new field, containing a check box, now appears in the datasheet. You may need to scroll to the right to see the new field.

Save

View

Entering Data Using an AutoForm

With the Carriers table now complete, Fred is ready to enter the data he's compiled for the first three carriers. You remind him that data should always be entered using a form, and you tell him that data entry forms are easy to create. Because his form is very basic, requiring no special formatting or controls, he can use the AutoForm feature to create the form.

> # important
> In the following exercise, you can edit as much as necessary within a record, but be careful not to delete a record and begin it all over again. If you enter one record, delete it, and then re-enter it, the CarrierID number will be different than intended. Understanding the data type of autonumber will explain this. An autonumber data type does the work of entering a unique, sequential number into a field. It increments by 1 for each record and never reuses a value once it is deleted. In the Carriers table, the CarrierID uses the autonumber data type. Since CarrierID is also the primary key field for the record, it is the unique identifier. When relating tables, the primary key field is used to link two tables that share a common field. The contents of the common field must be identical. For this reason, be careful in the following exercise not to delete a record in the Carriers table. You will learn more about protecting your data in Lesson 5, "Keeping Database Information Reliable."

Create an AutoForm and enter data

New Object:
AutoForm

❶ On the Datasheet View toolbar, click the New Object: AutoForm button.

The new Carriers form appears with (AutoNumber) already selected in the CarriersID field. The Table Design toolbar becomes the Form View toolbar and the Formatting toolbar appears below it. On the Form View toolbar, the New Object: AutoForm button becomes the New Object: Table button.

tip

The New Object toolbar button can create any Access 2000 object: AutoForm, AutoReport, AutoPage, table, query, form, report, page, macro, module, or class module. Like the View toolbar button, the New Object button and the corresponding ScreenTip change when you change views.

Because the CarriersID is already assigned in the Shipping table, the carriers must be entered in the same order to create a match.

❷ Press Tab to move to the CarrierName field, and type **Wild Fargo Carriers**

When you start typing, the CarriersID field is filled in automatically.

❸ Fill out the rest of the form, pressing Tab to move from field to field. (For this record, leave the AirDelivery check box clear to indicate No; press Tab twice to skip over it and start a new record.)

Address:	**410 NE 84th Street**
City:	**Chicago**
State:	**IL**
PostalCode:	**606574512**
AirDelivery:	No

The predefined PostalCode field is already formatted for ZIP+4—the numbers are automatically separated into two groups.

❹ Enter the information for the two remaining carrier records. To select the AirDelivery check box, press the Spacebar.

CarrierName:	**Grey Goose Express**	**Pegasus Overnight**
Address:	**100 Day Street**	**45908 Airport Way**
City:	**New York**	**Dallas**
State:	**NY**	**TX**
PostalCode:	**123781701**	**786545908**
AirDelivery:	Yes	Yes

AutoForm allows you to create a form whenever you need one. You can discard the AutoForm when you're finished with it.

5 Close the new Carriers form.

A message appears, confirming that you want to save the changes to the new form.

6 Click No.

The new Carriers form closes, and the Carriers table reappears in Datasheet view.

Refresh the table data

Fred is impressed with the AutoForm feature, but when the new Carriers form closes he's puzzled—the Carriers table is still empty! Where are the three new records you just entered?

You explain that because the Carriers table was still open while you were entering the data, the table displayed on the screen is no longer current. The simplest way to update the data in the table is to close and open the table.

1 Close the Carriers table.

2 In the tables list of the Database window, double-click Carriers.

The Carriers table appears, displaying three new records.

Improving Data Entry and Display

Access 2000 sets *properties*, or attributes, of a field to define the characteristics of the field and how data is entered and displayed in the field. When you create a table using the Table Wizard or a form using the Form Wizard or AutoForm, Access 2000 sets many of the field properties for you. For example, when you selected the predefined PostalCode field from the Table Wizard, the field was already formatted for ZIP+4. The most visible properties of a field are its data type and its display format.

The *data type* is another kind of attribute. It establishes the kind of data that the field can accept—text, numbers, dates and times, yes-or-no data, monetary amounts—or whether it can accept user-entered data at all. For example, the AutoNumber data type fills the field with a predetermined number that can't be changed.

Each data type has a set of associated properties. For example, the Text and Number data types have a Field Size property that sets the maximum number of letters or the type of number that you can store in the field. The Yes/No data type doesn't have a Field Size property, however, because it can accept only two values.

The *display format* determines how the data is displayed and printed. This format is often associated with the data type. For example, the Text, Memo, Number, Currency, Date/Time, and Yes/No data types have predefined formats that are also associated with the regional settings determined in the Control Panel. These predefined formats can be changed at any time or overridden entirely by changing the properties of the field in which the data is displayed. For example, by changing the Format field property, a Yes/No text box can be made to display True and False or On and Off instead.

Other properties might also affect the display format. For example, a field with a Yes/No data type can be displayed as a check box, a text box, or a combo box by changing the Display Control field property.

important

Changing the Display Control field property changes only the format of the data as it is entered into the form. The format in which data is presented to or accepted from the user is independent of the format in which Access 2000 processes it. For example, the currency format displays an entry as a monetary value of $4.81 even if it was entered as 4.8142. Access stores the value as entered and displays it according to the format.

Set field properties

Fred has a problem with the new Carriers table: it's too easy to accidentally select or clear the AirDelivery check box with a stray click of the mouse. He likes the idea of an either-or control, but he'd prefer that at least two steps be required to change it, not just a single mouse click or space bar. He'd also prefer to see the words *Yes* and *No* when looking up the information. In this exercise, you help Fred turn the check box into a combo box by changing the Display Control field property.

1. Verify that the Carriers table is displayed in Datasheet view.
2. Click the View button on the Table Datasheet toolbar.
3. In the grid, click anywhere in the AirDelivery row.

   The AirDelivery field properties appear in the Field Properties.

View

❹ In the Field Properties, click the Lookup tab.

Check Box appears in the Display Control property box.

❺ In the Display Control property box, select Combo Box.

After you have set the Display Control property to Combo Box, the default control in the table and on any new forms based on the table becomes a combo box. The Field Properties reflects this change, displaying nine other properties that apply to combo boxes (and not to check boxes).

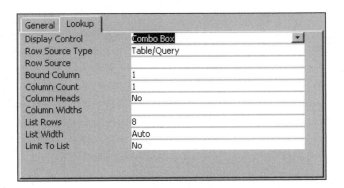

General	Lookup
Display Control	Combo Box
Row Source Type	Table/Query
Row Source	
Bound Column	1
Column Count	1
Column Heads	No
Column Widths	
List Rows	8
List Width	Auto
Limit To List	No

❻ In the Row Source Type property box, select Value List.

This tells Access 2000 to use a predefined list of values in the combo box.

❼ In the Row Source property box, type **No;Yes**

This creates the predefined list of values for the combo box: No or Yes, with No as the default value.

❽ Save your changes, and then click the View button on the Table Design toolbar to switch to Datasheet view.

The words *Yes* and *No* now appear in the AirDelivery field. You may need to scroll to the right to view the field.

New Object: AutoForm

❾ On the Table Datasheet toolbar, click the New Object: AutoForm button to create a form for testing the new AirDelivery combo box in Form view.

The AirDelivery field is now a combo box that lets you select Yes or No.

❿ Close the test form without saving it, and then close the Carriers table.

Connecting a New Table to a Database

When you add a new table, it's important that you understand how the new table will interact with existing tables. For the data in the table to be useful, you must incorporate it into the database by establishing logical links or *relationships* to other tables. Relationships are used to collect data from several tables and place them in a single form, report, or query. Once you do create a relationship between specific tables, you can use the relationship to combine data from one table with data in the other table, following the lines of that relationship.

For example, the relationships between the Bonbons, Basket Details, and Baskets tables allow information from the Bonbons and Basket Details tables to be combined into the Baskets subform and added to the Baskets form. When a bonbon ID for a given basket is selected in the Baskets subform, the corresponding bonbon name, chocolate type, filling type, nut type, and cost are drawn from the related Bonbons table, and the corresponding quantity is drawn from the related Basket Details table. The BonbonCost and Quantity fields are then used to calculate the total basket cost on the Baskets form.

Understanding Table Relationships

Access 2000 creates *relational databases:* databases that combine data from multiple tables. It does this by means of relationships between the various tables of a database. After you create tables and let Access 2000 set a primary key for each table, you can create relationships between the tables to collect data from several tables and place it all in a single form, report, or query.

Between two tables, you can create one of two types of relationship: one-to-many or one-to-one.

The most common relationship is the *one-to-many* relationship, in which one record in one table can be related to many records in another table. For example, one customer can place many orders; each record in the Customers table can therefore be related to many records in the Orders table. In a one-to-many relationship, the table on the "one" side is termed the *primary table*, and the table on the "many" side is the *related table*. In the above example, the Customers table is the primary table and the Orders table is the related table.

A table can be the related table in one relationship and the primary table in a different relationship.

The primary table in the relationship can have many matching records in the related table. Creating a link between the primary key field in the primary table and a field that has a matching value—called a *foreign key* field—in the related table is what establishes the relationship between the two. For example, the CarriersID field in the Carriers table matches the CarriersID field in the Shipping table, so a relationship can be made between the two tables. One carrier can have many different shipping charges, depending on where the item is being shipped, so the Carriers table is the primary table in a one-to-many relationship with the related Shipping table.

In the far less common one-to-one relationship, one record in the primary table can have at most one matching record in the related table. For example, a new table of bonbon recipes could only have a *one-to-one* relationship with the existing Bonbons table, because the recipe for each bonbon is unique.

For more information about creating and enforcing referential integrity, see Lesson 5, "Keeping Database Information Reliable."

Access 2000 uses a system of rules to create *referential integrity* between tables, which ensures that relationships between records in related tables are valid and that you don't accidentally delete or change related data. For example, you must match a carrier in the Carriers table for every shipping charge in the Shipping table to enable the relationship between the two tables to work properly. Referential integrity prohibits any changes to the primary table that would invalidate records in the related table. Referential integrity also prevents the entry of a related record that doesn't have an associated primary record. For instance, it prevents the entry of an order record for a customer that does not exist in the database. A record without an associated primary record is called an *orphan*.

After you create a relationship between two tables, you can't modify or delete the fields on which the relationship is based without first deleting the relationship.

Creating a Relationship

The primary tool for creating and managing relationships in Access 2000 is the Relationships window. It lets you create simple relationships, and it is ideally suited for creating complex relationships, especially when:

- Referential integrity is required.
- The primary key includes more than one field.
- There's no matching field common to the two tables.

The Relationships window allows you to join matching fields that have either the same or different names, and to see the relationships that you create in a graphical, "big picture" overview.

The Shipping table has information about the cost to ship from one region to another and the Carriers table has information about the shipping companies. To find out how much it costs to deliver a box of bonbons, you must know where and by whom it's being shipped. Since the shipping charge is the amount charged by a given carrier to ship to a given area, and each carrier ships to more than one area, the procedure for finding the charge is to look up the carrier, then the area, and then the charge. Each carrier serves many areas, with a different charge for each area, so there's a one-to-many relationship between the Carriers information and the Shipping information.

To combine the new information about the carriers with the existing information about the shipping charges, Fred must establish a relationship between the new Carriers table and the existing Shipping table. In the following exercises, you help Fred create a one-to-many relationship between the Carriers and Shipping tables, using the Relationships window and Relationship toolbar.

Show Table button

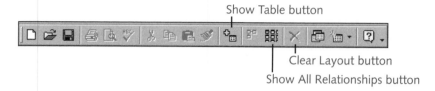

Clear Layout button
Show All Relationships button

Lay out tables in the Relationships window

Before Fred adds, alters, or deletes a relationship between the Carriers and Shipping tables, he needs to know what relationships (if any) already exist. In this exercise, you show Fred how to open the Relationships window and lay out the Carriers and Shipping tables. The Relationships window will show him how the two tables are related.

1 Verify that all tables and forms are closed.

2 On the Database toolbar, click the Relationships button.

The Relationships window opens. The Relationship toolbar replaces the Database toolbar.

Relationships

3 If anything appears in the Relationships window, click the Clear Layout button on the Relationship toolbar, and then click Yes in the confirmation message.

The Relationships window should be empty before you begin.

Clear Layout

4 On the Relationship toolbar, click the Show Table button.

The Show Table dialog box appears.

Show Table

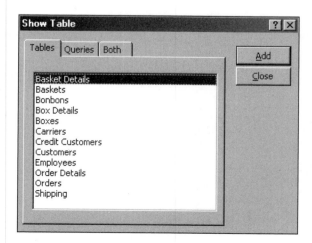

⑤ In the Show Table dialog box, be sure the Tables tab is active, and then double-click Carriers in the tables list.

The Carriers field list appears in the Relationships window, with the CarriersID primary key field selected.

⑥ In the Show Table dialog box, double-click the Shipping table.

The Shipping field list appears in the Relationships window, with the CarriersID primary key field selected. (This field will be the foreign key in this relationship.) If the table is not visible, drag the Show Table dialog box aside.

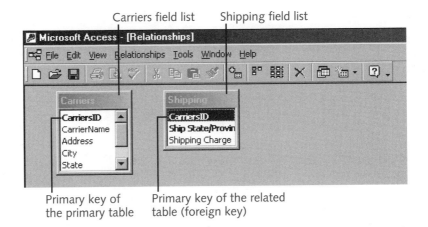

Carriers field list   Shipping field list

Primary key of   Primary key of the related
the primary table   table (foreign key)

⑦ Close the Show Table dialog box.

Create a relationship between two tables

To combine the new information about the carriers with the existing information about the shipping charges, Fred must establish a relationship between the new Carriers table and the existing Shipping table. In this exercise, you show Fred how to relate the Carriers and Shipping tables.

important

In this exercise, the direction in which you drag the key field determines which is the primary table and which is the related table. The table from which you drag the field is always set as the primary table, and the table to which you drag the field is always set as the related table.

Managing Database Change | 4

❶ In the Relationships window, drag the CarriersID field from the Carriers field list to the CarriersID field in the Shipping field list.

The Edit Relationships dialog box appears, and One-To-Many appears in the Relationship Type box.

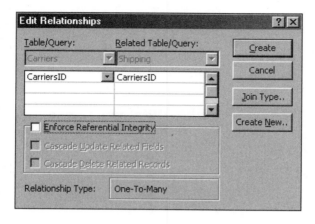

Referential integrity prevents orphan records.

❷ In the Edit Relationships dialog box, select the Enforce Referential Integrity check box.

❸ Click Create.

The Edit Relationships dialog box closes. The Carriers table is now related to the Shipping table, as indicated by a line linking the matching fields in both tables. Near the line, the *1* beside the Carriers field list and the ∞ (infinity symbol) beside the Shipping field list show that it's a one-to-many relationship. The relationship remains intact until you delete it.

To delete a relationship, click the line linking the related fields, and then press Delete.

The layout in the Relationships window is a visual aid. Saving or deleting the layout has no effect on the database.

❹ Close the Relationships window.

A message appears, confirming that you want to save changes to the Relationships layout.

❺ Click Yes.

The layout you just created is saved and will reappear whenever you open the Relationships window, until you clear or modify the layout and save those changes.

Relate a multiple-field primary key to a matching key

Now that he's created a relationship between the Carriers and Shipping tables, Fred realizes that a similar relationship between the Shipping table and the Orders table would make it possible to automate the process of looking up an order's shipping charge. The CarriersID and ShipStateOrProvince fields in the Orders table can be used to find the related carrier name in the Carriers table and the related shipping charge in the Shipping table.

To create a relationship between the Shipping and Orders tables, you must relate the primary key of the Shipping table to the related key in the Orders table. The primary key of the Shipping table consists of *two* fields—CarriersID and ShipStateOrProvince—because the primary key has to be unique. Shipping charges are based on both the carrier and the delivery area, so both must be included in the key. The Shipping table lists the same carrier and the same delivery area multiple times because each carrier has a different charge for each area. But because there's only one delivery route from a given carrier to a given area, the combination of carrier and area is unique.

To create a relationship when the primary table has a multiple-field primary key, you must relate all the fields of the primary key in the primary table to matching fields in the related table. (The related table must already have fields that match those of the primary table key.)

In this exercise, you show Fred how to create a relationship between the multiple-field primary key of the Shipping table and the matching data in the Orders tables.

1 On the Database toolbar, click the Relationships button.

2 On the Relationship toolbar, click the Show Table button.

The Show Table dialog box appears.

Show Table

3 In the Show Table dialog box, click the Tables tab, double-click the Orders table, and then close the Show Table dialog box.

The Orders field list appears in the Relationships window, with the OrderID primary key selected.

Fields with different names can be related as long as their data type and field size are the same.

4 In the Relationships window, drag the CarriersID field from the Shipping field list to the CarriersID field in the Orders field list.

The Edit Relationships dialog box appears, and Indeterminate appears in the Relationship Type box.

5 In the Table/Query list, click the first empty field below the CarriersID field.

A drop-down arrow appears next to the empty field.

You can relate any number of matching fields between the primary and related tables.

6 Click the drop-down arrow next to the empty field, and then select ShipStateOrProvince from the list.

7 In the Related Table/Query list, click the first empty field below the CarriersID field, and then select ShipStateOrProvince from the list.

One-To-Many appears in the Relationship Type box.

Because it's impossible to maintain full correspondence between the ShipStateOr Province fields in both tables here, Enforce Referential Integrity should not be selected.

8 In the Edit Relationships dialog box, click Create.

The Edit Relationships dialog box closes. The CarriersID and ShipStateOrProvince fields in the Shipping table are now related to the matching fields in the Orders table. You may have to scroll through or resize the Orders list to view the relationship between the two fields.

9 Close the Relationships window and save the layout.

One Step Further — Combining Data from Related Tables Using a Query

For more information about creating and using queries, see Lesson 7, "Using Queries."

Fred has created a relationship between the Carriers and Shipping tables and another relationship between the Shipping and Orders tables. Because of the interrelationships among these three tables, he can now automate the process of looking up a shipping charge by drawing upon information in all three tables simultaneously using a *query*. A query works much like a filter, showing only the fields that contain information of interest, but a query can combine fields from two or more tables by following the chain of relationships between them.

To automatically look up the appropriate shipping charge for a given order, Fred must create a query that combines related information from the Carriers, Shipping, and Orders tables. The query can use the CarrierID and ShipStateOrProvince fields in the Orders table to find the related carrier name in the Carriers table and the related shipping charge in the Shipping table.

Use a query to combine data from related tables

In this exercise, you show Fred how to combine data from the Carriers, Shipping, and Orders tables, using a query.

1 In the Database window, click Queries on the Objects bar to open the queries list.

2 In the queries list, double-click Create Query By Using Wizard.

The first page of the Simple Query Wizard appears.

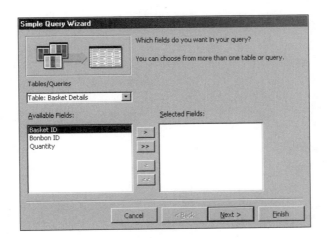

3 In the Tables/Queries list of the Simple Query Wizard, select Table: Orders.

The fields of the Orders table appear in the Available Fields list.

4 In the Available Fields list, double-click OrderID.

The OrderID field from the Orders table appears in the Selected Fields list.

Access 2000 uses the relationships you created to combine the fields from all of the related tables.

5 In the Tables/Queries list, select Table: Carriers, and then in the Available Fields list, double-click CarrierName.

The CarrierName field from the Carriers table appears in the Selected Fields list.

6 In the Tables/Queries list, select Table: Shipping, and then in the Available Fields list, double-click ShippingCharge.

The ShippingCharge field from the Shipping table appears in the Selected Fields list.

7   Click Next.

The second page of the Simple Query Wizard appears.

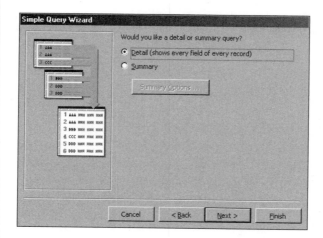

8   Be sure the Detail (Shows Every Field Of Every Record) option is selected, and then click Next.

The third page of the Simple Query Wizard appears.

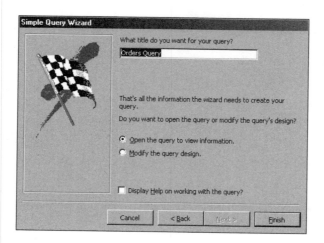

9   Be sure the Open The Query To View Information option is selected. In the What Title Do You Want For Your Query? box, type **Carriers Information** and then click Finish.

The new Carriers Information query opens, displaying the order ID, carrier name, and shipping cost for every order in the Orders table.

⑩ Close the Carriers Information query.

The query was saved automatically when it was created, so the Carriers Information query will appear in the queries list of the Database window.

Finish the lesson

❶ To continue to the next lesson, on the File menu, click Close.

❷ If you're finished using Access 2000 for now, on the File menu, click Exit.

Lesson 4 Quick Reference

To	Do this	Button
Create a table	In the Database window, click Tables on the Objects bar, double-click Create Table By Using Wizard, and follow the instructions.	
Add a field	Open the table in Design view, type a field name in the first empty row, and then select a data type.	
Create an AutoForm to add data to a new table	With the table in Datasheet view, click the New Object: AutoForm button on the Datasheet toolbar.	
Set a field property	In Table Design view, select a field in the grid, and then change the setting in the appropriate property box of the property sheet.	
Create a relationship between two tables	Click the Relationships button on the Database toolbar. Click the Show Table button on the Relationship toolbar. In the Show Table dialog box, add the primary and related tables. In the Relationships window, drag the primary key field from the primary table to the matching key field of the related table. In the Edit Relationships dialog box, select the Enforce Referential Integrity check box, and then click Create.	
Delete a relationship between two tables	In the Relationships window, click the line connecting the tables, and then press Delete.	
Combine data from related tables using a query	In the Database window, click Queries on the Objects bar. Double-click Create Query By Using Wizard, and follow the instructions.	

Managing Database Change

4

5

Keeping Database Information Reliable

In this lesson you will learn how to:

✔ *Add data validation checks and messages.*

✔ *Use form controls to increase data entry accuracy.*

✔ *Set field properties to strengthen data validation.*

✔ *Ensure related tables always contain correct data.*

✔ *View and edit related tables or queries in a subdatasheet.*

✔ *Recognize many-to-many relationships.*

"Garbage in, garbage out" is the motto of the data processing professional. The information that you get out of a database is only as good as the data you put into it. Bad data is often worse than no data at all. In Microsoft Access, database reliability is realized by conscientiously applying data validation and referential integrity.

Data validation is the system of rules that Access 2000 uses to reduce or even eliminate the possibility of error as data is being entered into a database. Data validation can be applied by using the appropriate controls on a form or by setting the appropriate properties on a field. For example, using a list box control on a form restricts the data that can be entered to one of the items on the list, greatly reducing the opportunity for error. Setting an AutoNumber data type property on a number field in a table automatically fills that field with the next sequential number, so there's no possibility of error.

To review information on creating database relationships, see Lesson 4, "Managing Database Change."

Referential integrity is the system of rules that Access 2000 uses to be sure that relationships between records in related tables are valid, and that changes made in one table are properly applied to a related table. For example, when you delete the record on a customer from the Customers table, all of the order records in the related Orders table should also be deleted, unless a related order is still pending.

To assist Sweet Lil's adoption of Microsoft Access 2000, Impact Public Relations' data manager Becky Sawyer conducted a complete audit of Sweet Lil's data processing operations. The database portion of Becky's research revealed that Sweet Lil's could improve a number of areas. Becky suggests applying data validation checks, or rules, to certain forms or fields, changing the way data is entered into certain forms or fields, enforcing referential integrity between related tables, and coordinating changes in related tables. Becky has asked you to help her implement these improvements.

Start Microsoft Access 2000 and reopen the database

● If Access 2000 isn't started yet, start it. Open the Sweet Lil's database. If the Microsoft Access window doesn't fill your screen, maximize the window.

   If you need help opening the database, see Lesson 1, "Using Forms."

Validating Data in a Form

Access 2000 displays data within graphical objects: forms, queries, reports, data access pages, and tables. These objects are made up of smaller objects—controls—that accept, display, or locate the data. Everything that you see on a form is a control. All data is entered into a form through a form control. By changing the properties of a form control or replacing one control with another, you can change the way data is entered into the form. For example, you can restrict the information that can be entered into a field by changing the field from a text box to a list box, in which only predefined items can be selected.
By limiting what can be entered, you reduce the opportunity for error.

Impact Public Relations' Becky Sawyer recommended a number of improvements to the Orders form that will both increase data validation and streamline data entry. In these exercises, you add a data validation check, replace a text box control with a list box control, set a default value, and change the tab order on the Orders form.

For a demonstration of how to add a data validation check to a form control, in the Multimedia folder on the Microsoft Access 2000 Step by Step CD-ROM, double-click Validation-Check.

Add a data validation check

Becky's research showed that credit transactions could be placed using expired credit cards. She recommended adding a validation rule to check credit card expiration dates as they're being entered into the Orders form. At Sweet Lil's you make the change, adding a data validation rule to the Expiration Date text box control on the Orders form.

> ## tip
>
> On the Orders form, the Expiration Date text box displays only the month and year. This format matches the expiration date format as it appears on the credit card, but you must enter a full date with a day, month, and year to satisfy the needs of the credit tracking program. Expiration dates will always be the first or fifteenth of the month.

1   In the Database window, click Forms on the Objects bar.

2   In the forms list, select Orders, and then click the Design button on the Database window toolbar.

The Orders form opens in Design view. The Form Design toolbar replaces the Database toolbar and the Formatting toolbar appears just below it.

If the toolbox is blocking your view, you can click its title bar and drag the toolbox out of your way.

If the Orders field list is open, close it.

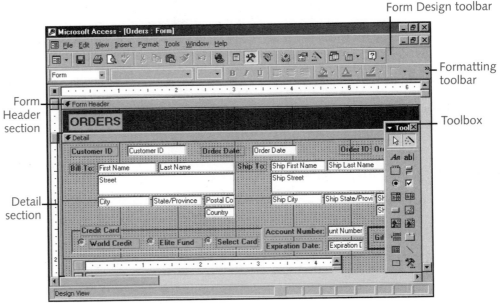

3 In the Orders form detail section, click the ExpirationDate text box.

Small blocks, called sizing handles, appear surrounding the text box and its label to select them.

Properties

4 On the Form Design toolbar, click the Properties button.

The Text Box property sheet appears.

5 In the property sheet, click the Data tab.

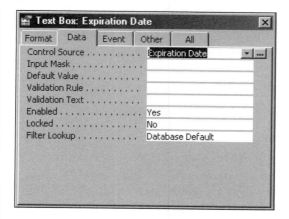

For more information on expressions and how to use them, see Appendix C, "Using Expressions" on the Microsoft Access 2000 Step by Step CD-ROM.

6 In the Validation Rule property box, type the expression **>=now** and press Enter.

The expression is converted to >=Now() to indicate that it's a function. The Now() function, which is built into Microsoft Access, retrieves the current date and time. In plain language, the validation rule is: "The expiration date must be either today or later."

7 In the Validation Text property box, type **Invalid date! Please check the order and re-enter.** and press Enter.

Whatever you type into the Validation Text property box appears as a message whenever the validation rule is broken.

Save

8 On the Form Design toolbar, click the Save button.

Access 2000 can now check any date entered in the Expiration Date field and display the validation text for any date in the past.

9 Close the Text Box property sheet.

The new validation rule and message are now in place.

Test the new data validation check

Testing is the only way to be sure that any change to a field property has the intended effect. In this exercise, you test the data validation check by entering invalid data.

View

New Record

① On the Form Design toolbar, click the View button to switch to Form view.

The Orders form reappears in Form view, and the Form View toolbar replaces the Form Design toolbar.

② On the Form View toolbar, click the New Record button.

A new blank record appears.

③ On the Orders form, type **9/1/98** in the Expiration Date field, and press Enter.

The validation text appears as a message.

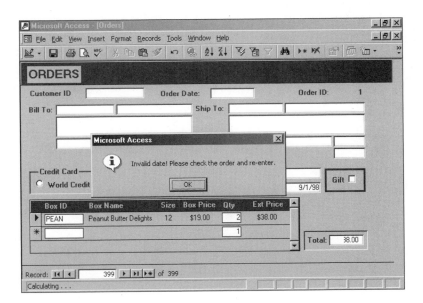

④ Click OK.

⑤ On the Orders form, type **12/1/04** in the Expiration Date field, and press Enter.

This entry is accepted as a valid date (December 01, 2004).

A message appears, telling you that Access 2000 can't find a record in the Customers table that matches one in the CustomerID primary key field. This happens because the test record is purposely incomplete and the key data is missing.

⑥ Click OK.

7 Close the Orders form.

The message appears again, telling you that Access 2000 can't find a record in the Customers table that matches one in the CustomerID primary key field.

8 Click OK.

A message appears, confirming that the new record won't be saved. This is a built-in Access 2000 safety feature that prevents you from adding records that are missing key information.

9 Click Yes.

The new record is discarded, and the Orders form closes.

tip

It's a good idea to set properties for a field in an underlying table before you create a form based on that table. Changing form control properties directly is a quick and easy way to improve data reliability on a particular form, but the benefit is usually confined to that form. If you change the property setting for a field in a table or query after you've created a form by using that field, the property setting for the control isn't updated, and you must update it manually. (However, if you change the field property settings for DefaultValue, ValidationRule, and ValidationText, these changes will be enforced in any controls based on these fields, even if the controls were created before you changed the field properties.)

Add a combo box control to a form

Becky's research showed that Sweet Lil's could streamline much of the data entry work by creating predefined lists instead of having the data entry staff enter the data manually each time. This is especially true of the customer information on the Orders form. Currently, the sales clerks must look up the customer by name in the Customers form to find the customer ID and other data for the Orders form. You can automate this process by using a combo box control that lists the customers by name and then enters the corresponding customer ID, name, and address into the form. At Sweet Lil's you make the change, replacing the CustomerID text box on the Orders form with a combo box.

Keeping Information Reliable 5

important

In addition to the behavioral properties that you're changing in this lesson, other properties govern the appearance of controls. When you create a control using the control wizards, the control is given the default settings in its appearance properties, which don't match the customized appearance of the forms in the practice database file. For the purposes of this lesson, you should disregard any differences in appearance between the control you are adding and the form to which you are adding it. The techniques for achieving a consistent appearance among the objects on a form are explained in Lesson 10, "Presenting a Form More Effectively."

1. In the Database window forms list, select Orders, and then click the Design button on the Database window toolbar.

2. In the Orders form, click the CustomerID text box, and then press Delete.

    When you click the text box, sizing handles appear around the CustomerID text box and its label to select them. When you press Delete, both objects disappear.

3. If the field list is not visible, click the Field List button on the Form Design toolbar.

Field List

    The field list appears.

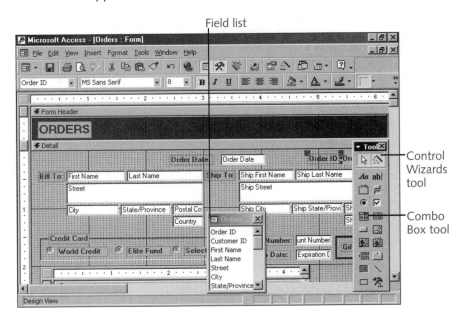

Field list

Control Wizards

Combo Box

4 In the toolbox, be sure that the Control Wizards tool is selected, and then click the Combo Box tool.

5 In the field list, drag the CustomerID field to the center of the empty space on the Orders form where the CustomerID text box used to be.

The mouse pointer becomes a field pointer. When you release the mouse button, a combo box and its label are added to the form and the first page of the Combo Box Wizard appears.

6 On the first Combo Box Wizard page, be sure the I Want The Combo Box To Look Up The Values In A Table Or Query option is selected, and then click Next.

The second page of the Combo Box Wizard appears.

7 In the View area, select the Queries option.

The queries list replaces the tables list.

8 In the queries list, select Customer List, and then click Next.

The third page of the Combo Box Wizard appears.

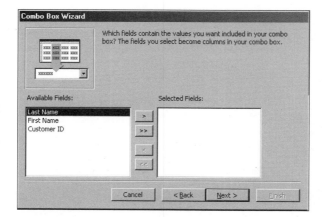

You select all the fields to be used and the order in which they appear.

9 In the Available Fields list, double-click CustomerID, LastName, and FirstName, in that order, and then click Next.

As you double-click each field name, the fields appear in the Selected Fields list in the same order in which you double-clicked them. When you click Next, the fourth page of the Combo Box Wizard appears.

10 Double-click the right edge of each of the three column selectors, and then click Next.

As you double-click each column selector, the width of each column adjusts to the best fit for the data it contains. When you click Next, the fifth page of the Combo Box Wizard appears.

⓫ Click CustomerID, the column that contains the data you want, and then click Next.

CustomerID is now bound to the combo box. When you click Next, the sixth page of the Combo Box Wizard appears.

⓬ Be sure that the Store That Value In This Field option is selected and that CustomerID is selected in the corresponding box, and then click Next.

Data from the CustomerID field is now listed in the combo box. When you click Next, the last page of the Combo Box Wizard appears.

⓭ Be sure that Customer ID is the label for your combo box (include a space before ID), and then click Finish.

The Orders form reappears in Design view. It now has a combo box, bound to the CustomerID field, in place of the text box.

⓮ Close the field list.

View

The names are listed alphabetically by last name, so you'll see 98 Palmer Faye in the actual list.

⓯ Save your changes and click the View button on the Form Design toolbar to switch to Form view.

⓰ In the new Customer ID combo box, select the name Faye Palmer.

The number 98 appears in the Customer ID combo box and the customer information for Faye Palmer appears in the Bill To area of the form.

Bound Controls

A bound control is a control on a form that's logically linked to a field in an underlying database table or query. For example, the new CustomerID combo box control on the Orders form is bound to the CustomerID field in the Customers List query. The information in the bound control on the form is drawn from the query to which it's bound.

When you insert a lookup column in a table, the Lookup Wizard appears and creates the lookup column combo box for you.

You can also add bound controls to tables. For example, you can add a lookup column to a table that works just like the new CustomerID combo box on the Orders form. The lookup column is a combo box that replaces a text box in a table. It is bound to a field in another table or in a query and displays the data in that column as a list in the combo box. Any form based on the lookup column automatically incorporates the field as a combo box control.

Keeping Information Reliable 5

Set a default value in a form

Becky's research showed that Sweet Lil's sales clerks often end up entering and selecting data unnecessarily, and that employees' data entry can be further streamlined by changing the default values of certain fields. The default value is a predefined item of data that's used if nothing else is entered or selected. Because the date that the sales clerks must enter into the Order Date combo box on the Orders form is always the date that the form is filled out, Becky has recommended changing the field so that it automatically fills in the current date. In this exercise, you make the change, setting the default value of the OrderDate field to the current date.

View

1 On the Form View toolbar, click the View button to switch to Form Design view.

2 In the Orders form detail section, click the OrderDate text box.

The text box and its label are selected.

Properties

3 On the Form Design toolbar, click the Properties button.

The property sheet for the text box appears.

4 In the Default Value property box, type the expression **=Date()**

The Date() function, which is built into Access, returns the current date. Today's date is now set as the default value for the OrderDate text box.

For more information on expressions and how to use them, see Appendix C, "Using Expressions" on the Microsoft Access 2000 Step by Step CD-ROM.

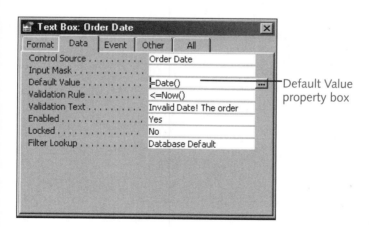

Default Value property box

5 Close the property sheet and save your changes.

Access 2000 now puts today's date in the OrderDate field of each record as the record is added to the Orders form.

View

6 On the Form Design toolbar, click the View button to switch to Form view, and then on the Form View toolbar, click the New Record button.

New Record

A new blank Orders form appears, with today's date in the OrderDate field.

7 Close the Orders form.

A message appears, asking if you want to save your changes.

8 Click Yes.

The new record is discarded, and the Orders form closes.

Change the tab order on a form

Becky's database research showed that the process for moving between fields on a form doesn't always follow the layout of the form. For example, on the Orders form, customer details are grouped in one area, shipping details in another, and credit information in a separate section, but the sales clerks must jump from one area to another as they fill out the form. The sequence in which the insertion point moves from field to field on a form is called the *tab order*. In this exercise, you help Liz implement Becky's form improvement recommendation, changing the tab order of the Orders form so that the data entry sequence flows smoothly from one area to another.

1 In the Database window forms list, select Orders, and then click the Design button on the Database window toolbar.

2 On the Orders form, click the CustomerID combo box.

The CustomerID combo box and label are selected.

3 On the View menu, click Tab Order.

The Tab Order dialog box appears. Because the CustomerID field was just changed, CustomerID is now last in the Custom Order list.

4 In the Tab Order dialog box, scroll to the bottom of the Custom Order list and click the field selector to the left of CustomerID.

5 Drag CustomerID to the top of the Custom Order list.

6 In the Custom Order list, drag Street up until it's just below LastName.

7 Drag ShipFirstName down until it's just below Country.

8 Continue rearranging the Custom Order list until the fields are in the following order.

CustomerID
OrderDate
OrderID
FirstName
LastName
Street
City
StateOrProvince
PostalCode
Country
ShipFirstName
ShipLastName
ShipStreet
ShipCity
ShipStateOrProvince
ShipPostalCode
ShipCountry
CreditCard
AccountNumber
ExpirationDate
Gift
Orders Subform
Subtotal

9 In the Tab Order dialog box, click OK.

The Tab Order dialog box closes. The new tab order is now saved.

10 On the Form Design toolbar, click the View button to switch to Form view.

The CustomerID field is selected.

View

11 Press Tab to move through the Orders form.

The new tab order moves in a logical progression across the top of the form, and then through the Bill To area, Ship To area, and Credit Card area before jumping to the subform.

12 Press Ctrl+Tab to move to the Total area in the main form.

13 Save your changes, and close the Orders form.

Validating Records Across Related Tables

To protect data in related tables from becoming disconnected, Access 2000 applies a system of rules called *referential integrity*. Referential integrity uses the relationships between tables to preserve data integrity and reliability. Changes made to one table are also made to the related tables, according to a set of rules that prohibit invalid relationships and prevent mismatches.

Referential integrity enforces the following basic rules:

The primary key field of the related table is also called the foreign key field.

- You can't enter a value in the foreign field of the related table unless that value already exists in the primary key field of the primary table. For example, you can't create a new order record in the Orders table unless you have a customer ID that matches a customer ID in the Customers table. (You can't place an order for a customer who doesn't exist.)

- You can't delete a record from the primary table if matching records exist in any related table. For example, you can't delete a customer record from the Customers table if there are matching orders for that customer in the Orders table. (You can't delete a customer while there are orders pending for that customer.)

- You can't change a primary key value in the primary table if there are any related records that refer to that value. For example, you can't change a customer ID in the Customers table if there are matching orders for that customer in the Orders table. (You can't change a customer's unique ID while there are orders pending for that customer.)

You can't establish referential integrity between an Access 2000 database and a linked data source, such as a table in Microsoft Excel format.

Referential integrity can't always be applied. You must ensure that your tables meet the following conditions before you can set or use referential integrity.

- The matching field from the primary table must be a primary key.

- Any value in the foreign field of the related table must already exist in the primary key field of the primary table.

- The related fields of both tables must have the same data type, which defines the kind of data (such as text, currency, or yes/no) that a field contains. The related fields must have the same field size.

- Both tables must belong to the same Access 2000 database. If the tables are in separate files that have been linked, the files must be in Microsoft Access database (.mdb) format, and the database in which the linked tables are stored must be open.

Cascading Update and Delete

Access 2000 offers a feature that lets you make an exception to the rules on deleting records or changing primary keys, without violating referential integrity. Changes made to the primary table are automatically applied to the related table through a process called *cascading*.

Cascading update applies any changes that you make in the primary table to the matching records in the related tables. For example, a change to the unique customer ID number in the Customers table "cascades" to the Orders table. Orders created using the old customer ID are automatically updated to the new customer ID, rather than being "orphaned" because they refer to a customer ID that no longer exists.

Apply cascading delete only when you're certain that the data should be removed.

Cascading delete removes all matching records in the related tables when a record in the primary table is deleted. For example, the deletion of a customer record from the Customers table cascades to the matching order records in the related Orders table, which cascades in turn to the matching detail records in the Order Details table. All matching order records in the Orders table are automatically deleted. Then, for each deleted order record in the Orders table, all matching detail records in the Order Detail table are also deleted. This would remove pending as well as fulfilled orders, however, so cascading delete should be used with caution.

Database research conducted by Impact Public Relations' Becky Sawyer revealed that data in the Customers and Orders tables could be deleted or changed in ways that might compromise data integrity and reliability. In these exercises, you apply referential integrity to the Sweet Lil's database, with cascading update between these related tables.

Set a field property to establish referential integrity

For a demonstration of how to establish referential integrity, in the Multimedia folder on the Microsoft Access 2000 Step by Step CD-ROM, double-click Referential-Integrity.

Becky's database research showed that it's possible to delete customer records from the Customers table while there are still pending order records in the Orders table. At Sweet Lil's, you prevent such deletions by applying referential integrity between the two tables. By applying referential integrity, and not choosing cascade delete, you can add the safety feature of making it impossible to delete customers who have pending orders.

Relationships

Clear Layout

Show Table

❶ In the Database window, click Tables on the Objects bar.

❷ On the Database toolbar, click the Relationships button.

The Relationships window opens. The Relationship toolbar replaces the Database toolbar.

❸ On the Relationship toolbar, click the Clear Layout button, clicking Yes to the message confirming that you want to clear the table layout.

The table layout in the Relationships window is cleared.

❹ On the Relationship toolbar, click the Show Table button.

The Show Table dialog box appears.

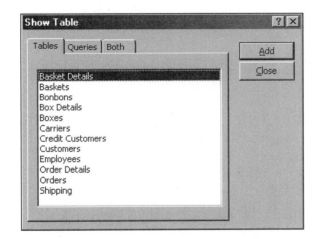

❺ In the Show Table dialog box, double-click Customers in the tables list, and then click Close.

The Show Table dialog box closes, and the Customers table appears in the Relationships window.

Show Direct Relationships

❻ On the Relationship toolbar, click the Show Direct Relationships button.

The Orders table appears in the Relationships window, with a line indicating a one-to-many relationship between the Customers table and the Orders table.

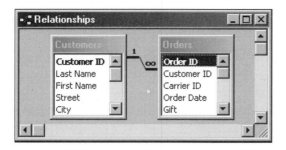

7 In the Relationships window, double-click the thin section of the line connecting the Customers table to the Orders table.

The Edit Relationships dialog box appears, with the CustomerID field selected for both the Customers (primary) table and the Orders (related) table.

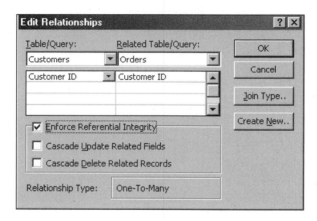

8 In the Edit Relationships dialog box, verify that the Enforce Referential Integrity check box is selected.

9 In the Edit Relationships dialog box, click Join Type.

The Join Properties dialog box appears.

10 In the Join Properties dialog box, be sure the Only Include Rows Where The Joined Fields From Both Tables Are Equal option is selected, and click OK.

The Join Properties dialog box closes.

11 In the Edit Relationships dialog box, click OK.

The Edit Relationships dialog box closes. Referential integrity is now in force between the Customers and Orders tables.

For a demonstration of how to apply cascading update, in the Multimedia folder on the Microsoft Access 2000 Step by Step CD-ROM, double-click FieldProperty.

Set a field property to keep primary keys consistent

Becky's database research showed that changes to the contents of the BoxID field in the Boxes table could break the relationship between the Boxes, Box Details, and Order Details tables, resulting in incorrectly filled orders. At Sweet Lil's, you prevent such mismatches by applying cascading update to the Box ID field.

1 On the Relationship toolbar, click the Clear Layout button, clicking Yes to the message confirming that you want to clear the table layout.

The table layout in the Relationships window is cleared.

2 On the Relationship toolbar, click the Show Table button.

The Show Table dialog box appears.

3 In the Show Table dialog box, double-click Boxes in the tables list, and then click Close.

The Show Table dialog box closes, and the Boxes table appears in the Relationships window.

4 On the Relationship toolbar, click the Show Direct Relationships button.

The Box Details and Order Details tables appear in the Relationships window, with lines indicating a one-to-many relationship between the Boxes table and the other two tables.

5 In the Relationships window, drag the Order Details table down and left until it's directly below the Box Details table.

The relationships are easier to see when the lines and tables don't overlap.

Clear Layout

Show Table

Show Direct Relationships

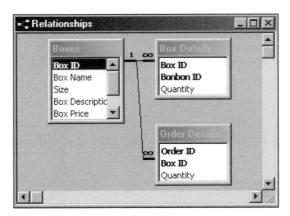

6 In the Relationships window, double-click the line connecting the Boxes table to the Box Details table.

The Edit Relationships dialog box appears, with the BoxID field selected for both the Boxes (primary) table and the Box Details (related) table.

*You can't
apply
cascading
update
without first
enforcing
referential
integrity.*

7 In the Edit Relationships dialog box, be sure that the Enforce Referential Integrity check box is selected.

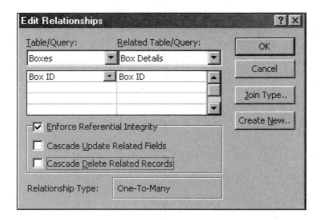

8 Select the Cascade Update Related Fields check box, and click OK.

The Edit Relationships dialog box closes. Cascading update is now applied between the Boxes table and the Box Details table.

9 In the Relationships window, double-click the line connecting the BoxID field in the Boxes table to the BoxID field in the Order Details table.

The Edit Relationships dialog box appears, with the BoxID field selected for both the Boxes (primary) table and the Order Details (related) table.

10 In the Edit Relationships dialog box, be sure that the Enforce Referential Integrity check box is selected, select the Cascade Update Related Records check box, and click OK.

The Edit Relationships dialog box closes. Cascading update is now applied between the Boxes table and the Order Details table.

11 Close the Relationships window, clicking Yes to confirm that you want to save your changes to the table layout.

Resolving Many-to-Many Relationships

A many-to-many relationship occurs when records in each related table can have more than one matching record in the other table. This can occur because, viewed from its own perspective, each side of the many-to-many relationship appears be a one-to-many relationship. For example, baskets and bonbons appear to have a one-to-many relationship because one basket can contain many different types of bonbons. The reverse, however, is also true: one type of bonbon can be contained in many different baskets.

The many-to-many relationship becomes evident only when you view such a relationship from both sides. It usually becomes apparent when you actually try to join such tables in a one-to-many relationship. Despite appearances, you can't make a one-to-many relationship between the two tables, no matter which table you set as the primary table. The only solution is to create a third table that links the other two: a junction table.

A *junction table* is an intermediate table that serves as a bridge between two tables with a many-to-many relationship. It uses the primary keys of the two other tables as its primary key (it is a multiple-field primary key); it is related to each table in a one-to-many relationship. It also contains at least one additional field that doesn't exist in either of the other two tables, but is relevant to both. The many-to-many relationship becomes a many-to-one and one-to-many relationship.

In the Sweet Lil's database, the Basket Details table is a junction table that resolves the many-to-many relationship between the BasketID and BonbonID fields of the Baskets and Bonbons tables. The primary key of the Basket Details table consists of the primary keys of two tables that the Basket Details table joins: the BasketID field of the Baskets table and the BonbonID field of the Bonbons table. The Quantity field of the Basket Details table resolves the many-to-many relationship by specifying the number of bonbons assigned to each basket.

View junction table relationships

As you make recommended changes to the database, you become more aware of the relationships between tables. You notice that the Basket Details table has only one unique field—Quantity. Why is a separate table necessary? In this exercise, you discover that the Basket Details table serves as a junction table between the Baskets and Bonbons tables to resolve a many-to-many relationship.

1 Verify that all tables and forms are closed.

Relationships

2 On the Database toolbar, click the Relationships button.

The Relationships window opens. The Relationship toolbar replaces the Database toolbar.

Clear Layout

3 On the Relationship toolbar, click the Clear Layout button, clicking Yes to the message confirming that you want to clear the table layout.

The table layout in the Relationships window is cleared.

Show Table

4 On the Relationship toolbar, click the Show Table button.

The Show Table dialog box appears.

5 In the tables list, double-click Basket Details, and then click Close.

The Basket Details table appears in the Relationships window, and the Show Table dialog box closes.

6 On the Relationship toolbar, click the Show Direct Relationships button.

The Baskets and Bonbons tables appear in the Relationships window, with lines indicating the one-to-many relationship between each of them and the Basket Details table.

7 Drag the Bonbons table down and left until it's directly below the Baskets table.

The relationships are easier to see when the lines and tables don't overlap.

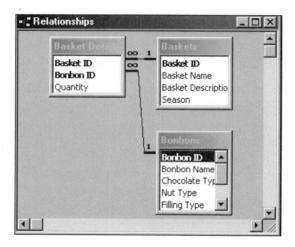

8 In the Relationships window, study the path from the Baskets table to the Basket Details table, and then from the Basket Details table to the Bonbons table.

You can now see the relationships among the three tables. The Baskets table has a one-to-many relationship with the Basket Details table through the primary key (BasketID field) of the Baskets table. The Basket Details table has a many-to-one relationship with the Baskets table through the multiple-field primary key (BasketID and BonbonID fields) of the Basket Details table. The Bonbons table has a one-to-many relationship with the Basket Details table through the primary key (BonbonID field) of the Basket Details table.

9 In the Relationships window, be sure the Bonbons table is selected. Then, on the Relationship toolbar, click the Show Direct Relationships button twice.

The Box Details and Boxes tables appear in the Relationships window, with lines indicating the one-to-many relationships between them and between the Box Details and Bonbons tables.

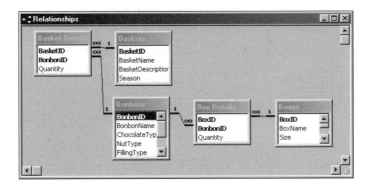

🔟 In the Relationships window, study the path from the Baskets table to the Basket Details table, and then from the Basket Details table to the Bonbons table.

You can now see that the relationships among the Boxes, Box Details, and Bonbons tables are exactly the same as those of the Baskets, Basket Details, and Bonbons tables. Basket Details is a junction table between the Bonbons and Baskets tables, and Box Details is a junction table between the Bonbons and Boxes tables.

⓫ Close the Relationships window without saving the layout.

One Step Further ## Using Subdatasheets

A table relationship can become visible in Datasheet view through a subdatasheet. A subdatasheet provides a hierarchical datasheet view, allowing you to browse and to edit related tables or queries from a single window. You view the primary data in the datasheet and related data in a subdatasheet, in much the same way that you view primary data in a form and related data in a subform.

For example, the relationship between the Baskets form and the Basket Details subform is now mirrored in the relationship between the Baskets table datasheet and the Baskets Subform Query subdatasheet. The parallel relationship between the Boxes form and Box Details subform is also mirrored in the relationship between the Boxes table datasheet and the Boxes Subform Query subdatasheet.

Keeping Information Reliable

5

You can insert any related table or query as a subdatasheet to any datasheet. For example, the Bonbons datasheet has the Bonbons By Box query as a subdatasheet. This allows you to go down the list of bonbons in the Bonbon datasheet and look up the boxes in which any given bonbon is shipped. If you want to look up the baskets in which each bonbon is shipped, you can substitute the Bonbons By Basket query as the subdatasheet and even switch back and forth between the two subdatasheets—all from within Datasheet view.

Now that you know how important and far-reaching the relationships between tables are, you browse through and insert subdatasheets to see exactly how data is related.

Open a subform and subdatasheet

In this exercise, you look at the mirrored relationship between Datasheet view with a subdatasheet for the Baskets table, and Form view with a subform view for the Baskets form.

1 In the Database window, click Forms on the Objects bar to display the forms list.

2 Double-click the Baskets form, and view the information displayed in the first record.

General information about the Summer Sampler basket appears in the main form. The subform displays details concerning the contents, four bonbon types, and their associated names: Bittersweet Blueberry, Bittersweet Strawberry, Bittersweet Raspberry, and Sweet Strawberry.

3 Close the Baskets form.

4 In the Database window, click Tables on the Objects bar to display the tables list.

5 Double-click the Baskets table.

The Baskets table displays the same information as the main Baskets form. You can't see all of the information in the form using just this datasheet.

6 To the left of the first record, click the plus sign (+).

The subdatasheet appears. It displays the same information as the Baskets subform. The datasheet plus the subdatasheet of the Baskets table shows you the same information as the main form plus the subform of the Baskets form. Moreover, the connection between the related tables is clearer with both forms showing in Datasheet view.

7 To the left of the first record, click the minus sign (–).

The Baskets subdatasheet closes.

8 Close the Baskets table.

Insert a subdatasheet

In this exercise, you find that it's easy to insert a different subdatasheet to browse through a different set of related data, all from within Datasheet view. You substitute the Bonbons By Basket query as a subdatasheet for the Bonbons By Box query on the Bonbons datasheet.

❶ In the Database window, double-click the Bonbons table.

The Bonbons table contains information about each individual bonbon. The bonbon name in the first record, Candlelight Ecstasy, is selected.

❷ In the first record, open the subdatasheet.

The Bonbons subdatasheet opens with the box name of the first record, Northwind Collection, selected. The subdatasheet links the Bonbons table to the Bonbons By Box Query table, which relates individual bonbons to the various boxes. You can see that the Candlelight Ecstasy bonbon is included in the Northwind Collection and Sweet Creams boxes, where it accounts for $1.20 and $1.80, respectively, of the total cost of the boxes.

❸ Close the subdatasheet.

❹ On the Insert menu, click Subdatasheet.

The Insert Subdatasheet dialog box appears.

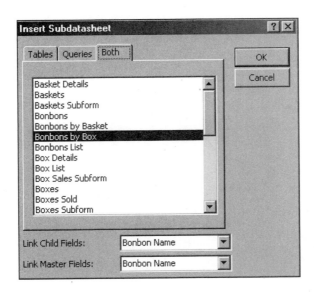

5   In the Insert Subdatasheet dialog box, select Bonbons By Basket from the list on the Both tab, and click OK.

The Master and Child boxes in the Insert Subdatasheet dialog box correspond to the related fields in the primary and related tables. You can see that the Bonbons and Bonbons By Basket Query tables are related through the Bonbon Name field.

6   In the third record, open the subdatasheet.

The Bonbons By Basket Query table is now attached as a subdatasheet to the Bonbons table, so you can now see that the Marzipan Oakleaf bonbon is included in the Summer Sampler basket, where it accounts for 40 cents of the total cost.

7   Close the subdatasheet, and then close the Bonbons table.

A message appears, confirming that you want to save the changes to the table layout.

8   Click Yes.

The Bonbons By Basket Query table will appear in the subdatasheet the next time you open the Bonbons table.

Finish the lesson

1   To continue to the next lesson, on the File menu, click Close.

2   If you're finished using Access 2000 for now, on the File menu, click Exit.

Lesson 5 Quick Reference

To	Do this	Button
Add a validation rule to a control	In Design view, click the control. Click the Properties button on the Form Design toolbar. In the property sheet, type the rule in the Validation Rule property box.	
Add a control to a form	In Design view, click the Field List button on the Form Design toolbar. Click the Control Wizards tool in the toolbox, and then click the tool for the control you want to add. Drag the field from the field list to the form.	
Set a default value for a field	In Design view, click the control. Click the Properties button on the Form Design toolbar. In the property sheet, type the value in the Default Value property box.	
Change the tab order on a form	In Design view, click a form control. Select Tab Order on the View menu. Rearrange the Custom Order list in the order you want.	
Establish referential integrity between two related tables	In the Relationships window, double-click the line between the related tables. In the Edit Relationships dialog box, select Enforce Referential Integrity.	
Apply cascading update	In the Relationships window, with one of the tables displayed, click the Show Direct Relationships button on the Relationship toolbar. Double-click the line between the related tables. In the Edit Relationships dialog box, select Enforce Referential Integrity and Cascade Update Related Fields.	
Apply cascading delete	In the Relationships window, double-click the line between the related tables. In the Edit Relationships dialog box, select Enforce Referential Integrity and Cascade Delete Related Fields.	
Use a junction table	Create a table containing the primary keys of both of the tables you want to join as a multiple-field primary key. Add a field that is relevant to both tables. Establish a one-to-many relationship between the junction table and the tables you want to join.	

LESSON

6

Working with External Data

ESTIMATED TIME 30 min.

In this lesson you will learn how to:

✔ *Link to other data sources.*

✔ *Work with external data in linked tables.*

✔ *Import data from another data source into a database.*

✔ *Export a table.*

No single database, however well designed, can serve every need. And Microsoft Access 2000 doesn't exist in a vacuum; there are other relational databases. As with word processors and most other computer programs, databases store information in a specific format that may be incompatible with other database programs that store data in different formats.

Databases are also not the only way to organize information. Most people use spreadsheets, not databases, as their first choice for organizing data. Access 2000 coexists with other databases better than most because of its ability to incorporate data from other database programs.

The independent financial firm of Ferguson & Bardell handles accounting and payroll for Sweet Lil's. Ferguson & Bardell stores Sweet Lil's assets data in the dBASE IV database format and tracks the payroll using a Microsoft Excel spreadsheet. Sweet Lil's would like to integrate these external data sources with their own Access 2000 database.

In this lesson, you link the external Assets table to the Sweet Lil's database and work with the data using Access. You also import the Payroll spreadsheet into the Sweet Lil's database.

Start Microsoft Access 2000 and reopen the database

● If Access 2000 isn't started yet, start it. Open the Sweet Lil's database. If the Microsoft Access window doesn't fill your screen, maximize the window.

If you need help opening the database, see Lesson 1, "Using Forms."

Gathering Data from External Sources

Data is shared between different databases by importing, exporting, and linking. When you *import* data, you incorporate a copy into your Access 2000 database. When you *export* data, you make a copy of the Access 2000 data and convert it into a format that the other database can either import or use directly.

An external data source does not need to be in a different format. You can also link one Microsoft Access database to another.

When you *link* data, you create a dynamic connection between one database, called a *data source*, and another, called a *destination*. The data is not copied or converted, just transmitted via the link from the source to the destination. Linked data appears to be part of the destination database, but it remains within the external data source in its original file format. This allows you to use the data in Access 2000 while the authors of the data source continue to use and update the data using the original database program.

In Access, you can import, export, or link data from a number of different database, spreadsheet, and text file formats:

- Database files, such as those created in Access itself. Access 2000 works with database files created in dBASE III or later, Microsoft Exchange, Microsoft Outlook, Paradox 3.0 or later, Microsoft Access 2000 projects, and the previous version of Microsoft Access.

- Open Database Connectivity (ODBC) links and Structured Query Language (SQL) tables, such as those used in Microsoft SQL Server. Access 2000 works with ODBC links and SQL tables created in Microsoft FoxPro 2.0 or later, Microsoft SQL Server, and Oracle.

- Hypertext Markup Language (HTML) lists and tables, such as those created in a Web page. Access 2000 works with lists created in HTML 1.0 or later, and tables created in HTML 2.0 or later, and can export tables and lists for use in Active Server Pages.

- Files in HTX and IDC formats, such as those created in Microsoft Internet Information Server. Access 2000 works with files created in Microsoft IIS 1.0 or later.

- Spreadsheet files, such as those created in Microsoft Excel. Access 2000 works with spreadsheet files created in Microsoft Excel and Lotus 1-2-3.

■ Rich Text files, such as those created in Microsoft Word. Access 2000 works with the Rich Text Format (RTF) used in all of the programs in Microsoft Office.

■ Text files, such as those created in a word-processing program or text editor. Access 2000 works with ASCII text, MS-DOS text, PC-8 text, plain text, and Windows-based American National Standards Institute (ANSI) text files that use either fixed-width or delimited fields.

In this lesson, you link to the external Assets database table to bring over the assets data. You also import an Excel spreadsheet to incorporate the external payroll data.

Creating a Link to an External Data Source

Linking to an external data source provides several benefits. The authors of the data source retain their ability to use and update the data using the original database program, while the users of the linked data source use it just as they would any other table in their own database. Because the data remains in the source, external processes acting through the database program that created the data source can update it. Access 2000 can create forms, queries, and reports based on the external table using the most current information. Linked data appears to be part of the destination database, but it remains within the external data source in its original file format.

The main disadvantage to data links is that the connection to the data source might occasionally become compromised or lost, blocking Access 2000 to the linked data until the connection is restored. And, while you can change the data in the fields, you can't add, delete, or change the layout of the fields themselves or make any other changes to the structure of the linked table.

Linking to an External Database Table

The financial firm of Ferguson & Bardell created the external Assets data table for Sweet Lil's in a dBASE IV database file. The data is stored in a file format known as DBF, which is used by a number of database programs besides dBASE, including Microsoft FoxPro. The Assets.dbf file contains a fixed-assets register that Sweet Lil's wants to integrate with its own database, but the data must remain in DBF format so that Ferguson & Bardell can maintain it.

Link to a table

To integrate the external Assets table into the Sweet Lil's database without changing the file format, you must link the database to this external data source.

1   On the File menu, point to Get External Data, and then click Link Tables.

The Link dialog box appears.

2   In the Look In box, click the drop-down arrow and select your hard disk, and then double-click the Access 2000 SBS Practice folder icon.

The Sweet Lil's database file, Sweetlil.mdb, appears in the Link file list.

3   In the Files Of Type list, select dBASE IV (*.dbf).

The external Assets database file, Assets.dbf, appears in the Link file list.

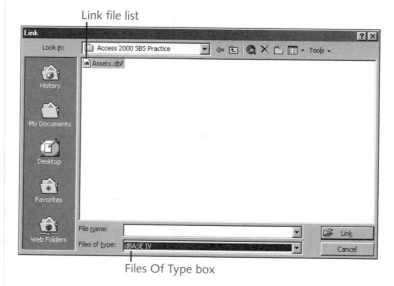

Link file list

Files Of Type box

4   Select Assets.dbf, and then click Link.

The Select Index Files dialog box replaces the Link dialog box.

5   Click OK.

6   In the Link dialog box, click Close.

In the Database window, the linked Assets table now appears in the tables list.

Linked Assets table

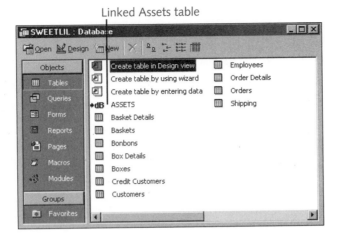

Working with a Linked Table

An icon reflecting the file type distinguishes linked tables from standard Access 2000 tables. For example, the linked Assets table has a ➡**dB** symbol, indicating that it's a linked dBASE file. Linked tables can be used just like any other table, except that you can't change the table structure. While you can't add, delete, or rearrange the fields, you can reset the field properties in Design view. Depending on the differences between the database formats, some other capabilities may also be lost. For example, some properties of the linked Assets table can't be modified in Access, because the dBASE format doesn't support those properties.

Change the field properties of the linked table

Now that you can view the linked Assets table, you discover that all the financial data is displayed as "raw" or unformatted numeric values, making it difficult to read. In this exercise, you change the properties of the book value (BOOK_VALUE) and purchase price (PURCHASE_P) fields to display the financial data as currency.

① In the Database window, verify that Tables on the Objects bar is selected.

② In the tables list, select Assets, click the Design button on the Database window toolbar, and then click Yes when alerted that you can't modify some properties of a linked table.

The Assets table opens in Design view.

Working with External Data
6

3   In the lower portion of the window, be sure the General tab of the field property sheet is active.

4   In the upper portion of the window, click in the Data Type cell of the BOOK_VALUE field row.

The properties of the BOOK_VALUE field appear in the field properties. The field description warns that the data type can't be changed.

You can't modify the Data Type field property in a linked table, but you can change the way the data in the field is displayed.

5   In the Format property box, select Currency.

The BOOK_VALUE field is reformatted to display numbers as currency.

The ASSESSED_V field can't be reformatted, because its data type is Text, not Number, and you can't change the data type.

Format property box

ASSETS : Table			_ □ ×
Field Name	Data Type	Description	
PURCHASE_D	Date/Time		
PURCHASE_P	Number		
ASSESSED_V	Text		
▶ BOOK_VALUE	Number	·	

Field Properties

General | Lookup

Field   property   sheet

Field Size	Double	
Format	Currency	
Decimal Places	General Number	3456.789
Input Mask	Currency	$3,456.79
Caption	Fixed	3456.79
Default Value	Standard	3,456.79
Validation Rule	Percent	123.00%
Validation Text	Scientific	3.46E+03
Required	No	
Indexed	No	

The display layout for the field. Select a pre-defined format or enter a custom format. Press F1 for help on formats.

6   Repeat steps 4 and 5 for the PURCHASE_P field.

The PURCHASE_P field is reformatted to display numbers as currency.

7   On the Table Design toolbar, click the Save button.

Your changes are saved.

Save

8   On the Table Design toolbar, click the View button to view the effect of your changes in Datasheet view.

View

The financial data in the BOOK_VALUE and PURCHASE_P fields now appears as currency values.

9   Close the Assets table.

Importing a Table

Imported data becomes part of the Access 2000 database; it is no different from a table you create yourself in Access, and it is always available. After the data is imported, there's no connection between the data source and the destination, so any changes made to one copy of the table won't be reflected in the other copy. For this reason, data should be imported only when you expect to assume control of it.

Because Sweet Lil's has a small staff, they decided to reassume the employee payroll deduction portion of the payroll accounting from Ferguson & Bardell. In this exercise, you help import the Microsoft Excel payroll deduction spreadsheet into the Sweet Lil's database.

Import a Microsoft Excel spreadsheet

1   On the File menu, point to Get External Data, and then click Import.

     The Import dialog box appears.

2   In the Look In box, click the drop-down arrow and your hard disk, and then double-click the Access 2000 SBS Practice folder icon.

     The Sweet Lil's database file, Sweetlil.mdb, appears in the Import file list.

3   In the Files Of Type list, select Microsoft Excel (*.xls).

     The Payroll spreadsheet file, Payroll.xls, appears.

Import file list

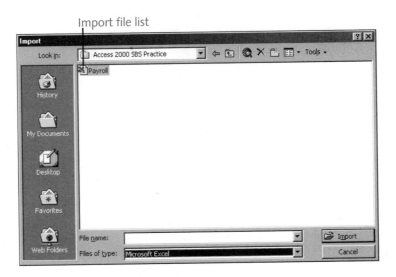

4 Select Payroll.xls, and then click Import.

The first page of the Import Spreadsheet Wizard appears, asking whether to use the spreadsheet's column headings as field names.

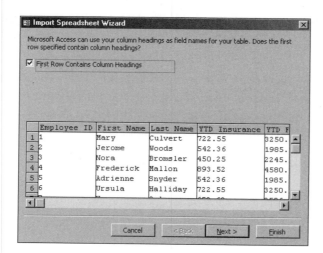

5 Be sure the First Row Contains Column Headings check box is selected, and then click Next.

The second page of the Import Spreadsheet Wizard appears, asking where to save the spreadsheet data.

6 Be sure the In A New Table option is selected, and then click Next.

The third page of the Import Spreadsheet Wizard appears.

7 Click Next again.

The fourth page of the Import Spreadsheet Wizard appears.

8 Select the Choose My Own Primary Key option, and then click Next.

The EmployeeID field will be selected as the primary key. The last page of the Import Spreadsheet Wizard appears.

⑨ Be sure the default name is Payroll, and then click Finish.

A message appears, confirming that the Payroll table was successfully imported.

⑩ Click OK.

The Payroll table appears in the tables list of the Database window.

One Step Further   Making Data Available to Other Sources

Just as Access 2000 can gather and work with data from other sources, it can also serve as a data source for other database programs. Data is shared between different databases by importing, exporting, and linking. Other data sources can link to Access 2000 in the same way that Access 2000 links to other data sources, and Access 2000 can export data in a format that other data sources can use.

Although Sweet Lil's is reassuming a portion of its payroll accounting, Ferguson & Bardell will continue to provide financial advice and support. In this exercise, you export a copy of the Payroll table as an Excel spreadsheet for Ferguson & Bardell to review.

Export a table to Microsoft Excel

① In the tables list of the Database window, select Payroll.

② On the File menu, select Export.

The Export Table dialog box appears.

③ Verify that the Access 2000 SBS Practice folder is shown in the Save In box.

The Sweet Lil's database file, Sweetlil.mdb, appears in the Export Table To file list.

4 In the Export dialog box, select Microsoft Excel 97-2000 (.xls) in the Save As Type list.

The Payroll spreadsheet file, Payroll.xls, appears in the Export Table To file list.

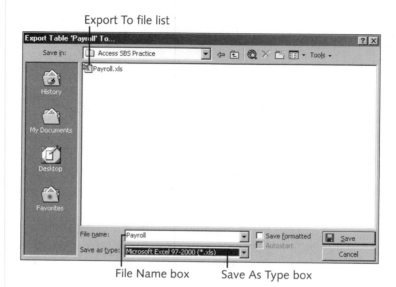

Export To file list

File Name box   Save As Type box

5 In the File Name box, delete Payroll and type **Payroll1** to distinguish the filename from the existing Payroll spreadsheet file.

6 Click Save.

The Payroll1.xls spreadsheet file is saved in the Access 2000 SBS Practice folder.

Finish the lesson

1 To continue to the next lesson, on the File menu, click Close.

2 If you're finished using Access 2000 for now, on the File menu, click Exit.

Sharing Data Within Microsoft Office

Microsoft Access 2000 can convert tables into Microsoft Excel 2000 spreadsheets directly using the drag-and-drop feature. You can drag any table from the Database window in Access 2000 to an open Excel 2000 workbook, and it automatically becomes an Excel 2000 spreadsheet.

Microsoft Access 2000 can also save copies of the database in the Access 97 format to share with others who are not yet ready to upgrade to Access 2000. On the Tools menu, point to Database Utilities, point to Convert Database, and then click To Prior Access Database Version. It's not necessary to share copies of the database with Access 97 users who can link to your Access 2000 database, because they can connect to the data directly, without regard for the differences in format.

Lesson 6 Quick Reference

To	Do this
Link to an external table	On the File menu, point to Get External Data, and then click Link Tables. Select the file type, find and select the file, and then click Link.
Change field properties of a linked table	Open the linked table in Design view. Select the field. In the field properties, click the property box for the field property you want to change.
Import a table	On the File menu, point to Get External Data, and then click Import. Select the file type, find and select the file, and then click Import. Follow the directions of any Import Wizard that might appear.
Export a table	Select a table in the Database window, and click Export on the File menu. In the Export dialog box, select the export file format for the table, and a destination folder, and then click Save.

Working with External Data

6

PART

2

Review & Practice

**ESTIMATED
TIME
20 min.**

You will review and practice how to:

✔ *Create a new database table.*

✔ *Create a relationship between tables.*

✔ *Change a field property to meet a business need.*

✔ *Create a form with a combo box control.*

✔ *Export a table as a spreadsheet.*

Before you move on to Part 3, which covers turning raw data into meaningful information, you can practice the skills you learned in Part 2 by working through this Review & Practice section.

Scenario

Sweet Lil's vice president of marketing, Mary Culvert, wants to promote selected boxes of bonbons during the next quarter. Mary will manage some of the promotions herself and delegate others to her subordinates Jerome Woods, Nora Bromsler, and Dale Wilson. To be sure that every promotion is assigned to one of these four people, Mary needs a database table for tracking the promotions and a form for making the assignments. Mary also wants to coordinate her efforts with Sweet Lil's vice president of planning, Rowen Gilbert, who prefers working with spreadsheets. You assist Mary in creating the Promotions table, relating it to the Employees table, setting the appropriate field properties, creating a form with the appropriate controls, and exporting the table as a spreadsheet.

Step 1:   Create a Table

You must complete steps 1 through 5 sequentially.

Mary Culvert needs a database table to track advertising promotions for different boxes of bonbons and the Sweet Lil's employee (Mary or one of her assistants) responsible for each promotion. Each promotion will be considered a separate project, with a unique name based on the bonbon box being promoted. You show Mary how to create the Promotions table, based on the Projects sample table in the Business category of the Table Wizard.

1 Create a new table with the following fields, renaming them as necessary.

Projects sample table	Promotions table
ProjectName	**PromotionName**
EmployeeID	**EmpID**
ProjectBeginDate	**StartDate**
PurchaseOrderNumber	**BoxID**

2 Name the table Promotions, and select the No, I'll Set The Primary Key option.

3 Set PromotionName as the field to hold unique data (primary key).

4 Select the Numbers And/Or Letters I Enter When I Add New Records option.

5 Do not set any relationships at this point. Finish and close table.

For more information about	See
Creating a table	Lesson 4
Selecting a data type	Lesson 4
Setting a primary key	Lesson 4

Step 2:   Create a One-to-Many Relationship Between Tables

Each promotion will be assigned to one of four Sweet Lil's employees—Mary Culvert, Jerome Woods, Nora Bromsler, or Dale Wilson—but any one of those four may be responsible for more than one promotion. You show Mary how to establish a one-to-many relationship between the Employees table and the new Promotions table, using the EmployeeID field as the matching key field.

1 Open the Relationships window and add the Employees and Promotions tables.

2 Create a one-to-many relationship between the Employees and Promotions tables by dragging EmployeeID to EmpID field.

3 Enforce referential integrity between the Employees and Promotions tables.

4 Close the Relationships window without saving the Relationships window layout.

For more information about	See
Using the Relationships window	Lesson 4
Creating relationships between tables	Lesson 4
Enforcing referential integrity	Lesson 5

Step 3: Change a Field Property

To ensure that every promotion has a unique and meaningful name, the PromotionName field must accommodate a sufficiently long string of text and must be a required entry that is not duplicated within the Promotions table. You assist Mary in setting the relevant properties of the PromotionName field.

1. Open the Promotions table in Design view, and change the Field Size property of the PromotionName field to 40.

2. Set the Required property of the PromotionName field to Yes.

3. Verify that the Indexed property of the PromotionName field is set to Yes (No Duplicates).

4. Save and close the table.

For more information about	See
Setting field properties	Lesson 5

Step 4: Create a Form and Add a Combo Box Control

Mary needs a form for entering and viewing data in the Promotions table. To reduce the chances for error, users should select the EmpID and BoxID values from lists instead of entering them manually. Both employee names and box IDs should appear in the list by name. You show Mary how to create and save an AutoForm, and then how to change a text box to a combo box, using the Combo Box Wizard.

1. Create an AutoForm based on the Promotions table, and then save it as Promotions.

2. Open the Promotions form in Design view, and then replace the EmpID text box with a combo box that looks up the employee ID, last name, and first name in the Employees table.

3. Replace the BoxID text box with a combo box that looks up the box ID and box name in the Boxes table.

For more information about	See
Using an AutoForm	Lesson 4
Adding a list control to a form	Lesson 5

Step 5:   Export a Table

Mary also wants to coordinate her efforts with Sweet Lil's vice president of planning, Rowen Gilbert, who prefers working with spreadsheets. You show Mary how to export the Promotions table as a Microsoft Excel spreadsheet.

● Export the Promotions table in the Microsoft Excel 97-2000 (*.xls) format.

For more information about	See
Exporting a table	Lesson 6

Finish the Review & Practice

1. To continue to the next lesson, on the File menu, click Close.
2. If you're finished using Access 2000 for now, on the File menu, click Exit.

PART 3

Turning Data into Meaningful Information

7

Using Queries

**ESTIMATED
TIME
25 min.**

*For a review
of creating
and using
filters, see
Lesson 3
"Using Filters
and Reports."*

In this lesson you will learn how to:

✔ *Use the Query Wizard to simplify a search.*
✔ *Create and modify a query in Design view.*
✔ *Set criteria for queries.*
✔ *Sort data and hide fields in a query.*
✔ *Use a query to combine data from multiple tables.*
✔ *Refine the results of a query.*

Using Queries

You have organized detailed information about Sweet Lil's into a series of easily managed tables. You now want to know how to use the information to your best advantage. There are many possible reasons why you might want to retrieve only certain data from your tables. You might want to be able to predict sales trends, or the marketing department may be considering a sales campaign by region. You might also want to track sales trends by season, area, or type of item. When the key ingredient of a certain bonbon changes, you might want to quickly locate the nearest supplier of that ingredient.

Microsoft Access 2000 offers flexible methods of data retrieval that allow you to find the information you need to answer specific questions. The two most useful methods are filters and queries. *Filters* allow you to exclude irrelevant data, giving you a clear view of the data you want. *Queries* work much the same as filters, showing only the fields that contain information of interest, but queries can draw information from more than one table and preserve that view permanently.

Mary Culvert, vice president of marketing at Sweet Lil's, takes a look at the company's quarterly report and realizes the company needs to cut expenses in order to increase its profit margin in time for the annual report. She wants to review the data on the highest priced bonbons to help her determine how best to reduce overall costs. Among the data Mary needs to find is pricing information, information on the distribution of the highest priced bonbons, and sales data on baskets and boxes that include those bonbons.

In this lesson, you show Mary how to create queries, set query criteria, use the Query Wizard, sort data within query fields, and refine the results of queries, and print query results.

Understanding Queries

Posing questions as simple as "How many boxes and baskets of bonbons were sold in New York in May?" can help you learn how to make sense of the raw data available in tables. Queries are questions that you pose in Access 2000, asking "What data meets these criteria?" Queries can help you find the specific information you need.

Access 2000 offers two methods for creating queries. The first method is to use query wizards, step-by-step guides that take you through the process of creating a query. There are four Access 2000 query wizards: the Simple Query Wizard, the Crosstab Query Wizard, the Find Duplicates Query Wizard, and the Find Unmatched Query Wizard. The Simple Query Wizard is the easiest to use and is covered in this lesson. The Crosstab Wizard is discussed in Lesson 8, "Analyzing Your Data." The other two wizards, Find Duplicates and Find Unmatched, are not discussed in this book, but their names describe what they do.

Working directly in Query Design view, the second method for writing queries, allows you to develop a query from scratch and to modify existing queries. While the query is open in Query Design view, you can add new fields, insert criteria, set parameters, define sort order, and total the information in fields.

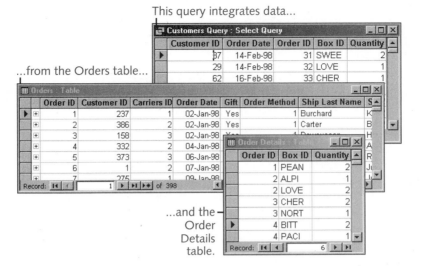

This query integrates data...

...from the Orders table...

...and the
Order
Details
table.

While filters can extract details from one table, queries allow you to extract information from several different tables at the same time. Queries can also be saved and used again.

Start Microsoft Access 2000 and reopen the database

●　If Access 2000 isn't started yet, start it. Open the Sweet Lil's database. If the Microsoft Access window doesn't fill your screen, maximize the window.

　　If you need help opening the database, see Lesson 1, "Using Forms."

Creating a Query with the Query Wizard

The easiest way to construct a new query in Access 2000 is to use the Simple Query Wizard. You simply choose the table you want to work with and then select the fields that contain the information you need. The Simple Query Wizard collects the information you request and presents it to you as a datasheet. With the results of your query in front of you, you can then modify the query until it suits your needs and answers your questions. Once it's given you the information you need, you can save the query for future use.

Before you begin using the Simple Query Wizard, you should carefully consider what types of information you would like to receive from your query. It will save you time and energy if you plan ahead, focusing on which fields to select for the data you need. Of course, you can also modify a query at any time.

Create a query

To identify the highest priced bonbons, Mary Culvert needs a list of available bonbons, in order according to the cost of each, from the Bonbons table. In the following exercise, you help her create a simple query to identify the highest-priced bonbons at Sweet Lil's and print the list for future reference.

For a demonstration of how to create a query with the Simple Query Wizard, in the Multimedia folder on the Microsoft Access 2000 Step by Step CD-ROM, double-click CreateQuery.

1 In the Database window, click Queries on the Objects bar to display the queries list.

2 On the Database window toolbar, click the New button.

The New Query dialog box appears.

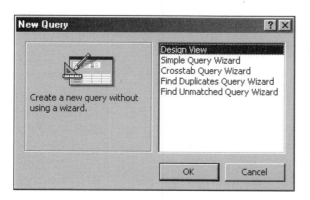

③ Double-click Simple Query Wizard in the list.

The first page of the Simple Query Wizard appears.

④ Click the Tables/Queries drop-down arrow, and then select Table: Bonbons.

The Bonbons fields are displayed in the Available Fields list.

You can also select the field and then click the Select button (>) to add the field to the Selected Fields list.

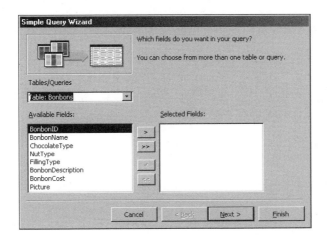

⑤ In the Available Fields list, double-click BonbonName.

BonbonName moves from the Available Fields list to the Selected Fields list.

⑥ In the Available Fields list, double-click ChocolateType, NutType, FillingType, and BonbonCost.

The four fields move to the Selected Fields list.

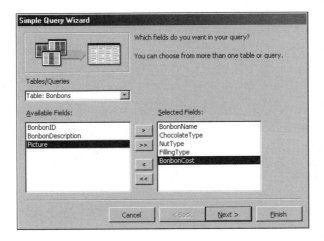

Using Queries

7   Click Next.

The second page of the Simple Query Wizard appears, asking whether you want a detail or a summary query.

8   Select the Detail option, and then click Next.

The third page of the Simple Query Wizard appears, asking you to enter a title for your query.

9   Type **Bonbon Stats For Mary** and then verify that the Open The Query To View Information option is selected.

10   Click Finish.

The Simple Query Wizard closes, and the Bonbon Stats For Mary query opens in Datasheet view.

Print the query as a datasheet

Print

1   With the Bonbon Stats For Mary query open in Datasheet view, click the Print button on the Query Datasheet toolbar.

The Print dialog box appears.

2   Click OK.

The Print dialog box closes, and the query datasheet is printed.

3   Close the query.

Modifying a Query in Design View

With your query open in Query Design view, you can add fields and controls. Query Design view lets you design the layout of your query. This is where you place controls and modify them if necessary. You can also add, rearrange, rename, and remove fields. Most of these tasks cannot be accomplished while the query is open in Datasheet view, which is where you view the results of your query in a simplified row-column format.

In addition, while working in the upper portion of the Query window in Query Design view, you can insert new tables and fields that broaden the scope of the query. These modifications can be made at any time in Query Design view.

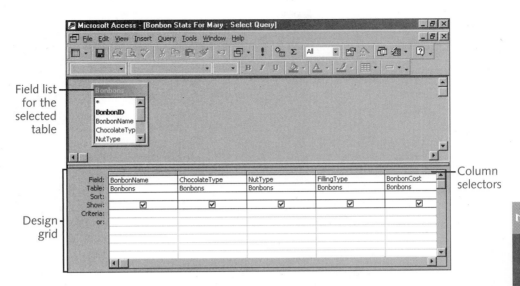

Field list for the selected table

Column selectors

Design grid

Mary Culvert reviews the query and sees the need for a few changes. She needs a description of each bonbon and, because she places more importance on the cost of the bonbons than the chocolate type, she'd like to shift the BonbonCost field to the left, between ChocolateType and BonbonName.

Add a field to an existing query

1. In the Database window, verify that Queries on the Objects bar is displayed.

2. In the queries list, verify that Bonbon Stats For Mary is selected, and then click the Design button on the Database window toolbar.

   The Bonbon Stats For Mary query opens in Design view.

3. Drag the BonbonDescription field from the Bonbons field list in the upper portion of the window to the empty field at the right of the BonbonCost field in the design grid. You may need to scroll in the field list to find the BonbonDescription field.

   The BonbonDescription field appears in the design grid.

Drag the BonbonDescription field from the Bonbons field list...

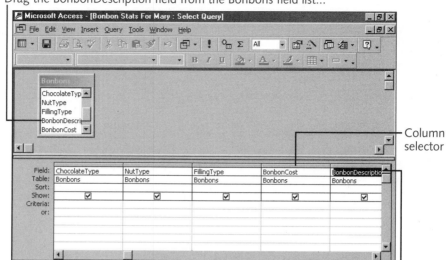

...to the empty field in the design grid.

Rearrange fields within a query

1 Click the BonbonCost column selector at the top of the design grid.

As you point to the column selector, the pointer changes to a down black arrow. Click. The BonbonCost column is selected.

2 Click the column selector again, and drag the column to the left until the border between the BonbonName column and the ChocolateType column thickens.

The BonbonCost column appears between the BonbonName and ChocolateType columns in the design grid.

New position

Remove fields from a query

Deleting a field in Query Design view does not affect the data itself, just the current view of the data.

Mary realizes that she's primarily interested in fillings, the most variable element of the bonbon product line. She asks that you remove the Chocolate Type field altogether.

1 Click the ChocolateType column selector at the top of the design grid.

The ChocolateType column is selected.

2 Press Delete.

The ChocolateType field is deleted from the query.

3 On the Query Design toolbar, click the Save button.

4 Close the Bonbon Stats For Mary query.

Save

Refining a Query with Criteria

The results of the current Bonbon Stats For Mary query show the cost of each bonbon, listed by filling type and nut type. Today, Mary Culvert receives news that almond prices are now skyrocketing. Mary wants to identify the bonbons that are already the most costly to produce and, in light of the news, those that contain almonds. She can do both by setting the appropriate criteria for her query.

For more information on how to establish query criteria, see Appendix C "Using Expressions" on the Microsoft Access 2000 Step by Step CD-ROM.

Access 2000 uses a technique called *Query By Example* (QBE) to set criteria. You select the field that contains the information you want to see. The field and contents you select serve as an example: "Show me records that look like this." In some cases, you can use an expression to match the data against a value that you select.

An *expression* is a mathematical formula used to calculate a value. Expressions can be used to establish criteria for queries. Mary will need to use an expression to find the bonbons that cost more than 25 cents to produce.

Specify criteria

1 In the Database window, verify that Queries on the Objects bar is selected.

2 In the queries list, select Bonbon Stats For Mary, and then click the Design button on the Database window toolbar.

The Bonbon Stats For Mary query opens in Design view.

Quotation marks appear around new text criteria but not around numerical criteria.

3 In the NutType column of the design grid, click the Criteria cell.

4 Type **Almond** and press Enter.

Quotation marks appear around the text.

5 In the Bonbon Cost column of the design grid, type **>.25** in the Criteria cell, and press Enter.

Find bonbons that
cost more than
25 cents to produce...

Field:	BonbonName	BonbonCost	NutType	FillingType	BonbonDescription
Table:	Bonbons	Bonbons	Bonbons	Bonbons	Bonbons
Sort:					
Show:	☑	☑	☑	☑	☑
Criteria:		>0.25	"Almond"		
or:					

...and that contain almonds.

View

6 On the Query Design toolbar, click the View button.

The refined query results appear in Datasheet view.

Bonbon Name	Bonbon Cost	Nut Type	Filling Type	Bonbon Description
Almond Supreme	$0.30	Almond	None	Whole almond hand-dipped
Almond Fudge Mocha	$0.44	Almond	Amaretto	Classic almond in amaretto.

Add more criteria

While examining the results, Mary Culvert notes that many of Sweet Lil's bonbons contain marzipan, and that marzipan is made of almonds. In light of the sudden increase in the cost of almonds, Mary decides that she will have to include the marzipan-filled bonbons in her cost-cutting analysis. You add another criterion to her query.

View

1 With the Bonbon Stats For Mary query in Datasheet view, click the View button on the Query Datasheet toolbar.

The Bonbon Stats For Mary query reappears in Design view.

2 In the FillingType column of the design grid, click the Or cell.

3 Type **Marzipan** and press Enter.

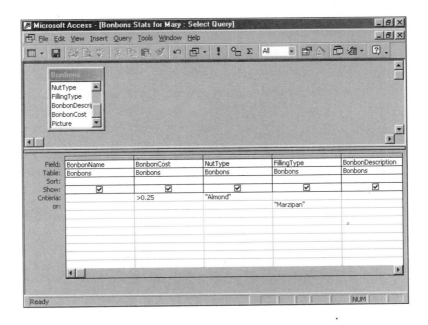

And vs. Or

Typing **Marzipan** in the Or row of the Filling Type column lets your search uncover any bonbons that contain either almonds *or* marzipan. If you type **Marzipan** in the same row as Almond, you find only bonbons that contain both almonds *and* marzipan. Access 2000 assumes that all entries on the same row in the design grid of the Query window are additional search criteria.

Save

④ On the Query Design toolbar, click the Save button.

⑤ On the Query Design toolbar, click the View button.

The query results reappear in Datasheet view.

Bonbon Name	Bonbon Cost	Nut Type	Filling Type	Bonbon Description
Marzipan Oakleaf	$0.40	None	Marzipan	Marzipan shaped in the form
Almond Supreme	$0.30	Almond	None	Whole almond hand-dipped
Almond Fudge Mocha	$0.44	Almond	Amaretto	Classic almond in amaretto.
Marzipan Delight	$0.38	None	Marzipan	Delicious marzipan with dark
Marzipan Finch	$0.32	None	Marzipan	Finch-shaped marzipan with
Marzipan Maple	$0.37	None	Marzipan	Marzipan shaped in the form
Marzipan Marvel	$0.33	None	Marzipan	Almond-shaped marzipan wi
Marzipan Swallow	$0.34	None	Marzipan	Swallow-shaped marzipan w

Using Queries

Presenting a Query More Effectively

A well-designed query can answer not just one but a number of related questions, simply by varying the presentation. The results of a query can be sorted to make it easier to find the information you need immediately. To find a particular bonbon ingredient, for example, you could sort the bonbons alphabetically by filling. To find a specifically priced bonbon, you could sort the records by cost.

For a cleaner presentation, you can also hide unnecessary information. You can hide fields within your query if you don't need them to appear in your current results, but you do require them in order to produce the desired results. For example, you may want to sort the bonbons by their unique ID numbers but keep those numbers hidden.

Sorting the query results in Datasheet view leaves the original query intact; sorting in Design view is a change to the query itself, allowing the sort to be saved along with the query.

In these exercises, you show Mary how to sort and hide fields in Query Design view.

Sort records alphabetically in Datasheet view

1   Verify that the Bonbon Stats For Mary query is open in Datasheet view.

2   Click any field in the Filling Type column.

Sort Ascending

3   On the Query Datasheet toolbar, click the Sort Ascending button.

The records in the query reappear, sorted alphabetically by filling type.

Bonbon Name	Bonbon Cost	Nut Type	Filling Type	Bonbon Description
Almond Fudge Mocha	$0.44	Almond	Amaretto	Classic almond in amaretto.
Marzipan Swallow	$0.34	None	Marzipan	Swallow-shaped marzipan w
Marzipan Marvel	$0.33	None	Marzipan	Almond-shaped marzipan wi
Marzipan Maple	$0.37	None	Marzipan	Marzipan shaped in the form
Marzipan Finch	$0.32	None	Marzipan	Finch-shaped marzipan with
Marzipan Delight	$0.38	None	Marzipan	Delicious marzipan with dark
Marzipan Oakleaf	$0.40	None	Marzipan	Marzipan shaped in the form
Almond Supreme	$0.30	Almond	None	Whole almond hand-dipped

4   On the Query Datasheet toolbar, click the Print button to print the query results.

Print

Sort records by two fields in Design view

Recalling that bonbons containing nuts are nearly always the most expensive types, Mary decides to sort the query by cost and by nut type. This will make it easy for her to identify the higher-priced bonbons, because they'll be ranked first by cost, and then by nut type within each cost level. By setting up the sort in Design view, Mary can save the new sort order as part of the query.

View

① With the Bonbon Stats For Mary query in Datasheet view, click the View button.

The Bonbon Stats For Mary query reappears in Design view.

② In the design grid, click the Sort box of the NutType column.

A drop-down arrow appears in the Sort box.

③ Click the Sort drop-down arrow, and then select Ascending.

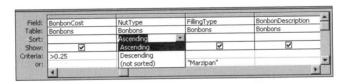

④ Click the Sort cell of the BonbonCost column, click the Sort drop-down arrow, and then select Descending.

View

⑤ On the Query Design toolbar, click the View button to switch to Datasheet view.

The query results are now sorted by cost, with the most expensive bonbons first. Any items with the same cost are then sorted alphabetically by nut type.

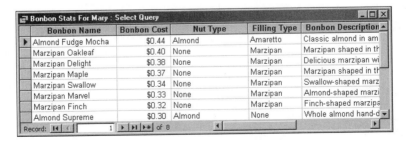

⑥ On the Query Datasheet toolbar, click the Print button.

The query results are printed.

Hide a field

Mary decides that she doesn't really need to see the nut type, just the cost. Since nut type is a factor in determining the cost, it must be included in the query, but it need not appear in the results. Hiding the field will return the desired results without including the field in those results.

View

1 With the Bonbon Stats For Mary query in Datasheet view, click the View button.

The Bonbon Stats For Mary query reappears in Design view.

2 In the NutType column, clear the Show check box.

> Clear the Show check box
> to hide the NutType field.

Field:	BonbonName	BonbonCost	NutType		FillingType	BonbonDescription
Table:	Bonbons	Bonbons	Bonbons		Bonbons	Bonbons
Sort:		Descending	Ascending			
Show:	☑	☑	☐		☑	☑
Criteria:		>0.25	"Almond"			
or:					"Marzipan"	

View

3 On the Query Design toolbar, click the View button to switch to Datasheet view.

In Datasheet view the NutType field is no longer visible, but the query is still sorted by nut type within cost, and the NutType field has not been deleted from the query.

4 Close and save the Bonbon Stats For Mary query.

Joining Related Tables in the Query Window

Relationships between tables are discussed in Lesson 4, "Managing Database Change."

When you create a query that involves more than one table, Access 2000 needs to know the fields by which the tables are related: the field or fields they have in common. Access 2000 uses these table relationships to combine related data from multiple tables. When fields of more than one table are used in a query, a join line appears between the related fields.

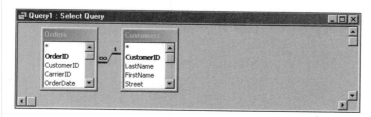

Creating a Query Using Related Tables

The executive staff ask Mary Culvert for a detailed analysis of the company's orders for the first quarter of 1998, to compare with this year's orders to date. Mary decides to include order IDs, customer names, and the date of the orders. Some of this information is contained in the Orders table and some in the Customers table. The two tables are related through the Customer ID field.

Set up a query with two tables

In this exercise, you help Mary create a new query in Query Design view using the Orders and Customers tables, setting criteria to list sales for the last quarter of 1998.

1   In the Database window, click Queries on the Objects bar.

2   On the Database window toolbar, click the New button.

The New Query dialog box appears.

3   In the New Query dialog box, double-click Design View.

The Query window opens, and the Show Table dialog box appears.

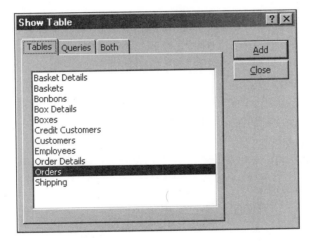

4   In the tables list, double-click Orders, and then double-click Customers.

The Orders table and Customers table field lists appear in the upper portion of the Query window.

5   Close the Show Table dialog box.

In the upper portion of the Query window, a join line connects the CustomerID fields of the Orders field list and the Customers field list.

Add fields to a query using multiple tables

1 In the Orders field list of the Query window, double-click CustomerID, OrderID, and OrderDate.

The three fields appear in the design grid.

2 In the Customers field list, double-click LastName.

The LastName field is added to the design grid.

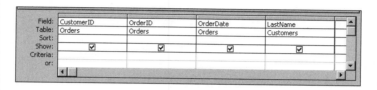

3 On the Query Design toolbar, click the Save button.

The Save As dialog box appears.

Save

4 In the Query Name box, type **Order Information**, and then press Enter.

Set criteria for the query

1 In the Criteria cell of the OrderDate column, type **Between 1-Oct-98 And 31-Dec-98** and press Enter.

Between #10/1/98# and #12/31/98# appears in the OrderDate Criteria cell of the design grid.

2 In the OrderDate column selector at the top of the design grid, double-click the right border of the column selector.

The right border moves to the right, and the column is resized to show the complete expression.

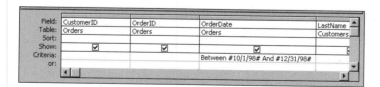

3 On the Query Design toolbar, click the Save button.

View

④ On the Query Design toolbar, click the View button.

The datasheet appears, with order IDs, customer IDs, order dates, and last names of the customers who placed orders in the last quarter of 1998.

⑤ Close the Order Information query.

One Step Further ## Fine-tuning Queries

Access 2000 provides additional ways to help you refine queries for your intended audience. You can change the field labels to clarify the information within your fields. This assists everyone who sees the query results. For example, an ID field can be given a more informative column heading. And when you want to filter out all but the most significant information, you can use the Show Top filter to limit the available information within each field to the first few rows or a percentage of the rows.

Change a field label

Mary wants to clarify the column headings on some of the field names in her query. In this exercise, you rename a field column heading by setting the Field Caption property for the CustomerID field.

① In the Database window, verify that Queries on the Objects bar is selected.

2 In the queries list, select Order Information, and then click the Design button on the Database window toolbar.

The Order Information query opens in Design view.

3 In the CustomerID column of the design grid, click the Field cell.

4 On the Query Design toolbar, click the Properties button.

The property sheet for the CustomerID field opens.

Properties

5 In the Caption property box, type **Winter Customers**

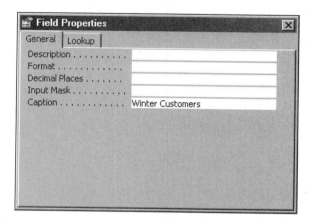

6 Close the property sheet.

7 On the Query Design toolbar, click the View button to switch to Datasheet view.

The CustomerID field is renamed Winter Customers.

View

8 Double-click the right border of the Winter Customers column selector to view the entire field name.

Display only the top values

After taking another look at the Order Information query, Mary decides that she'd now like to see a list of only the 25 most recent orders. You use the Top Values property to limit the query to the top 25 values in the Order Date column.

View

1 With the Order Information query in Datasheet view, click the View button.

The Order Information query reappears in Design view.

2 In the OrderDate column, click the Sort row, click the drop-down arrow, and then select Descending.

The order dates are sorted in descending order, with the most recent dates at the top.

You can also use Top Values to select a given percentage of the available records.

3 On the Query Design toolbar, click the Top Values drop-down arrow, and then select 25.

4 On the Query Design toolbar, click the View button to switch back to Datasheet view.

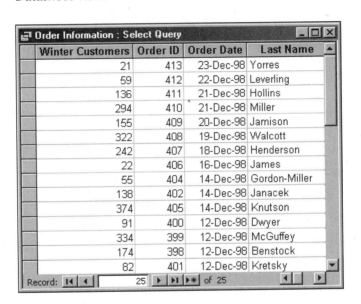

5 Save and close the query.

Finish the lesson

1 To continue to the next lesson, on the File menu, click Close.

2 If you're finished using Access 2000 for now, on the File menu, click Exit.

Lesson 7 Quick Reference

To	Do this	Button
Create a query	In the Database window, click Queries on the Objects bar, and then click the New button on the Database window toolbar. Double-click Simple Query Wizard, and follow the instructions.	
Print a query	With the query open in Datasheet view, click the Print button on the Query Datasheet toolbar, and click OK.	🖨️
Add a field to a query	In Design view, in the upper portion of the Query window, double-click the field in the appropriate field list.	
Rearrange fields	In Design view, in the design grid, click the column selector and drag the column to the new position.	
Remove a field from a query	In Design view, in the design grid, click the appropriate column selector, and press Delete.	
Set criteria	In Design view, enter criteria in the appropriate Criteria cells of the design grid.	
Sort records in a query	In Datasheet view, click the field or fields you want to sort, and then click the Sort Ascending or Sort Descending button on the Query Datasheet toolbar.	A↓ Z↓
Hide a field in a query	In Design view, in the design grid, clear the Show check box of the field you want to hide.	
Add two tables to a query	In the Database window, click Queries on the Objects bar, and then click the New button on the Database window toolbar. In the New Query dialog box, double-click Design View, and then double-click the two tables in the tables list.	
Set field properties	In Design view, select the field in the design grid. Click the Properties button on the Query Design toolbar. Change the appropriate property in the property sheet.	📑
Display the top values of a query	In Design view, sort the column whose values you want to display. Click the Top Values drop-down arrow, select the number of values you want, and then switch to Datasheet view to top display the values.	

8

Analyzing Your Data

ESTIMATED TIME 40 min.

In this lesson you will learn how to:

✔ *Arrange data into groups and summaries.*

✔ *Create descriptive query column headings.*

✔ *Add a calculated field to a query.*

✔ *Use a crosstab query to analyze data.*

✔ *Work with parameter values.*

✔ *Present the results of a query in a chart.*

Queries put the "access" into Microsoft Access 2000. Without queries, the information stored in your database is little more than rows and columns of raw data. By writing queries carefully, you can access and analyze the data, which can then be put to use. Queries are also used to create new data.

You can take three different approaches to data analysis by query in Access 2000. The first is to summarize and group data from selected fields. The second is to construct calculations on the data within the fields of the query. The third is to create a crosstab query, which can combine the previous two approaches.

Summary queries can be used when you need information on groups of records taken as a whole, rather than on the individual records themselves. For example, a list of every order ever placed is not particularly useful; if volume is high, a complete list might even be counterproductive. But a summary of those orders, containing only totals or averages and grouped by region or product, can help you plan your next marketing campaign.

You can create a *calculated field* by adding a more complex expression to a field that holds numeric information. There are many types of calculations you can perform in a query. For example, you can calculate the sum or average of the values in one field, multiply the values in two fields, or calculate the date three months from the current date. You can use a predefined calculation that Access 2000 provides or custom calculations that you define. For example, you can use the predefined Totals calculation to compute the sum, average, count, minimum, maximum, standard deviation, or variance for groups of records or for all the records combined.

tip

When you display the result of a calculation in a field, the result isn't actually stored in the underlying table. Instead, Access 2000 reruns the calculation each time you run the query so that the result is always based on the most current data in the database. Therefore, you can't manually update the calculated result.

A *crosstab query* displays summarized values (sums, counts, and averages) from one field in a table, grouping them by one set of facts listed down the left side of the datasheet and another set of facts listed across the top of the datasheet. For example, you can use a single crosstab query for two related tasks: to group sales by product and to show total sales values for those products in a "cross-tabulated" or spreadsheet-like view.

All three approaches to data analysis by query can be used to find answers to requests made by Fred Mallon, the shipping coordinator at Sweet Lil's. Fred needs to know how many orders customers in Canada and the United States placed in 1998. These numbers will let him reorganize his shipping schedule for the remainder of 1999 and create a draft version of the upcoming holiday shipping schedule.

In this lesson, you find answers to Fred's requests by using the summarization capability of Access queries.

Start Microsoft Access 2000 and reopen the database

● If Access 2000 isn't started yet, start it. Open the Sweet Lil's database. If the Microsoft Access window doesn't fill your screen, maximize the window.

If you need help opening the database, see Lesson 1, "Using Forms."

Turning Raw Data into Meaningful Information

Raw data, as it appears in a database table, is just rows and columns of information with some semblance of order but no immediately obvious connection. Queries allow you to select the specific data you need, arrange and view that data in different ways, and manipulate existing data to create entirely new information.

In these exercises, you find the information Fred needs by first modifying an existing query to list the number of 1998 orders made by customers in Canada and the United States. The final query will perform calculations, group the query results, and then present a simple answer to this request in two easy-to-read fields.

Use an existing query to create a summary query

You could begin a new query, but in most cases it's easier to modify an existing query that already provides some of the information you want. You use the existing Order Review query to create a new query that provides more specific information. The Order Review query is a list of the orders made by each Sweet Lil's customer. It draws from the Orders and Customers tables as its source tables, and it lists orders by order ID. In addition, it displays the order date and the customer's first and last name. In this exercise, you group this information by country and then summarize it to extract information about the grouped data.

❶ In the Database window, click Queries on the Objects bar to display the queries list.

2 In the queries list, select Order Review, and then click the Design button on the Database window toolbar.

The Order Review query opens in Design view.

Field lists for the
Customers and
Orders tables

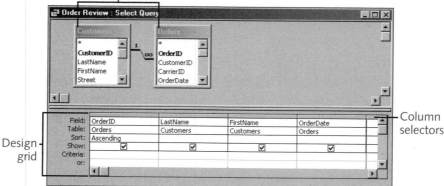

Column
selectors

Design
grid

3 On the File menu, click Save As.

The Save As dialog box appears.

4 In the Save Query 'Order Review' To box, type **Total Orders By Country**

5 In the As box, click the drop-down arrow, select Query, and click OK.

The name of the new query appears in the Query window title bar and in the Database window queries list.

Add a field to the query

In this exercise, you add the Country field that lets Fred group the data according to the country of origin.

In the upper portion of the Query window, double-click the Country field in the Customers field list.

The Country field appears in the design grid.

Rearrange fields within the query

The Country field provides the information you need to group the records, so it should be the first field processed by the query. Fields are processed as they appear in the design grid, reading from left to right. In this exercise, you move the Country field to the leftmost position in the design grid.

1 Click the Country column selector at the top of the design grid.

The Country column is selected.

2 Drag the column selector to the first column on the left.

Drag from here...

...to here.

The Country field appears as the first column in the design grid.

Delete fields from the query

The LastName, FirstName, and OrderDate fields are no longer needed in the new query, since you are searching for the total number of orders made in the United States and Canada. In this exercise, you remove the fields.

1 Click the LastName column selector, and then drag across the FirstName and OrderDate column selectors.

The three columns are selected.

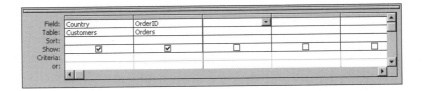

2 Press Delete.

The LastName, FirstName, and OrderDate columns are deleted from the query. The Country and OrderID columns remain in the design grid.

Perform calculations and group the query results

The data you need for your summary is now specified within the query. In this exercise, you group the data by country and add an expression that counts the number of orders in each group in order to fulfill Fred's request.

Totals

1 On the Query Design toolbar, click the Totals button.

A row called Total appears in the design grid. The words *Group By* appear in the Total cells of each column.

2 In the OrderID column, click the Total cell, click the drop-down arrow, and then select Count.

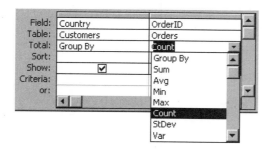

The Count function counts the total number of orders.

View

3 On the Query Design toolbar, click the View button.

The Total Orders By Country query reappears in Datasheet view.

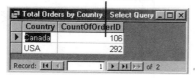

The datasheet shows the total number of orders for each country. CountOfOrderID becomes the second column, in place of OrderID. You may need to widen the field to see the full field name.

Group totals by two fields

Being able to get the group total of two fields is a very useful tool. So far in this lesson, you have found the total number of orders. But Fred is considering dividing the customers into regional zones. He asks you for a further breakdown into states and provinces. To answer this request, you group by a second field in this exercise.

View

① With the query in Datasheet view, click the View button on the Query Datasheet toolbar.

The Total Orders By Country query reappears in Design view.

② In the upper portion of the Query window, click the StateOrProvince field of the Customers field list and drag it to the OrderID column in the design grid.

The StateOrProvince column appears in the design grid between the Country and OrderID columns. The words *Group By* appear in the Total cell of the StateOrProvince column.

View

③ On the Query Design toolbar, click the View button.

The Total Orders By Country query reappears in Datasheet view.

Sort Ascending

④ On the Query Datasheet toolbar, click the Sort Ascending button.

The query results are grouped first by country (because Country is the first column in the design grid) and then by state or province. The totals are calculated, not by country, but for each state or province within each country.

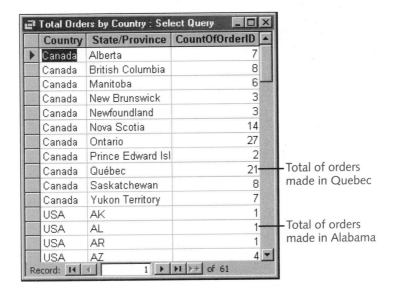

Total of orders made in Quebec

Total of orders made in Alabama

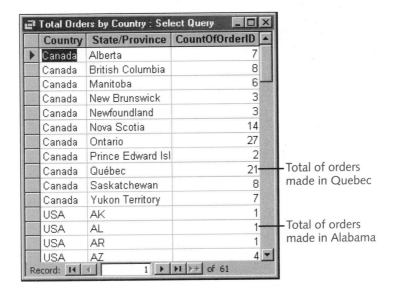

(sidebar) Analyzing Your Data

5 Close the Total Orders By Country query, clicking Yes when you are prompted to save changes.

Creating Descriptive Column Names

Columns in a query are fields that can be used in a form, a report, or even other queries. You should make sure that the column names are short and succinct, but descriptive of their content.

CountOfOrderID is a generic field name used by Access 2000, one of many designed to be temporary placeholders. Such names can be easily changed. If different groups of people are going to read the results of a query, as is often the case at Sweet Lil's, being able to make field names more meaningful is a useful feature. In this case, the Total Orders By Country query will be used by the shipping department to help reorganize its shipping schedule, and by the marketing department to conduct research on new international marketing tactics.

Change a column heading

1 In the Database window, verify that Queries on the Objects bar is selected.

2 In the queries list, select Total Orders By Country, and then click the Design button on the Database window toolbar.

The Total Orders By Country query opens in Design view.

Access 2000 automatically inserts a space after the colon to make the column heading more readable.

3 In the design grid, place the insertion point just to the left of the OrderID field name.

4 Type **Total Orders:**

The Total Orders: OrderID field appears in the design grid.

5 Double-click the right border of the column selector.

The right border moves to the right, and the column is resized to show the complete expression.

View

6 On the Query Design toolbar, click the View button to switch to Datasheet View and examine your results.

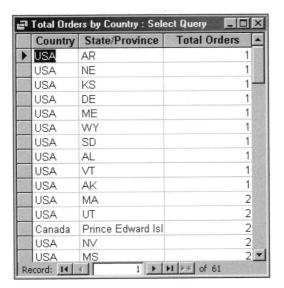

7 Close the Total Orders By Country query, clicking Yes when you are prompted to save changes.

Using Queries with Calculated Fields to Analyze Data

With the help of Impact Public Relations, the marketing department at Sweet Lil's is putting the finishing touches on an advertising campaign for the summer of 1999. Mary Culvert, vice president of marketing, is optimistic that the ad campaign will result in increased sales of Sweet Lil's bonbon boxes and baskets. She estimates that, as a result of the ad campaign, the company can raise prices by 25 percent without damaging sales.

Mary asks you to present her with some facts on paper. She would like to have a list of the new box prices after a 25 percent increase.

Using a query to list the results of price increases is a convenient way to plan for future changes. If Mary changes her mind and wants to raise prices further, or decides that 25 percent is too high, you can easily amend the query.

In these exercises, you create a new query based on the Boxes table, insert a calculated field into the query in response to Mary's request, and make a few quick improvements.

Create a new query

1   In the Database window, click Queries on the Objects bar.

2   In the Database window, click the New button.

The New Query dialog box appears.

3   Double-click Design View.

The Query window opens, and the Show Table dialog box appears.

4   In the tables list, select Boxes, and then click Add.

The Boxes table field list appears in the upper portion of the Query window.

5   Close the Show Table dialog box.

The Query window remains open.

6   In the Boxes field list, double-click BoxName and then BoxPrice.

The BoxName and BoxPrice fields appear in the design grid.

View

7   On the Query Design toolbar, click the View button.

The query reappears in Datasheet view, displaying the price for each box of chocolates.

Box Name	Box Price
Alpine Collection	$20.75
Bittersweets	$27.75
Cherry Classics	$16.25
Fudge Mocha Fantasy	$18.00
Heavenly Hazelnuts	$15.75
International	$34.00
Island Collection	$35.00
Lover's Hearts	$17.50
Marzipan Marvels	$32.25
Northwind Collection	$33.25
Pacific Opulence	$21.00
Peanut Butter Delights	$19.00
Supremes	$18.25
Sweet Creams	$23.00
Sweet and Bitter	$27.75

Record: |◄ ◄ | 1 | ► ►| ►* | c

Boxname

For more information on expressions, see Lesson 9, "Merging Data onto One Form."

View

Add a calculated field

In this exercise, you insert an expression into a field to show what the results would be if bonbon prices were raised by 25 percent, in accordance with Mary's predictions.

1 With the query in Datasheet view, click the View button on the Query Datasheet toolbar.

The Query1 query reappears in Design view.

2 Click the empty cell to the right of the BoxPrice cell in the Field row.

3 Type the expression **[BoxPrice]*1.25** and then press Enter.

4 To see the whole expression, double-click the right border of the Expr1: [BoxPrice]*1.25 column selector.

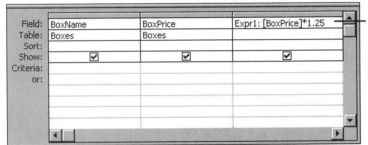

The expression field calculates a projected 25 percent increase.

Field:	BoxName	BoxPrice	Expr1: [BoxPrice]*1.25
Table:	Boxes	Boxes	
Sort:			
Show:	☑	☑	☑
Criteria:			
or:			

View

5 On the Query Design toolbar, click the View button to switch to Datasheet view and examine the results.

Box Name	Box Price	Expr1
▶ Alpine Collection	$20.75	25.9375
Bittersweets	$27.75	34.6875
Cherry Classics	$16.25	20.3125
Fudge Mocha Fantasy	$18.00	22.5
Heavenly Hazelnuts	$15.75	19.6875
International	$34.00	42.5
Island Collection	$35.00	43.75
Lover's Hearts	$17.50	21.875
Marzipan Marvels	$32.25	40.3125
Northwind Collection	$33.25	41.5625
Pacific Opulence	$21.00	26.25
Peanut Butter Delights	$19.00	23.75
Supremes	$18.25	22.8125
Sweet Creams	$23.00	28.75
Sweet and Bitter	$27.75	34.6875
*	$0.00	

Customize the calculated field

Mary asks if you can change the generic, "placeholder" field name, Expr1, to New Price and display it as dollars and cents. In this exercise, you use the property sheet to change the format to Currency, add a meaningful description of the expression, and change the name to New Price.

View

Properties

1 With the query in Datasheet view, click the View button on the Query Datasheet toolbar.

The query reappears in Design view.

2 Verify that the Expr1 Column is active. On the Query Design toolbar, click the Properties button.

The field property sheet appears.

3 Click the Description property box, and then type **Shows prices raised by 25 percent**

4 Click the Format property box, click the drop-down arrow, and then select Currency.

The contents of the field will appear as dollars and cents in Datasheet view.

5 Click the Caption property box, and then type **New Price**

New Price will appear as the column heading in Datasheet view.

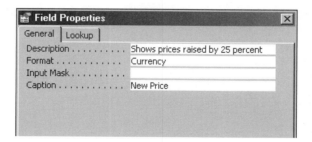

6 Close the property sheet.

7 Select Expr1 and type NewPrice.

8 Examine the design grid now.

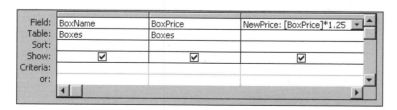

9 Close the query, clicking Yes when you are prompted to save changes.
The Save As dialog box appears.

10 In the Query Name box, type **Price Increases**, and then press Enter.
The new query Price Increases closes and appears in the Database window queries list.

Summarizing and Calculating with a Crosstab Query

A crosstab query uses the same row-and-column format as a table to provide a summary analysis of information. A crosstab query, however, also includes a calculating column that provides additional information through automatic calculation.

Crosstab queries can be used in a variety of ways. They are especially useful in calculating sales totals or sums of values.

When designing a crosstab query, you must decide whether you want to base the crosstab query on tables, queries, or both. If you select both, the list of tables and queries will be combined alphabetically into one list that appears in the query window.

The Crosstab Query Wizard allows you to choose the fields that will be the source of the data in the rows and columns of your query. You also can specify the data that will be placed at the intersection of the rows and columns, and whether you want that data to be used to perform a calculation. As you respond to the wizard, a diagram of the query appears in the wizard.

Rowen Gilbert, vice president of planning, has been considering Mary's intention to raise prices 25 percent. He's concerned that perhaps the current quality of the ingredients in the bonbons isn't high enough to justify such a large price increase. He says that, to maintain the company's reputation, Sweet Lil's must first ensure that the product is worthy of the price.

Rowen wants to be able to view the total sales for each box of bonbons produced by Sweet Lil's during 1998 so that he can see how profitable sales were for each type of box and decide which chocolates justify more expensive ingredients. In these exercises, you create a crosstab query that provides a year's worth of sales totals for the boxed bonbons.

Create the query with the Crosstab Query Wizard

1 In the Database window, click Queries on the Objects bar.

2 On the Database window toolbar, click the New button.

The New Query dialog box appears.

3 In the list of the New Query dialog box, double-click Crosstab Query Wizard.

The first page of the Crosstab Query Wizard appears.

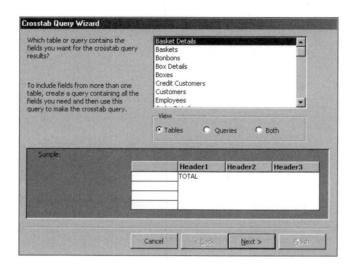

4 In the View area, select the Queries option.

5 Scroll down, select Sales By Box from the list of queries, and then click Next.

The second page of the Crosstab Query Wizard appears, with the fields of the Sales By Box query displayed in the Available Fields list.

6 In the Available Fields list, double-click BoxName, and then click Next.

BoxName appears in the Selected Fields list. The values of BoxName become the row headings for the crosstab query: *BoxName* becomes the leftmost column heading, *BoxName1* becomes the second row heading, and so on.

Then the third page of the Crosstab Query Wizard appears.

7 Select OrderDate from the list of query fields, and then click Next.

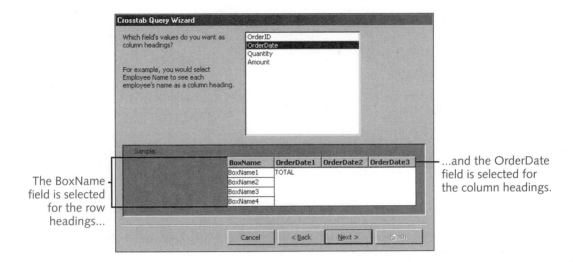

The BoxName field is selected for the row headings...

...and the OrderDate field is selected for the column headings.

The fourth page of the Crosstab Query Wizard appears.

8 Select Date from the list of possible intervals, and then click Next.

The Order Date field is grouped by date.

Then the fifth page of the Crosstab Query Wizard appears.

9 Select Amount from the Fields list.

Avg(Amount) appears in the crosstab query calculated field.

Avg appears as the function only because it's first on the list of available functions. Choose your desired function in the next step.

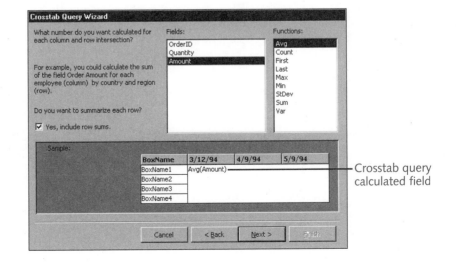

Crosstab query calculated field

10 Select Sum from the Functions list.

Sum appears in the crosstab query calculated field as the calculation to be performed.

11 Click Next.

The last page of the Crosstab Query Wizard appears, with the query name Sales By Box_Crosstab displayed in the title bar.

12 Accept the name Sales By Box_Crosstab by clicking Finish.

The Crosstab Query Wizard closes, and the first Enter Parameter Value dialog box appears.

Complete the crosstab query

The first parameter value is the beginning date in the range of dates you want the query to cover.

1 In the first Enter Parameter Value dialog box, type **1-Jan-98**, and then press Enter.

The second Enter Parameter Value dialog box appears.

The second parameter value is the ending date in the range of dates you want the query to cover.

2 Type **31-Dec-98**, and then press Enter.

The crosstab query Sales By Box_Crosstab appears in Datasheet view.

Box Name	Total Of Amou	1/10/98	1/12/98	1/15/98	1/17/98	1/18/98
Alpine Collection	$1,867.50					$41.50
Bittersweets	$5,577.75				$27.75	
Cherry Classics	$1,348.75					
Fudge Mocha Fantasy	$2,358.00	$18.00				$36.00
Heavenly Hazelnuts	$1,858.50				$31.50	
International	$2,278.00					
Island Collection	$2,170.00					
Lover's Hearts	$3,797.50					
Marzipan Marvels	$1,354.50	$64.50				
Northwind Collection	$7,082.25		$66.50			
Pacific Opulence	$1,428.00		$21.00	$21.00		
Peanut Butter Delights	$1,691.00				$19.00	
Supremes	$876.00				$36.50	
Sweet and Bitter	$4,634.25			$55.50	$27.75	$83.25
Sweet Creams	$2,047.00					$23.00

Record: 14 4 | 1 | ▶ ▶I ▶* of 15

3 Close the Sales By Box_Crosstab query.

The Sales By Box_Crosstab query appears in the Database window queries list.

The query now displays the total sales for each box of bonbons produced by Sweet Lil's. Total sales for each type of box sold during 1998 are displayed in the Total Of Amount column. Rowen can look at the query to see how profitable sales were for each box of chocolates. By studying the results, he can decide which chocolates justify ingredient upgrades.

One Step Further Presenting Data in a Chart

As you have seen, queries allow you to take the raw data in your tables and rework it into useful information in a format that is easy to read and easy to understand. With Access 2000, you can go one step further by presenting the same information graphically. Very few people are able to spot trends by looking at a column of numbers, but when the same data is presented as a graph, trends often become immediately obvious.

Access 2000 provides a collection of 20 chart types in its Chart Wizard, ranging from bubble charts to doughnut charts to simple column or bar charts. The charts offer vertical, horizontal, spherical, and conical diagramming. Brilliant colors represent the different cells or fields in the table or query as they appear in chart form.

In these exercises, you help Rowen convert data from the Sales By Box query into a graphical format. Once the query is converted, Rowen can quickly identify the high and low points in sales totals of Sweet Lil's boxed bonbons.

Create the chart with the Chart Wizard

1. In the Database window, click Reports on the Objects bar.
2. On the Database window toolbar, click the New button.

   The New Report dialog box appears.

You can type S to jump to tables that start with S.

3. In the reports list at the top of the dialog box, select Chart Wizard.
4. In the Choose The Table Or Query Where The Object's Data Comes From box, click the drop-down arrow, select the Sales By Box query from the list, and click OK.

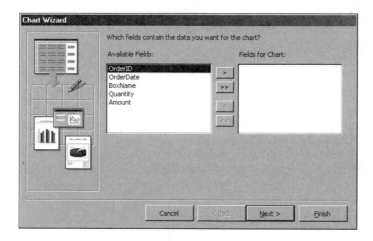

The first page of the Chart Wizard appears.

5   In the Available Fields list, double-click OrderDate, BoxName, and Quantity.
The three fields move to the Fields For Chart list.

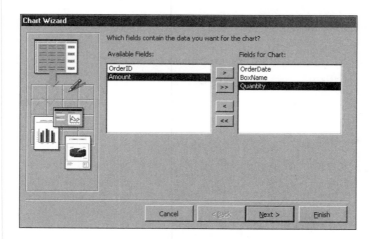

6   Click Next.

The second page of the Chart Wizard appears, displaying 20 graphical chart presentations.

Line Chart

7   Click the Line Chart button (the third button in the third row), and then click Next.

The third page of the Chart Wizard appears.

SumOfQuantity is the field currently displayed on the vertical axis of the chart.

8 Double-click SumOfQuantity.

The Summarize dialog box appears.

9 In the Summarize 'Quantity' By list, select Count, and click OK.

The Summarize dialog box closes, and the third page of the Chart Wizard reappears, with SumOfQuantity replaced by CountOfQuantity.

Preview the chart in the Chart Wizard

Preview Chart

1 On the third page of the Chart Wizard, click the Preview Chart button.

Both the Sample Preview dialog box and the first Enter Parameter Value dialog box open.

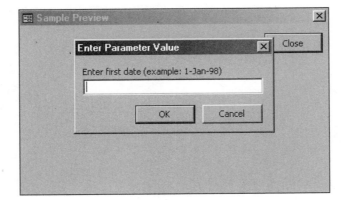

2 In the first Enter Parameter Value dialog box, type **1-Jan-98**, and then press Enter.

The second Enter Parameter Value dialog box appears.

3 In the second Enter Parameter Value dialog box, type **31-Dec-98**, and then press Enter.

The Sample Preview dialog box displays a preview of the Sales By Box chart for 1998.

Bonbon boxes

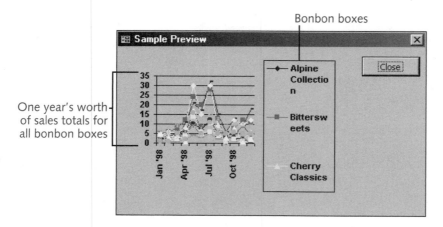

One year's worth of sales totals for all bonbon boxes

④ Close the Sample Preview dialog box to return to the third page of the Chart Wizard.

Change the parameters of the chart

The Sales By Box chart, as it appears in the Sample Preview dialog box, is rather difficult to read. With all four quarters of 1998 visible, too much information is displayed in a small amount of space. In this exercise, you reduce the parameters of the chart to make it easier to read and to improve its use as an analytical tool.

① Double-click the OrderDate By Month box.

The Group dialog box appears.

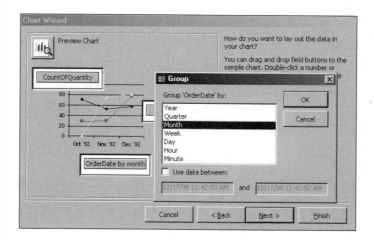

2 In the Group 'OrderDate' By list, select Quarter, and click OK.

The Group dialog box closes, and the OrderDate By Quarter box replaces the OrderDate By Month box.

3 Click Preview Chart.

The first Enter Parameter Value dialog box appears.

4 Type **1-Jan-98**, and then press Enter.

The second Enter Parameter Value dialog box appears.

5 Type **31-Mar-98**, and then press Enter.

The second Enter Parameter Value dialog box closes, and the Sample Preview dialog box appears. The Sales amounts for the first quarter of 1998 appear in a row. Each box of bonbons is represented by a different color and shape on the chart.

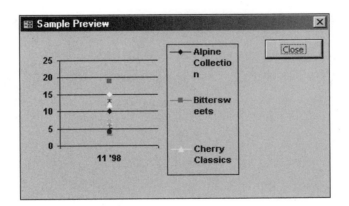

Close the Chart Wizard

1 Click Close to return to the third page of the Chart Wizard.

2 Click Finish.

The first Enter Parameter Value dialog box appears.

3 Type **1-Jan-98**, and then press Enter.

The second Enter Parameter Value dialog box appears.

4 Type **31-Mar-98**, and then press Enter.

The second Enter Parameter Value dialog box closes, and the final version of the chart appears.

5 Close the chart, clicking Yes when you are prompted to save changes.

6 Type **Sales By Box Chart**, and then press Enter.

Finish the lesson

① To continue to the next lesson, on the File menu, click Close.

② If you're finished using Access 2000 for now, on the File menu, click Exit.

Lesson 8 Quick Reference

To	Do this	Button
Create a new query by modifying an existing query	Open an existing query in Design view. On the File menu, click Save As to rename the query. Make any changes to the new query.	
Add a field to a query	In Design view, double-click the field in the field list.	
Rearrange fields in a query	In Design view, click the column selector in the design grid and drag the column to the new position.	
Delete a field from a query	In Design view, click the column selector in the design grid, and press Delete.	
Group the results of a query	In Design view, click the Totals button on the Query Design toolbar. Click the Total cell for the field you want to group by. Click the cell arrow, and select the basis for the grouping.	Σ
Change a column heading	In Design view, click the Properties button on the Query Design toolbar, and type the new name in the Caption property box for the selected field.	
Add a calculated field to a query	In Design view, type an expression in the Field row of a blank column in the design grid.	
Customize a calculated field	In Design view, click the Properties button on the Query Design toolbar, and make changes in the property sheet.	
Create a crosstab query	In the Database window, click Queries on the Objects bar, and then click the New button. Select Crosstab Query Wizard, and follow the instructions.	
Create a chart based on a query	In the Database window, click Reports on the Objects bar, and then click the New button. Select Chart Wizard. Click the Tables And Queries drop-down arrow, select a query, and follow the instructions.	

LESSON 9

Merging Data onto One Form

ESTIMATED TIME
20 min.

In this lesson you will learn how to:

✔ *Use the Form Wizard to create custom forms.*

✔ *Create subforms.*

✔ *Use a table or a query as the basis for a form.*

✔ *Merge data from multiple tables by using forms.*

✔ *Create expressions that can be inserted as calculated controls.*

The marketing department at Sweet Lil's uses several forms for tracking the contents of bonbon-filled baskets and boxes. The Bonbons form identifies each bonbon, the ingredients of that bonbon and the individual cost. The Baskets and Boxes forms identify the bonbon collections, the number and type of bonbons in those collections, and the collective cost.

To review subforms, see Lesson 2 "Using Tables and Subforms.".

But as the company grows, so do its tracking needs. The management team has studied the situation and decided that it would like to see a wider range of forms that are able to interact with each other and with the data stored in the database tables. Sweet Lil's will also require a simpler method for navigating through the forms.

Many Sweet Lil's employees now use queries to track information within the Sweet Lil's database. Queries and the defined relationships between tables help users gather specific information for analysis. In a similar way, Microsoft Access 2000 forms and subforms allow data to be entered simultaneously in several places. Subforms are forms within forms that let you work with records from two separate tables or queries at the same time, within a single form. The fields in the main form contain data from one table or query, while the subform contains data from another table or query. Information in the two tables or queries is separate, but the relationship between them is maintained by using this form-within-a-form structure.

Hans Orlon, vice president of operations, is responsible for organizing and streamlining the information management system at Sweet Lil's. He meets with you to discuss ways in which the forms and subforms currently in use can be further refined to meet these goals. In this lesson, you help Hans learn more about Access 2000 form refinements and how they can be put to use in getting Hans the improvements he needs. First, you get him started building forms with subforms on his own and help him create a form that combines a table with a query. Later, you add a calculated field that uses information from a form to calculate data in a subform.

Start Microsoft Access 2000 and reopen the database

● If Access 2000 isn't started yet, start it. Open the Sweet Lil's database. If the Microsoft Access window doesn't fill your screen, maximize the window.

If you need help opening the database, see Lesson 1, "Using Forms."

Creating Custom Forms with the Form Wizard

The data necessary for Hans and you to create forms is stored in the various tables of the Sweet Lil's database. With Access 2000, you can create custom forms that bring together specific information you need from different tables and place it in one easy-to-use format.

To search for a particular customer in the Customers form, click the Find button on the Form View toolbar.

Sweet Lil's is overwhelmed with telephone orders during the holiday season. Many of the callers are longtime customers of Sweet Lil's who want to increase the amount of their order or to repeat past orders. Some callers find that they can't remember the items they ordered in years past but would like to order them again. In these exercises, you'll use the Form Wizard to create a form that lets the sales clerks see all orders placed by a particular customer.

Use the Form Wizard to create a custom form and subform

In this exercise, you use the Form Wizard to modify the Customers form by adding a subform based on the Orders Form query. With the new subform in place, Sweet Lil's employees can identify the boxes or baskets ordered by customers in the past.

① In the Database window, click Forms on the Objects bar, and then click the New button in the Database window.

The New Form dialog box appears.

② In the list in the upper portion of the dialog box, click Form Wizard.

③ Click the Tables/Queries drop-down arrow, select the Customers table, and click OK.

The first page of the Form Wizard appears. Table: Customers appears in the Tables/Queries box, and the fields of the Customers table are displayed in the Available Fields list.

④ In the Available Fields list, double-click CustomerID.

CustomerID appears in the Selected Fields list.

Choose the table you want to use...

...and then select a field.

⑤ Repeat step 4 with LastName and FirstName.

The three fields are displayed in the Selected Fields list.

Microsoft Access 2000 distinguishes fields with the same name but from different tables by adding the name of the underlying table, separated by a period, in front of the field names.

⑥ Click the Tables/Queries drop-down arrow, and then select the Orders Form query.

Query: Orders Form appears in the Tables/Queries box, and the fields of the Orders Form query are displayed in the Available Fields list.

⑦ In the Available Fields list, double-click CustomerID, OrderID, and OrderDate.

The CustomerID, OrderID, and OrderDate fields are displayed in the Selected Fields list.

8 Click Next.

The second page of the Form Wizard appears, asking how you want to view your data.

9 Select the By Customers option and the Form With Subform(s) option, and then click Next.

The third page of the Form Wizard appears, asking you to choose a form layout option.

10 Select Datasheet as the preferred layout option, and then click Next.

The fourth page of the Form Wizard appears, asking you to choose from several style options.

11 Select Standard, and then click Next.

The final page of the Form Wizard appears, asking you to name the form and subform.

12 Accept the names that appear, select the Open The Form To View Or Enter Information option, and then click Finish.

The form and subform open in Form View.

13 Resize the form and subform as necessary so that both navigation bars are visible.

Customers form

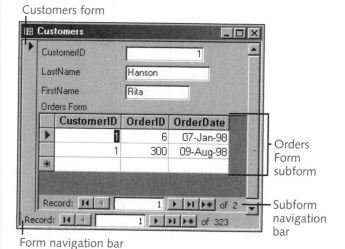

Orders Form subform

Subform navigation bar

Form navigation bar

Examine the records

In this exercise, you check the relationship between the Customers table and the Orders Form query.

Next Record

1 In the Customers form, click the Next Record button on the navigation bar at the bottom of the window.

The record for the second customer, Stephen Pence, should appear in the main Customers form, and his associated orders should appear in the Orders Form subform.

You can also click in the Last Name box and use the Find button.

2 In the Customers form, continue to move through the records until you locate and check the record for Jim Hernandez.

3 Close the form.

The new subform is saved, and it appears in the Database window forms list.

Adding a Calculated Control to a Form

After hearing news about worldwide almond shortages, vice president of marketing Mary Culvert is faced with the decision of whether to eliminate bonbons filled with marzipan and almond. Such bonbons are contained in at least three of the prepackaged boxes of bonbons. If the bonbons containing almonds are removed from inventory, the contents of many of the boxes must also change, which might eventually affect sales.

Before making the decision, Mary needs more facts about the current value of each box and basket. Total sales and averaged sales values are available from the Box Sales form. The quantity sold is listed in a column in the Box Sales subform, but this column does not show the total number of bonbons sold, an important piece of data that would help Mary make her decision. Mary asks you to redesign the Box Sales Subform to include the total number of boxes sold. You'll find the numbers she needs by using calculated controls.

Understanding Calculated Controls

For more information on the Expression Builder, see Appendix C, "Using Expressions" on the Microsoft Access 2000 Step by Step CD-ROM.

Specifically designed *calculated controls* add value to forms. Calculated controls can summarize the information available in the tables connected to forms, or they can perform standard mathematical calculations on any numerical content within forms. Access 2000 includes a group of mathematical functions in its Expression Builder. With the *Expression Builder*, a Microsoft Access feature that helps you construct expressions using predefined building blocks, you create and place mathematical functions inside your forms where they perform mathematical calculations.

9

Merging Data

The formula that is used to calculate a value within a control is called the *control source*. The control source can be created with the Expression Builder, or it can be entered as a mathematical formula.

In these exercises, you redesign the Box Sales subform so that it includes a calculated control that totals the number of boxes sold.

Add a calculated control to the Box Sales Subform

In this exercise, you create a text box for the calculated control.

1 In the Database window, verify that Forms on the Objects bar is selected.

2 Select Box Sales Subform, and then click the Design button on the Database window toolbar.

The Box Sales Subform opens in Design view.

Text Box

3 In the toolbox, click the Text Box tool, and then click in the Box Sales Subform just below the Sales Average box. (If necessary, increase the size of the Box Sales Subform by clicking the lower edge of the subform and dragging the sizing handle downward.)

A text box and its label appear on the form; the label consists of the word *Text* followed by a number (for example, *Text21*).

The Text Box tool creates an unbound text box. Unbound means that the contents of the box are not stored in a table. The contents are calculated for display only, not storage.

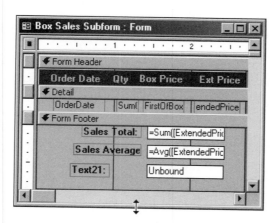

Properties

④ Click in the new text box.

⑤ On the Form Design toolbar, click the Properties button.

The text box property sheet opens.

⑥ In the text box property sheet, click the Data tab, and then click the Control Source property box.

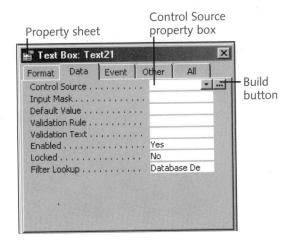

Create a calculated control using expressions

You use the Expression Builder to construct a calculated control that totals the number of bonbon boxes sold. In this exercise, you build an expression for the new text box that calculates the total for the quantities listed in the Quantity column of the Box Sales subform.

Build

*All expres-
sions begin
with the
equal sign.*

① In the property sheet, click the Build button next to the Control Source property box.

The Expression Builder opens.

② In the row of operator buttons below the Expression box, click the equal sign (=) button.

The equal sign appears in the Expression box.

9

Merging Data

3 Double-click the Forms folder in the left list of the Expression Builder.

The two subfolders Loaded Forms and All Forms are displayed under the Forms folder. To build an expression, you first select a folder from the left list.

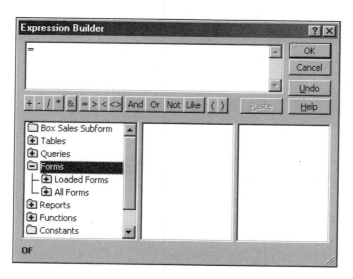

The Expression Builder

At the top of the Expression Builder is the Expression box, where the expression is displayed as you build it. Directly below the Expression box is a row of shortcut operator buttons that you can use in your expression. They are provided by Access 2000 to save you the trouble of typing.

The three boxes below the operator buttons contain expression elements. When you first open the Expression Builder, all three boxes show every choice possible. As you select items in the left and middle boxes, you successively restrict the number of selections available in the box to the right.

To build an expression, you first select a folder from the list on the left. Then you select the constant, operator, or type of function from the center list, which displays the contents of the folder you selected in the left list.

(continued)

continued

The list on the right displays the possible values or functions associated with the item you chose in the center list. Select items from the right list and click the operator buttons to assemble the elements of your expression in the Expression box.

For instance, if you choose the Operators folder on the left, you have several choices of types of expressions to choose from in the center. If you then choose *Arithmetic* in the center, a list of the arithmetic expressions appears in the right list.

Operator buttons   Expression box

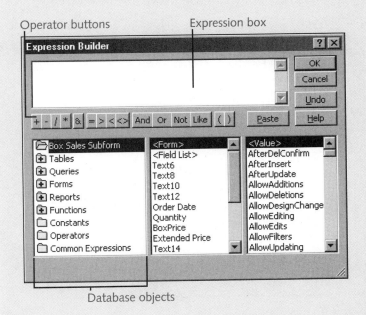

Database objects

The expressions available in the Expression Builder, along with examples of expressions used in calculated controls, calculated fields, query criteria fields, and field validation rules are listed in Appendix C, "Using Expressions."

④ Double-click the Loaded Forms subfolder, and then click the Box Sales Subform subfolder.

All the fields and other objects contained in the Box Sales Subform are displayed in the center list. You select the constant, operator, or type of function from the center list.

⑤ Select <Field List> in the center list.

The name of the field, SumOfQuantity, appears in the right list. You select items from the right list and click the operator buttons to assemble the elements of your expression in the Expression box.

The square brackets identify the word as a field.

⑥ Select SumOfQuantity in the right list, and then click Paste.

[SumOfQuantity] appears after the equal sign in the Expression box.

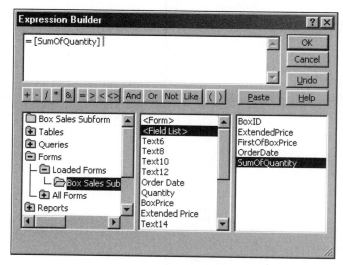

⑦ In the Expression box, type **Sum** between the equal sign and *[SumOfQuantity]*.

You can also type the expression yourself without using the Expression Builder.

⑧ Enclose *[SumOfQuantity]* in parentheses to identify it as the mathematical formula used as the calculated control, and click OK.

The Expression Builder closes, and the expression appears in the Control Source property box.

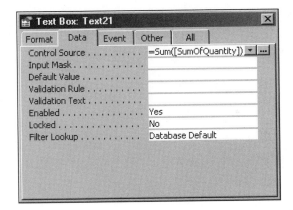

9 Close the property sheet.

The expression appears in the new text box on the Box Sales subform.

Edit control properties

You have added the calculated control Mary needs to the Box Sales subform, but now she wants you to edit the properties of the label next to the text box so that it is consistent with the rest of the form. You return to the property sheets to make these changes.

1 In the Box Sales Subform, click the new label.

The label located to the left of the last text box is selected.

Properties

2 On the Form Design toolbar, click the Properties button.

The property sheet for the new label appears.

3 On the property sheet, click the Format tab.

4 Click the Caption property box, type **Total Quantity Sold:** and press Enter.

5 Close the property sheet.

The caption of the label is reset to Total Quantity Sold:

6 Point to a sizing handle on the left side of the label, and then drag to resize the label so that the new text fits.

Merging Data

7 Close the Box Sales Subform.

The Microsoft Access dialog box appears.

8 Close the Microsoft Access dialog box, clicking Yes to save changes.

Verify the calculated control

You confirm that the calculated control you added to the Box Sales Subform also appears in the Box Sales form.

1 In the Database window, click Forms on the Objects bar to open the forms list.

2 In the forms list, double-click the Box Sales form.

The Box Sales form opens, with the new text box displaying the total of the Quantity column.

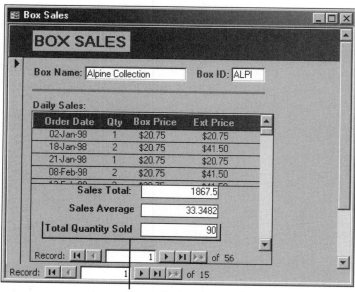

New calculated control and
its label, Total Quantity Sold.

3 Close the form.

Finish the lesson

1 To continue to the next lesson, on the File menu, click Close.

2 If you're finished using Access 2000 for now, on the File menu, click Exit.

Lesson 9 Quick Reference

To	Do this	Button
Create a custom form with the Form Wizard	In the Database window, click Forms on the Objects bar, and then click the New button. Select Form Wizard, and follow the instructions.	
Create a subform with the Form Wizard	Use the Form Wizard to select the fields from the necessary related tables. On the second page of the Form Wizard, select the Form With Subform(s) option, and follow the wizard instructions.	
Insert a calculated control in a form or subform	In Design view, add a text box to the form or subform, and then click the Properties button on the Form Design toolbar. In the property sheet for the text box, click the Data tab, click the Control Source property box, and then click the Build button. Use the Expression Builder to create an expression. Close the Expression Builder and the property sheet.	

PART

3

Review & Practice

You will review and practice how to:

✔ *Use the Simple Query Wizard to create a new query and establish criteria.*

✔ *Sort information and find a range of data in a query.*

✔ *Create a query that uses data from related tables.*

✔ *Summarize the data from the tables within a query.*

✔ *Use the Form Wizard to create a form based on a query.*

✔ *Use the Chart Wizard to create a chart based on a query.*

ESTIMATED TIME 20 min.

Before you move on to Part 4, which covers streamlining data entry and customizing reports and forms, you can practice the skills you learned in Part 3 by working through this Review & Practice section on creating queries and forms as a way to gather information from a database. You review how to use Microsoft Access 2000 wizards for queries, forms, and charts; insert calculated fields; and sort, summarize, and hide data within queries.

Scenario

Mary Culvert, the vice president of marketing, wants to raise prices across the board. Quality should improve, says Rowen Gilbert, vice president of planning, but Sweet Lil's prices must not rise. In response, vice president of operations Hans Orlon insists that a more cost-effective and efficient administration system will help keep costs down, which will in turn help prevent price increases. All departments need your help in creating queries that lead them toward more profitable results.

Step 1:   Create a New Query and Establish Criteria

The marketing department wants to increase prices, so it's been trying to collect information by analyzing the buying patterns of Sweet Lil's customers. The focus is on big spenders. The marketing executives ask you to create a query that identifies bonbon boxes weighing more than 12 ounces and costing more than 20 dollars.

1   Using the Simple Query Wizard, create a new query with the Boxes table.

2   Add the fields for the bonbon box name, size, and price to the query.

3   Save the query as Expensive Boxes.

4   Include an expression that identifies boxes that weigh more than 12 ounces.

5   Include an expression that identifies boxes that also cost more than 20 dollars.

6   Run the query.

7   Close the query, saving the changes.

For more information about	See
Creating a query	Lesson 7
Establishing criteria in a query	Lesson 7
Using an expression in a query	Lesson 7

Step 2:   Sort and Find a Range of Data Within a Query

As in past years, there's an overstock of boxes that cost between 15 and 25 dollars. Sweet Lil's must sell these boxes, so you develop a reusable query that will find all medium-priced boxes (between 15 and 25 dollars) for which there is an inventory of more than 200 boxes.

1   Using the Simple Query Wizard, create a new query with the Boxes table.

2   Add to the query the fields for the names, prices, and quantities of the boxes on hand.

3   Save the query as Medium-priced Boxes.

4   Include an expression that uses comparison operators to find the boxes priced between 15 and 25 dollars.

5   Include an expression that shows only those selections of which there are more than 200 boxes in stock.

6   Sort the query alphabetically by box name.

7   Run the query.

8   Close the query, saving the changes.

For more information about	See
Sorting data in a query	Lesson 7
Adding a calculated field to a query	Lesson 8

Step 3:

You must complete Steps 3, 4, and 5 sequentially.

Create a Query Using Data from Related Tables

The marketing department insists on an analytical approach, targeting customers who order bonbons as gifts during the months just before last year's holiday season—between October 1 and December 1. You assist by creating a simple query that lists the last name of all customers who purchased bonbons as gifts during those two months.

1 Using the Simple Query Wizard, create a new query with the Orders and Customers tables.

2 Add the following fields to the query: the order identification number, the gift status, the order date, the customer identification number, and the customer's last name (from the customers table).

3 Save the query as Holiday Gift Orders 1998.

4 Include an expression that shows only the orders placed between October 1, 1998, and December 1, 1998.

5 Include an expression that shows only the orders placed as gifts.

6 Hide the Gift field.

7 Run the query.

8 Close the query, saving your changes.

For more information about	See
Creating a query with data from related tables	Lesson 7
Hiding a field	Lesson 7

Step 4:

You must complete Steps 3, 4, and 5 sequentially.

Summarize Data in a Query

Now that it has a list of Sweet Lil's gift-giving customers for the fall of last year, the marketing department wants to know the total revenue for those gift orders. You deliver the information by modifying the Holiday Gift Orders 1998 query to show the total value of the orders.

1 Open the Holiday Gift Orders 1998 query in Design view.

2 Add the Order Details and Boxes tables to the query.

3 Add a new field called OrdersTotal that uses the formula [Quantity]*[BoxPrice].

④ Add the Total row to the design grid, and select Sum in the Total cell of the OrdersTotal column.

⑤ Run the query.

⑥ Close the query, and save your changes as Holiday Gift Revenue 1998.

For more information about	See
Summarizing data in a query	Lesson 8
Saving a modified query with a new name	Lesson 8

Step 5:   Create a Form with a Subform Based on a Query

You must complete Steps 3, 4, and 5 sequentially.

Hans Orlon wants the order entry staff to be able to quickly review the customers who ordered gifts last holiday season, along with those who received their gifts. You help him by creating a form that includes a subform based on the Holiday Gift Orders 1998 query.

① Open the Holiday Gift Orders 1998 query in Design view.

② Add to the query the shipping address fields for last name, first name, city, and state or province located in the Orders field list.

③ Close the query, saving your changes.

④ Using the Form Wizard, create a new form based on the Customers table.

⑤ Add the fields for last name, first name, city, and state or province.

⑥ Create a subform based on the Holiday Gift Orders 1998 query.

⑦ Add all the fields from the Holiday Gift Orders 1998 query to the subform, and choose a datasheet, standard layout.

⑧ Name the form Quick Gift Orders Dec-98.

⑨ Close the form.

For more information about	See
Creating a form or subform that presents data from multiple tables independently	Lesson 9

Step 6:   Create a Chart Based on a Query

Rowen Gilbert is gathering data to determine whether the company should consider increasing the number of white chocolate bonbons. He asks you to prepare a chart showing the number of white chocolate bonbon types as compared to other types of chocolate bonbons currently manufactured by Sweet Lil's.

1   Use the Chart Wizard to create a pie chart based on the Chocolate Types query.

2   Save the chart, and name it Chocolate Types.

For more information about	See
Using the Chart Wizard to create a chart	Lesson 8

Finish the Review & Practice

1   To continue to the next lesson, on the File menu, click Close.

2   If you're finished using Access 2000 for now, on the File menu, click Exit.

PART 4

Turning Data into Meaningful Information

10

Presenting a Form More Effectively

ESTIMATED TIME
30 min.

In this lesson you will learn how to:

✔ *Add a headline to a form.*

✔ *Standardize the format of a form.*

✔ *Refine the format and layout of a form.*

✔ *Add a picture to a form.*

✔ *Use AutoFormat to speed custom formatting of your forms.*

A polished and elegant appearance is the hallmark of good design. A database form should not only work well; it should also present a distinctive and uniform appearance that reflects its purpose. Such refinement conveys professionalism, inspiring confidence that similar care has been taken throughout the product. Presentation has a big impact on how a product is perceived.

The best way to develop professional-looking forms is to let Microsoft Access 2000 do as much of the design work as possible, by using the Form Wizard or the AutoForm feature to create a basic form and then applying a unified design scheme. The judicious use of color, type styles, layout, and pictures can give even the most basic form an air of distinction, of being an integral part of a grand design.

In this lesson, you use various Access 2000 tools to refine the look of the Credit Customer form so that it fits into the Sweet Lil's design scheme.

Start Microsoft Access 2000 and reopen the database

● If Access 2000 isn't started yet, start it. Open the Sweet Lil's database. If the Microsoft Access window doesn't fill your screen, maximize the window.

If you need help opening the database, see Lesson 1, "Using Forms."

Enhancing Form Wizard and AutoForm Forms

To review using AutoForm, see Lesson 4. To review using the Form Wizard, see Lesson 9, "Merging Data Onto One Form."

The Microsoft Access 2000 Form Wizard and AutoForm make creating a serviceable, basic form simple. On their own, though, they can't give a form all the refinements you might need. After you've created and tested a new form, you can use built-in Access 2000 design tools to modify the appearance of this basic form so that it reflects the image of your enterprise.

All forms have three basic areas: a header section, a detail section, and a footer section. The detail section is the main body of the form, in which each record is displayed. The header and footer sections are optional display areas above and below the detail section. They present ancillary information and are ideal for corporate logos and other distinctive design elements. The Form Wizard and AutoForm create the detail section and add all the necessary form controls, but the header and footer sections are left empty and closed, visible only in Design view, until you manually create a header or footer.

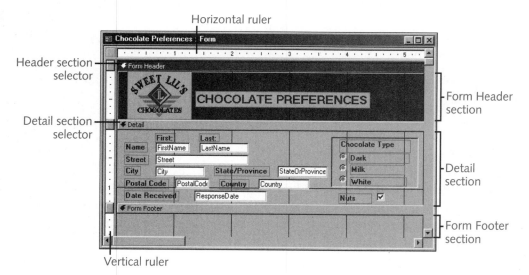

Adding a Headline to a Form Header

Every form appears in a window with an identifying title bar, but placing a headline in the form header and using a uniform color scheme and layout make the form both distinctive and immediately identifiable. In the following exercises, you add a label control to the Sweet Lil's form and modify the format of that label to create a headline that matches the Sweet Lil's design scheme.

Add a label control to a form header

For a demonstration of how to add and modify a headline on a form, in the Multimedia folder on the Microsoft Access 2000 Step by Step CD-ROM, double-click FormHeader.

The Credit Customer form is based on the Credit Customers table. The actual title of the form, displayed on the title bar of the form window—Check Credit—is set separately with the Caption property. In this exercise, you open the form header section and add a label control that matches the actual title.

1. In the Database window, click Forms on the Objects bar to display the forms list.

2. In the forms list, select Credit Customer.

3. On the Database window toolbar, click the Design button.

   The Credit Customer form opens in Design view. The Form Design toolbar replaces the Database toolbar, and the Formatting toolbar appears just below it.

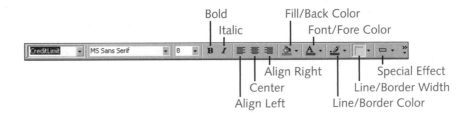

Toolbox

Properties

Label

4. If the toolbox and the property sheet aren't displayed, on the Form Design toolbar, click the Toolbox button and the Properties button.

5. Position the mouse pointer on the detail section selector. When the mouse pointer changes to a double-headed arrow, drag it down to the 1-inch mark on the vertical ruler.

   An inch-high header section appears above the detail section.

6. In the toolbox, click the Label tool, and then move the mouse pointer to the header section.

   The mouse pointer changes to a capital *A*.

7 In the header section, just inside the upper-left corner, drag down and to the right to create a new label covering the left half of the header section.

8 Type **Check Credit** in the label, and then press Enter.

The text appears in the upper-left corner of the new label, in the default font color and weight. The label remains selected.

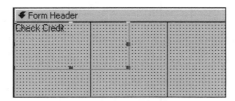

9 On the Formatting toolbar, click the Font Size drop-down arrow, and then select 14.

The text of the new label increases in size to 14 points.

10 Position the mouse pointer on the center sizing handle at the top edge of the label. When the mouse pointer changes to a double-headed arrow, double-click the sizing handle.

The label area shrinks to match the size of the text.

11 Position the mouse pointer at the top edge of the detail section selector. When the mouse pointer changes to a double-headed arrow, drag it up until it's the same distance below the new label as the label is below the header section selector.

The header is now perfectly sized to serve as a headline for the form.

12 Save the form.

Modify the format of a form header

In this exercise, you use the formatting tools to modify the background color of the form header and the foreground color of the headline.

1 Click the header section selector.

The header section darkens to indicate that it's selected.

*Fill/Back
Color*

2 On the Formatting toolbar, click the Fill/Back Color drop-down arrow.

The Fill/Back Color palette opens. It contains 40 colors arranged in five rows of eight boxes.

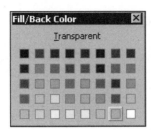

*As you apply
formatting,
note the
changes that
occur on the
Format tab of
the property
sheet.*

3 On the Fill/Back Color palette, click the first color in the second row.

The background of the header becomes chocolate brown, and the Fill/Back Color palette closes.

4 In the header section, click the headline label.

The foreground and background colors of the headline label change to match the header. You want the color scheme of the headline label to be the reverse of the header color scheme.

5 On the Formatting toolbar, click the Fill/Back Color drop-down arrow, and then click the last color in the fourth row.

The background of the headline label becomes light gray, matching the color of the detail section.

Bold

6 On the Formatting toolbar, click the Bold button.

The headline label text becomes bold.

7 On the Formatting toolbar, click the Font/Fore Color drop-down arrow.

The Font/Fore Color palette opens.

*Font/Fore
Color*

8 On the Font/Fore Color palette, click the first color in the second row.

The text of the headline label becomes chocolate brown.

9 Resize the label as necessary.

10 Save and close the form.

Presenting a Form Effectively   10

Maintaining the Consistency of Form Formatting

The Form Wizard and AutoForm create forms with a uniform format, based on the default format properties of the Access 2000 "standard" form. You could use this default format without any changes, and all your forms would have a unified design scheme, but they wouldn't be very distinctive or reflect the image you wish to project.

When you make changes to any form control, you introduce new design elements and risk losing the uniformity of your design. To reduce this risk, Access 2000 has a Format Painter tool that allows you to copy formatting properties from one form control to another, maintaining the consistency of the form.

The Format Painter copies the following formatting properties between controls:

BackColor	DisplayWhen	ForeColor
BackStyle	FontItalic	LabelX
BorderColor	FontName	LabelY
BorderStyle	FontSize	SpecialEffect
BorderWidth	FontWeight	TextAlign

For a demonstration of how to use the Format Painter, in the Multimedia folder on the Microsoft Access 2000 CD-ROM, double-click FormFormatting.

A Sweet Lil's form has one distinctive feature: the labels are colored a bold chocolate brown. The Credit Customer form has five labels. In this exercise, you reformat one label and then apply the new formatting to the other four using the Format Painter.

Apply a standardized format

❶ In the Database window, verify that Forms on the Object bar is selected.

❷ In the forms list, select Credit Customer, and then click the Design button on the Database window toolbar.

The Credit Customer form opens in Design view.

❸ In the detail section, click the CustID label.

Sizing handles appear around the label.

❹ On the Formatting toolbar, click the Bold button.

The label text becomes bold.

Bold

Font/Fore Color

The Color palette also includes the eight most recently selected colors in an extra row at the bottom of the palette.

5 On the Formatting toolbar, click the Font/Fore Color drop-down arrow.
The Font/Fore Color palette opens.

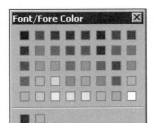

6 On the Font/Fore Color palette, click the first color in the second row.
The text color of the label becomes chocolate brown.

7 On the Form Design toolbar, double-click the Format Painter button.

Because you're going to paste the same format properties several times, you double-click the Format Painter to activate it.

Format Painter

If you want to paste properties only once, click the Format Painter just once to select the current format.

8 Click each of the other four label controls: CreditLimit, Balance, PastDue, and AvailableBalance.

The text of the CreditLimit, Balance, PastDue, and AvailableBalance labels becomes bold chocolate brown.

9 Press the Esc key.
The Format Painter becomes inactive.

Refining the Appearance of a Form

The Credit Customer form now has the proper color scheme, but there are still a few refinements to make before it can be considered a finished product. The alignment of the text box controls and their labels is unbalanced. Also, the automatically generated labels are not sufficiently descriptive and may confuse the user. Finally, the calculated field isn't set apart in any way from the other fields.

In these exercises, you put the finishing touches on the form by adjusting the size and position of the form controls, changing the text of the labels, and adding a colored line to set off the calculated field.

Presenting a Form Effectively 10

Adjust the size and position of form controls

To balance the form, all of the controls should be the same size, and all of the text in the labels and data in the fields should be aligned the same way. In this exercise, you size and position the form controls using the built-in formatting tools.

Snap To Grid aligns form controls to an underlying grid that is visible only in Design view.

1 On the Format menu, be sure that Snap To Grid is selected.

Field size isn't one of the properties that Format Painter can copy.

2 In the detail section of the form, click the CustID text box.

Sizing handles appear around the text box and its label.

3 Point to the center sizing handle on the right edge of the CustID text box. When the pointer changes to a double-headed arrow, drag it to the left until it lines up with the 2-inch mark on the horizontal ruler.

The text box becomes smaller as you drag to the left.

To resize the remaining four text boxes to match the CustID text box, select all five, on the Format menu, point to Size, and select To Narrowest.

4 Resize the remaining four text boxes to match the CustID text box.

5 On the Edit menu, click Select All.

Every control on the form is selected.

6 In the form header, click the Check Credit label while pressing the Shift key.

All but the check credit label remain selected.

Align Left

7 On the Formatting toolbar, click the Align Left button.

The text in both the labels and the text boxes shifts all the way to the left.

8 Point to the center of the selected group of controls. When the pointer changes to a hand, drag the grouped controls toward the center of the form.

All of the selected controls move together. When you see the same amount of space on all four sides of the group, the entire group is centered.

9 Click anywhere on the form outside the selected group to cancel the selection.

10 Save the form.

Change the text of a label

The labels on the Credit Customer form (except AvailableBalance) were generated from the field names. They aren't sufficiently descriptive and may even confuse the user. In this exercise, you change the text of these five labels.

Because the Available Balance text box contains a calculated field, its content is the underlying expression that computes the available balance: =[CreditLimit]–[Balance].

1 In the detail section of the form, click the CustID label.

2 In the CustID label, select *CustID* and type **Customer ID:**

The text of the label changes from *CustID* to *Customer ID:*.

❸ Select the CreditLimit label and change it to **Credit Limit:**

❹ Select the Balance label and change it to **Previous Balance:**

❺ Select the PastDue label and change it to **Past Due:**

❻ Select the AvailableBalance label and change it to **Available Balance:**

❼ Resize labels as necessary, extending them all the same distance to the right to maintain alignment.

❽ Save the form.

Add a colored separator line

The calculated field on the Credit Customer form isn't set apart sufficiently from the other fields. In this exercise, you add a colored line above the Available Balance label and control to separate them visually from the rest of the form controls.

Line

❶ Close the property sheet if it is displayed.

❷ In the toolbox, click the Line tool.

The pointer changes to a diagonal line.

❸ In the detail section of the form, click and drag a line above the Available Balance label and text box.

A flat line is added to the form between the Past Due and Available Balance text boxes. The line is selected.

Line/Border Width

❹ On the Formatting toolbar, click the Line/Border Width drop-down arrow.

The Line/Border Width palette opens. It contains seven width selections, from 0 to 6 pixels.

❺ On the Line/Border Width palette, click 3.

The line width changes to 3 pixels, and the Line/Border Width palette closes.

Line/Border Color

❻ On the Formatting toolbar, click the Line/Border Color drop-down arrow.

The Line/Border Color palette opens.

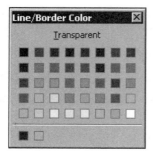

❼ On the Line/Border Color palette, click the first color box in the second row.

The line color changes to chocolate brown, and the Line/Border Color palette closes.

❽ Save the form.

View

❾ On the Form Design toolbar, click the View button to switch to Form view and review your work.

Your remodeled form should look similar to this.

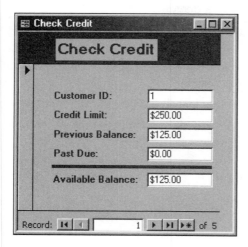

❿ Close the Credit Customer form.

Adding a Picture to a Form

Access 2000 can store or display external to pictures, sounds, media clips, Microsoft Excel charts, and many other objects that can enhance a form. When you store or *embed* an object, it becomes a permanent part of the database, which can significantly increase the size of the database file. When you connect to or *link* an object, it remains external to the database file, minimizing file size, but the object will become disconnected from the database if the linked object is later moved to another location.

The Sweet Lil's logo, used in the form header of the Chocolate Preferences form, is a Microsoft Paint bitmap picture file named Sweetlil.bmp, located in the Access 2000 SBS Practice folder. You can add a logo to another form by embedding this picture file in the other form's header.

Add a picture to a form

In this exercise, you add the Sweetlil.bmp picture to the Presenting Bonbons form.

For a demonstration of how to add and modify a picture on a form, in the Multimedia folder on the Microsoft Access 2000 Step by Step CD-ROM, double-click FormatPicture.

① In the Database window, click Forms on the Objects bar.

② In the forms list, select Presenting Bonbons, and then click the Design button on the Database window toolbar.

The Presenting Bonbons form opens in Design view. The Form Design toolbar replaces the Database toolbar, and the Formatting toolbar appears just below.

③ If the toolbox is not displayed, on the Form Design toolbar, click the Toolbox button.

Toolbox

④ In the toolbox, click the Unbound Object Frame tool.

The mouse pointer changes to a picture.

⑤ In the header section of the form, click just to the right of the Presenting Bonbons headline label.

The Insert Object dialog box appears.

Properties

⑥ In the Insert Object dialog box, select the Create From File option, and then click Browse.

The Browse dialog box appears.

⑦ In the Look in box, click the drop-down arrow and select your hard disk. Double-click the Access 2000 SBS Practice folder.

All of the Sweet Lil's practice files are displayed in the Browse file list.

Unbound Object Frame

⑧ Double-click the filename Sweetlil.bmp.

The Browse dialog box closes, and *C:\Access 2000 SBS Practice\ Sweetlil.bmp* appears in the File box.

⑨ Click OK.

The Sweet Lil's logo appears in the header section to the right of the headline label.

⑩ Point to the Sweet Lil's logo. When the mouse pointer changes to a hand, drag the logo until it's balanced beside the headline label.

View

⓫ Restore the form header to its original size, if necessary, by dragging the bottom edge back up.

⓬ On the Form Design toolbar, click the View button to switch to Form view and review your work.

Your remodeled form should look similar to this.

Modifying a Picture on a Form

If the object is embedded, your changes to the object apply only to that particular form. If the object is linked, your changes apply to all forms linked to that object.

The Sweet Lil's logo is embedded in the Presenting Bonbons form. Whether the object is embedded or linked, it can be modified on the form if a program capable of modifying that object is installed on your computer. Since Microsoft Paint is included with Microsoft Windows, you can change this logo even after it's been added to a form.

Changes to an embedded object are made only to the object on the form—the original file remains as it was. You can, however, copy the modified object embedded in one form and paste it into another form, so you need only make the changes once.

The Sweet Lil's logo is bright blue, rather than the signature chocolate brown. You can change the color of the lettering on the logo by modifying the Sweet Lil's logo picture on the Presenting Bonbons form using Microsoft Paint.

Edit a picture on a form

Objects embedded in a form can be modified using the same tools that created the original object. In this exercise, you use the Microsoft Paint toolbox and color box to change the Sweet Lil's logo embedded in the Presenting Bonbons form.

❶ Click the View button to switch to Design view, and then double-click the Sweet Lil's logo on the Presenting Bonbons form.

A frame with vertical and horizontal scroll bars appears around the logo. The Microsoft Paint toolbox and color box open in the Microsoft Access window.

Microsoft Paint toolbox

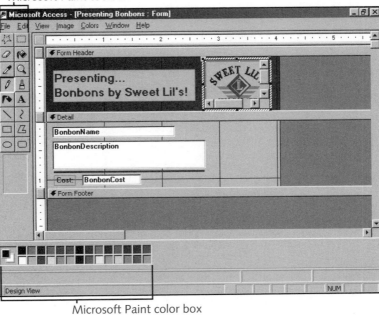

Microsoft Paint color box

② In the Microsoft Paint color box, click the third color box in the first row.

The foreground color in the color box changes to chocolate brown.

③ In the Microsoft Paint toolbox, click the Magnifier tool.

Magnifier

Due to the small size of the Sweet Lil's logo, you'll need to zoom in on it to make the changes you want.

④ On the Presenting Bonbons form, click of the *S* in *Sweet Lil's* on the Sweet Lil's logo.

The view zooms in until the letter *S* fills the frame.

⑤ In the Microsoft Paint toolbox, click the Fill With Color tool.

Fill With Color

If you make a mistake, click Undo on the Edit menu to undo your last change.

The pointer becomes a paint bucket.

⑥ On the Presenting Bonbons form, point with the tip of the pouring paint, and then click the *S* on the Sweet Lil's logo.

The color changes from blue to chocolate brown.

⑦ Scroll up and right until the *W* is centered in the frame, and then click the *W*. Continue scrolling and clicking until all of the blue lettering is chocolate brown.

⑧ When all of the lettering is chocolate brown, click the Presenting Bonbons form anywhere outside the frame.

The Microsoft Paint toolbox and color box close.

Presenting a Form Effectively   10

9   On the Form Design toolbar, click the View button to switch to Form view and review your work.

Your remodeled form should look similar to this.

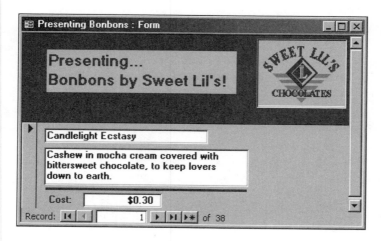

10   Save and close the Presenting Bonbons form.

One Step Further   Using AutoFormat

The Form Wizard and AutoForm use the standard color scheme when creating new forms, but Access 2000 has a number of formats, any of which can be selected while creating a form with the Form Wizard or applied later using AutoFormat.

To avoid reinventing the wheel every time a new form is created, you can add the Sweet Lil's color scheme to the list of formats in the Form Wizard and AutoFormat. In these exercises, you create a custom AutoFormat and apply it to a form.

Create a custom AutoFormat

1   In the Database window, verify that Forms is selected on the Objects bar.

2   In the forms list, select Employees, and then click the Design button on the Database window toolbar.

The Employees form opens in Design view. The Form Design toolbar replaces the Database toolbar, and the Formatting toolbar appears just below it.

AutoFormat

③ On the Form Design toolbar, click the AutoFormat button.

The AutoFormat dialog box appears.

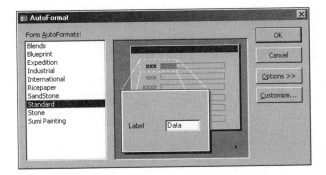

④ In the AutoFormat dialog box, click Customize.

The Customize AutoFormat dialog box appears.

⑤ In the Customize AutoFormat dialog box, select the Create A New AutoFormat Based On The Form 'Employees' option, and click OK.

The New Style Name dialog box appears, with *AutoFormat1* selected.

⑥ In the New Style Name dialog box, type **Sweet Lil's** and then press Enter.

The AutoFormat dialog box reappears, with *Sweet Lil's* added to the Form AutoFormat list.

⑦ Close the AutoFormat dialog box.

⑧ Close the Employees form.

Apply AutoFormat to a form

Once a custom format has been added, it will appear in the Form Wizard format list, from which you can select it when you create a new form. In this exercise, you apply a custom format to an existing form using AutoFormat.

① Open the Order Details form in Design view.

② On the Form Design toolbar, click the AutoFormat button.

The AutoFormat dialog box appears.

③ In the Form AutoFormat list, select Sweet Lil's.

④ Click OK.

The Sweet Lil's color scheme is applied to the Order Details form.

⑤ On the Order Details form, click between the header and detail section selectors, drag down, and then drag back up again to view the header section.

The Sweet Lil's color scheme is also applied to the form header.

⑥ Save and close the Order Details form.

Finish the lesson

① To continue to the next lesson, on the File menu, click Close.

② If you're finished using Access 2000 for now, on the File menu, click Exit.

Lesson 10 Quick Reference

To	Do this	Button
Add a headline to a form header	In Design view, click the Label tool in the toolbox. Drag a label in the header section, and type the desired headline text.	*Aa*
Change the background color of a form section	In Design view, click in the form section. Click the Fill/Back Color drop-down arrow on the Formatting toolbar, and select the desired color.	
Change the text color of a form control	In Design view, select the form control. Click the Font/Fore Color drop-down arrow on the Formatting toolbar, and select the desired color.	A
Change the text formatting of a form control (bold or italic)	In Design view, click the form control, and then click the Bold or Italic button on the Formatting toolbar.	B / *I*
Add a line to a form	In Design view, in the click the Line tool toolbox. Click in the form where you want the line to begin, and then drag.	\\
Change the width of a line	In Design view with the line selected click the Line/Border Width drop-down arrow on the Formatting toolbar, and select the width you want.	
Change the color of a line	In Design view, select the line. Click the Line/Border Color drop-down arrow on the Formatting toolbar, and select the color you want.	

Lesson 10 Quick Reference

To	Do this	Button
Add a picture to a form	In Design view, click the Unbound Object Frame tool in the toolbox. Click in the form where you want the picture. In the Insert Object dialog box, select the picture file you want.	
Modify an embedded picture on a form	In design view, double-click the picture. Use Microsoft Paint drawing tools to make changes. Click the form to return to Access 2000.	
Create a custom AutoFormat	Open a form with the desired format in Design view. Click the AutoFormat button on the Form Design toolbar. Click Customize, select Based On The Form, and click OK. Enter the name of the new AutoFormat style.	
Apply an AutoFormat to a form	With an existing form open in Design view, click the AutoFormat button on the Form Design toolbar. Select the AutoFormat style you want to apply.	

LESSON 11

Presenting an Effective Report

ESTIMATED TIME
25 min.

In this lesson you will learn how to:

✔ *Use the AutoReport Wizard to create reports.*

✔ *Customize headers and footers.*

✔ *Modify and move elements within a report.*

✔ *Add calculations to a report.*

✔ *Conceal duplicate values within a report.*

✔ *Create an "instant" AutoReport and refine it with AutoFormat.*

For more information on basic report production, see Lesson 3, "Using Filters and Reports."

Once you have collected relevant information and organized it into tables, queries, and forms, you need a way to produce easy-to-read reports containing the information. With the report creation functions of Microsoft Access 2000, you can produce professional-quality reports in minutes from information stored within the database.

In this lesson, you help produce a report for all Sweet Lil's departments. Your information sources are the tables and queries in the database. You use the Access 2000 AutoReport Wizard to create the report, customize it, and adjust headers and footers. By the end of the lesson, you will have produced a professional-looking report.

Start Microsoft Access 2000 and reopen the database

● If Access 2000 isn't started yet, start it. Open the Sweet Lil's database. If the Microsoft Access window doesn't fill your screen, maximize the window.

If you need help opening the database, see Lesson 1, "Using Forms."

Summarizing Data by Using a Detail Report

Tables and queries can be printed as datasheets or viewed as forms, or they can be reformatted into easy-to-read reports. Reports—the processed information, rather than the data itself—are often the only database objects that some people see. A *detail report* displays the same information as a table or query, but it presents the data more attractively, listing the selected records along with summary information such as totals and percentages. A *summary report* is a detail report without the details—the summary information is presented without the underlying records.

Detail reports are created from tables or queries and contain the same information as these sources. However, detail reports also include report headers, page headers, and page footers, which help you find information more quickly. The AutoReport Wizard creates "instant" basic reports using a standard columnar layout. The Report Wizard lets you choose from a number of layouts. You can also create a report from scratch or refine a report created with either wizard by opening the report in Report Design view.

This is where the Access 2000 report customizing features come in. The many presentation styles available in the Report Wizard can be quickly customized. For example, you might want to use a more elegant font or a different date format for a report being presented publicly than for a report that's used only privately.

You can create reports in either columnar or tabular format. A columnar report shows all the data in a single column, while a tabular report shows the data as a table.

Single column style   Tabular report style

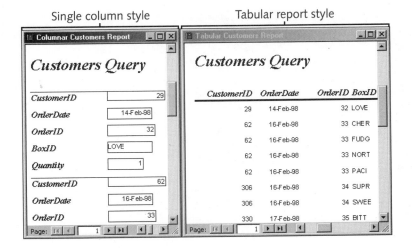

The Sweet Lil's marketing department has developed a new promotion called the CocoaNuts Club, in which members get discounts of up to 30 percent, depending on the amount of chocolate ordered and the number of orders made over the past year. You create a report listing all of the customers and their orders for presentation at the next executive meeting.

Create an AutoReport with the AutoReport Wizard

In this exercise, you create a tabular AutoReport in an easy-to-read format based on the Customers Query that lists customers and the orders they have made.

1 In the Database window, click Reports on the Objects bar.

2 On the Database window toolbar, click the New button.

The New Report dialog box appears.

3 In the New Report dialog box, select AutoReport: Tabular.

4 Click the drop-down arrow in the Choose The Table Or Query Where The Object's Data Comes From box, and select Customers Query from the list.

5 Click OK.

The AutoReport Wizard creates a tabular report named Report1 from the Customers Query. The report opens in Print Preview view with the heading *Customers Query*.

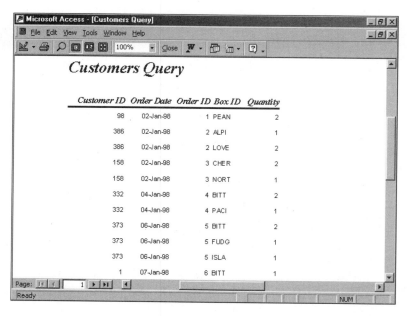

6 On the File menu, click Save As.

The Save As dialog box appears.

7 In the Save Report 'Report1' To box, type **Discount Club Report** then press Enter.

The report is saved as Discount Club Report.

8 Preview the report to be sure it's complete, and then print it.

9 Close the report.

Understanding the Design of the Report

To review previewing and printing reports, see Lesson 3, "Using Filters and Reports."

One of the benefits of the AutoReport Wizard is that it does most of the report design work for you. When you review a report, for example, you'll see that headers and footers are automatically inserted.

AutoReports include:

- A *report header* at the top of the first page that displays the title of the report.

- A *page header* at the top of every page that displays the heading for each column of data.

■ A *page footer* at the bottom of every page that shows the page number, the total number of pages, and the date the report was printed.

■ An optional *report footer* that contains any summary information relevant to your report (such as a grand total), added to the last page of the report.

■ The *detail section*, located between each page header and page footer, displays the records from the table or query.

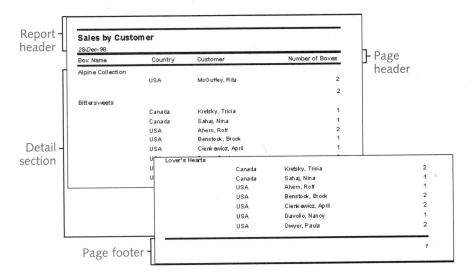

The AutoReport Wizard does more than just add headers and footers. It also creates additional information-rich sections within your report, places data in the appropriate sections, aligns the columns, adds divider lines between sections of the report, and selects fonts and font sizes.

All of these elements can be included in a report that you build from scratch, but using the AutoReport Wizard can save you time and work. Moreover, if you don't like the report design elements preselected by Access 2000, you can customize them.

Presenting Effective Reports

11

Customizing the Design of a Report

After reviewing the first draft of the Discount Club Report created with the AutoReport, the Sweet Lil's marketing department presents you with a list of refinements for you to make. They would like new labels, more information in the footer, and the total number of orders added to the last page as a reference point. They also want you to remove the repetition of the order ID numbers in the Order ID column.

All of these changes are possible with the report customizing features of Design view in Access 2000. In Design view, you're able to see the elements of the report. Each element is distinctively labeled. The detail section shows how the records from the selected table or query will look in the final design.

In these exercises, you change the name of a label, move a text box, and add information to the page footer and the report footer.

Open the report

1. In the Database window, verify that Reports is selected on the Objects bar.

2. In the reports list, select Discount Club Report, and then click the Design button on the Database window toolbar.

   Discount Club Report opens in Design view.

Change a label in the page header

If the field list is displayed, close it.

1. In the page header, click the Quantity label.

   Sizing handles appear around the label.

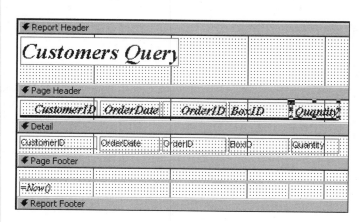

2 Click inside the label to the right of the word *Quantity*.

The background of the label changes, and within the label, the mouse pointer changes to a vertical line.

3 Press the space bar, type **Sold**, and press Enter.

The label name becomes Quantity Sold.

4 If necessary, use the sizing handles to resize the label.

Move a report label

For more information on expressions and how to use them, see Appendix C, "Using Expressions" on the Microsoft Access 2000 Step by Step CD-ROM.

In this exercise, you adjust the position of the label that contains the =Now() expression, which retrieves the current date and time. To make the report a little easier to read, you move the =Now() label from the page footer to the report header.

1 In the page footer, click the =Now() label, and then move the mouse pointer until it changes to a small, black hand.

2 Drag the =Now() label up to the report header section, placing it below the lower-left corner of the Customers Query label in the report header.

The page header section moves downward to make space for the new =Now() label.

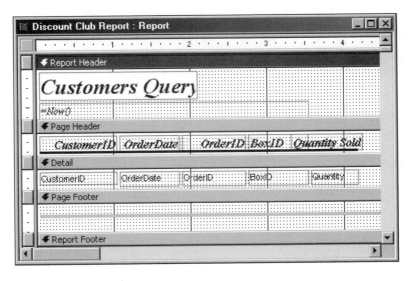

View

3 On the Report Design toolbar, click the View drop-down arrow, and then select Layout Preview.

A sample of the report appears in Layout Preview view, and the report printing date appears in the page header.

Add a label to the page footer

Inserting more information in the page footer will help the marketing department identify the purpose of the report. In this exercise, you add a subtitle, Customer Data for Marketing Meeting, to the page footer.

View

1 On the Print Preview toolbar, click the View button to switch to Design view.

The report reappears in Design view.

Toolbox

2 If the toolbox is not visable, on the Report Design toolbar, click the Toolbox button.

The toolbox appears.

Label

3 In the toolbox, click the Label tool.

4 Click the left side of the page footer, below the gray line.

A placeholder for a label appears in the section.

5 Type **Customer Data for Marketing Meeting** and press Enter.

The text is added to the page footer as a label.

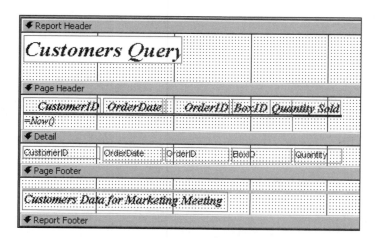

Format the page footer

The format of the text you inserted should match that in the other footer label to the right. In this exercise, you use the Format Painter to reformat the new text, and you then reposition the label.

1 On the right side of the page footer, click the text box, which contains a page numbering expression.

The text box is selected.

Format Painter

2 On the Report Design toolbar, click the Format Painter button, and then click the Customer Data for Marketing Meeting label.

The font of the Customer Data for Marketing Meeting label changes to match the font in the page numbering text box to the right.

Align Left

3 Click the Customer Data for Marketing Meeting label, and on the Formatting toolbar, click the Align Left button.

The text in the Customer Data for Marketing Meeting label is aligned to the left side of the label.

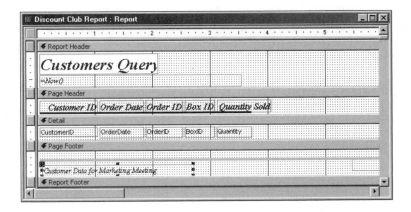

For a demonstration of how to add a calculation to a report, in the Multimedia folder on the Microsoft Access 2000 Step by Step CD-ROM, double-click AddCalculation.

Add a calculation to the report footer

To literally sum up the content of the report, you've been asked to add the total number of orders to the last page. In this exercise, you add a text box to the report footer of the report that has an expression calculating the total quantity of orders.

1 Scroll to the right to view the edge of the report. In the toolbox, click the Text Box tool, and then click below the Report Footer section selector at the 8-inch mark.

A grid area appears in the report footer area to encompass the new text box and its label.

Text Box

2 Double-click the new text box.

The text box property sheet appears.

3 In the property sheet, click the Data tab, and then in the Control Source property box, type **=sum([Quantity])** and press Enter.

For more
information
on expressions
and how to
use them,
see Appendix
C, "Using
Expressions"
on the
Microsoft
Access 2000
Step by Step
CD-ROM.

The expression =Sum([Quantity]) adds the total orders for each group, calculated in their Quantity fields, to calculate the grand total of all orders.

4 In the property sheet, click the Format tab.

5 In the Format property box, click the drop-down arrow, and then select General Number.

General Number becomes the format property for the text box. All numbers will be displayed exactly as entered, with no additional or special formatting (such as decimal alignment for Currency format) being applied.

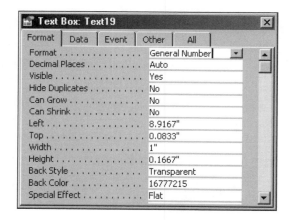

6 Close the property sheet.

7 Double-click the label to the left of the text box.

8 On the label property sheet, click the Format tab, and then click in the Caption property box.

9 In the Caption property box, select the default label text, type **Grand Total** and press Enter.

Grand Total is entered as the Caption property of the label.

10 Close the property sheet.

Grand Total appears as the label for the new =Sum([Quantity]) text box.

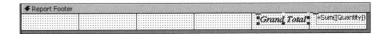

11 Double-click the sizing handles to resize the label so all the label text is visible.

Change a font style

Bold

You can use any of the tools on the Formatting toolbar to modify your reports.

1 Click the new =Sum([Quantity]) text box in the report footer. Be careful to select only the text box, not the text within the box.

2 On the Formatting toolbar, click the Bold button.

The =Sum([Quantity]) expression in the report footer appears in bold.

View

3 On the Report Design toolbar, click the View button.

The report reappears in Print Preview view.

4 Click the Last Record navigation button to view the new page footer and the grand total on the last page of the report.

Last Record

5 Close the report, clicking OK to save changes when you are prompted.

Hiding Duplicated or Unnecessary Information

The report you've created for the CocoaNuts Club membership list includes Sweet Lil's prime customers along with details about their purchasing history. In its current state, it is easy to read and looks professional enough for presentation at the upcoming executive meeting. However, the repeated order ID numbers are used only to order the data and are otherwise unnecessary, so you've been asked to remove them. In this exercise, you hide the unnecessary duplicate values that appear within columns of the report.

Hide duplicate values

1 In the Database window, verify that Reports is selected on the Objects bar.

2 In the reports list, select Discount Club Report and then click the Design button on the Database window toolbar.

Discount Club Report opens in Design view.

3 In the detail section, double-click the OrderID text box.

The text box property sheet appears.

4 In the property sheet, click in the Hide Duplicates property box, click the drop-down arrow, and then select Yes.

5 Close the property sheet.

View

6 On the Report Design toolbar, click the View button to switch to Print Preview view.

Each order ID now appears only once in the report preview.

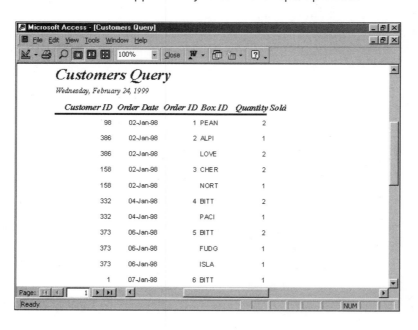

Save and close the report

View

1. On the Print Preview toolbar, click the View button to switch back to Design view.

Save

2. On the Formatting toolbar, click the Save button.

3. Close the report.

<table>
<tr><td>**One Step Further**</td><td></td></tr>
</table>

One Step Further — Creating and Refining a Custom AutoReport

The marketing department is doing a great job of promoting Sweet Lil's. Because of banner ad placement on several culinary Web sites, a German hotel chain wants to order several hundred cases of bonbons in all varieties. The sales representative working on the order needs a report showing all the bonbon varieties listed by chocolate type e-mailed to him immediately.

You can create a new report instantly by selecting a table or query and launching AutoReport without the AutoReport Wizard. This creates a columnar report based on the selected table or query, using the Standard format and layout. Once you have the new report, you can refine it quickly by applying an AutoFormat and hiding duplicate values.

Create an "instant" AutoReport

In this exercise, you create an AutoReport for the sales representative using the Standard style and layout.

1. In the Database window, click Queries on the Objects bar.

2. Double-click Chocolate Types in the queries list.

   The Chocolate Types query opens in Datasheet view.

New Object:
AutoForm

③ On the Query Datasheet toolbar, click the New Object: AutoForm drop-down arrow, and then select AutoReport from the list.

The Chocolate Types query appears as an AutoReport in Print Preview.

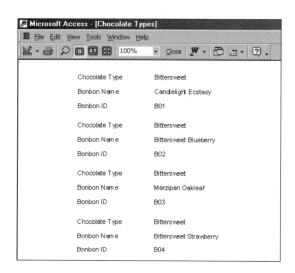

Refine the AutoReport using AutoFormat

You've created the Chocolate Type report for the sales representative to the German hotel chain, but it has no pizzazz, because AutoReport currently uses the Standard style and layout. You apply the Bold style to spice up the look of the report.

View

① On the Print Preview toolbar, click the View button.

The report reappears in Design view.

AutoFormat

② On the Report Design toolbar, click the AutoFormat button.

The AutoFormat dialog box appears.

③ In the Report AutoFormats list, select Bold, and click OK.

The report now appears in Bold style.

All reports that you create here-after with AutoReport will be in Bold style until you again apply AutoFormat using a different style.

④ In the detail section, double-click the ChocolateType text box.

The text box property sheet appears.

⑤ In the property sheet, click the Hide Duplicates property box, click the drop-down arrow, and then select Yes. Close the property sheet.

View

⑥ In the Report Design toolbar, click the View button to switch to Print Preview view.

The report appears using the colorful Bold AutoFormat color and style, which approximates Sweet Lil's chocolate brown.

Chocolate Type	**Bittersweet**
Bonbon Name	Candlelight Ecstasy
Bonbon ID	B01
Bonbon Name	Bittersweet Blueberry
Bonbon ID	B02
Bonbon Name	Marzipan Oakleaf
Bonbon ID	B03
Bonbon Name	Bittersweet Strawberry
Bonbon ID	B04

⑦ Close the report, and accept Chocolate Types as the report name when the Save As dialog box appears.

The Chocolate Types report appears in the Database window reports list.

⑧ Close the Chocolate Types query.

Finish the lesson

❶ To continue to the next lesson, on the File menu, click Close.

❷ If you're finished using Access 2000 for now, on the File menu, click Exit.

Presenting Effective Reports

11

Lesson 11 Quick Reference

To	Do this	Button
Create a quick detail report using the AutoReport Wizard	In the Database window, click Reports on the Objects bar, and then click the New button on the Database window toolbar. Select AutoReport: Tabular or AutoReport: Columnar, and then select the table or query that will provide the data for the report.	
Change a report label	In Design view, click the label. Drag the sizing handles to make the label larger or smaller. Select the text, and use the tools on the Formatting toolbar to change the font or alignment.	
Move a report label	In Design view, click the label, move the mouse pointer until it changes to a hand, and then drag the label to the new location.	
Add a report label	In Design view, click the Label tool in the toolbox, click where you want the label to appear, and then type the text of the label.	Aα
Apply a consistent format to new elements of a report	In Design view, click any existing report element that has the desired format. Click the Format Painter button on the Formatting toolbar, and then click the element you want to reformat.	
Add a calculation to a report	In Design view, click the Text Box tool in the toolbox, and then click the report where you want to add the calculation. In the text box, type an expression that calculates the desired result.	ab|
Hide duplicate values in the detail section of a report	In Design view, click the control for which you want to hide duplicates. Open the property sheet, and set the Hide Duplicates property to Yes.	
Create an "instant" AutoReport using the Standard format	Open the table or query containing the data for the report, click the New Object drop-down arrow, and select AutoReport.	
Apply an AutoFormat	In Design view, click the AutoFormat button on the Report Design toolbar. Select the format you want to apply, and click OK.	

12

Presenting Grouped Data in a Report

In this lesson you will learn how to:

ESTIMATED TIME 30 min.

✔ *Create a grouped report for summarizing data.*

✔ *Customize the group header and footer.*

✔ *Apply a new sort order to a group.*

✔ *Keep related groups together.*

✔ *Customize page numbering.*

✔ *Set properties and add expressions to a group header.*

Information stored in your database is simply rows and columns of text and numbers. Making sense of this raw data can be difficult, because the relevant connections between facts are not readily apparent in datasheet format. A *report* is a formatting tool for presenting information more clearly. You can use a report to summarize and group data to make it more meaningful. For example, when you're reviewing regional sales patterns, a simple datasheet presenting sales data alphabetically by state or province is not much help. A report that includes sales subtotals for each state or province, topped off by a grand total, would convey more information and be more useful.

Using report wizards, you can create *grouped reports*. A *group* is a collection of records that share a common value, such as a geographical region. A grouped report displays records (such as orders) in groups (such as states and provinces), along with introductory and summary information about each group. For example, a grouped report of orders by region presents a list of regions, each of which contains an indented list of orders from that region, with a header and footer for each region. The group header identifies the region, and the group footer summarizes the records in the group. The report footer at the end of the report summarizes the groups. For example, a report of regional orders might present totals for the orders within each region in the respective group footers and the grand total of all orders in the report footer.

The Sweet Lil's marketing department likes the idea of a members-only CocoaNuts Club, which offers its members discounts of up to 30 percent on all purchases. The executive staff wants the criteria for membership into the discount club to be established by region. They would like you to help initiate the club by first offering membership to customers living in areas that had high sales volume in the past. In this lesson, you create a grouped report containing sales totals by region for sales made in the United States and Canada.

Summarizing Data by Grouping Records

A grouped report contains summary information about a specified collection of records. It is a convenient way to organize similar information taken from one or more tables or queries so that the reader can quickly understand the impact of the relationships among the data.

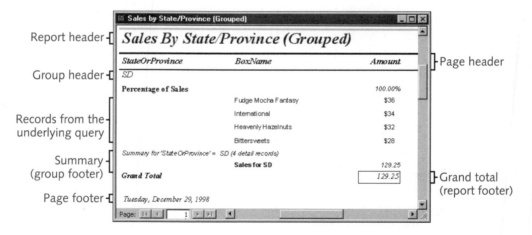

There are several sections in a grouped report, which are then organized into separate areas that contain introductory and summarized information.

- The *report header* and *report footer* include information associated with the report as a whole, such as report titles and grand totals.

- The *page header* and *page footer* include information associated with each page of the report, such as page numbers and print dates.

■ The *group header* and *group footer* include any information pertaining to each group as a whole.

■ The detail sections contain information pertaining to the individual records in the groups within the report.

The Sweet Lil's executive staff foresees instances when they can use this type of report, particularly when planning marketing strategy. The first report they request is an analysis of sales made in both the United States and Canada, grouped by state and province, with subtotals of sales made and a grand total of all sales.

Start Microsoft Access 2000 and reopen the database

● If Access 2000 isn't started yet, start it. Open the Sweet Lil's database. If the Microsoft Access window doesn't fill your screen, maximize the window.

If you need help opening the database, see Lesson 1, "Using Forms."

Summarizing Data with a Grouped Report

With the information you collect in the grouped report on regional sales totals, the marketing department can quickly understand where it has made the most sales and will be able to better determine requirements for membership into the CocoaNuts Club. In these exercises, you use the Access 2000 Groups/Totals Report Wizard to create a report based on the Sales By State Or Province query. The report calculates both a sum total of all sales and what percentage each region's sales are of the sum.

This Report Wizard lets you group records in your report and adds a group header and footer within the report that lets you quickly analyze the information within. (By contrast, the AutoReport Wizard creates "instant" basic reports with no grouping.)

Create a new report using the Report Wizard

In this exercise, you use the Report Wizard to create a report based on the Sales By State Or Province query.

1 In the Database window, click Reports on the Objects bar, and then click the New button on the Database window toolbar.

The New Report dialog box appears.

2 In the New Report dialog box, select Report Wizard.

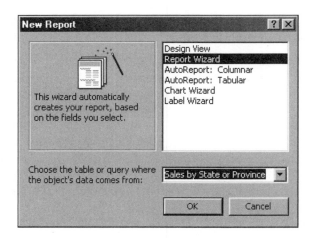

3 In the Choose The Table Or Query Where The Object's Data Comes From box, click the drop-down arrow, and select the Sales By State Or Province query, and then click OK.

The first page of the Report Wizard appears, and Query: Sales By State Or Province appears in the Tables/Query box and the query fields are displayed in the Available Fields list.

4 Double-click StateOrProvince.

The StateOrProvince field appears in the Selected Fields list.

5 Double-click BoxName, and then double-click Amount.

The three fields are displayed in the Selected Fields list.

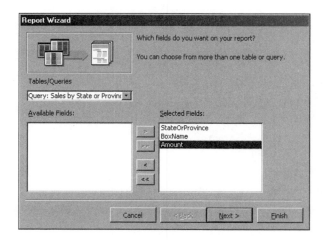

Group and sort the query data using the Report Wizard

In this exercise, you use the Report Wizard to add grouping levels to the report, select a sort order, and define the type of summary the report will present.

1   In the first page of the Report Wizard, click Next.

The second page of the Report Wizard appears, asking whether you want any grouping levels.

2   Double-click the StateOrProvince field in the left box to group the query results by state and province, and then click Next.

The third page of the Report Wizard appears, asking you to select a sort order and summary information.

3   In the first sort box, click the drop-down arrow, and select BoxName.

The Sort button to the right of the box indicates that the boxes of bonbons will appear in alphabetical order by name within the report.

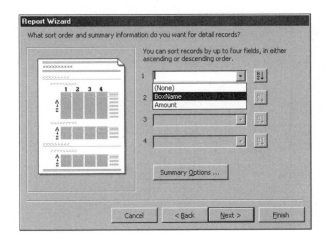

4   Click Summary Options.

The Summary Options dialog box appears, offering summary values to choose from within the Amount field.

5   In the Amount row, select the Sum check box. In the Show area, verify that the Detail And Summary option is selected. Select the Calculate Percent Of Total For Sums check box, and click OK.

The Summary Options dialog box closes, and the third page of the Report Wizard reappears.

Format the report using the Report Wizard

1 In the third page of the Report Wizard, click Next.

The fourth page of the Report Wizard appears, asking how you want to lay out the report.

2 Verify that the Stepped and Portrait options are selected the Adjust The Field Width So All Fields Fit On A Page check box is selected, and then click Next.

The fifth page of the Report Wizard appears, asking you what style you want for your report.

3 Select Corporate, and then click Next.

The final Report Wizard page appears.

4 Type **Sales By State/Province (Grouped)**, verify that the Preview The Report option is selected, and then click Finish.

The Report Wizard closes and your grouped report opens in Print Preview view.

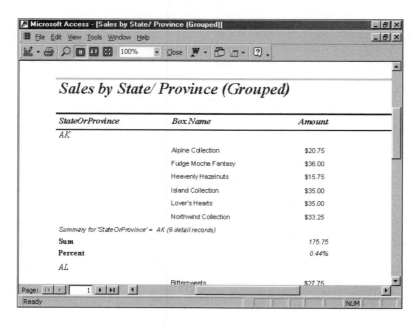

5 Close the grouped report.

Customizing a Group Header and Footer

The Report Wizard automatically adds a number of elements to your report, including the following:

For more information on expressions and how to use them, see Appendix C, "Using Expressions" on the Microsoft Access 2000 Step by Step CD-ROM.

- **Group headers and group footers.** Group headers and footers are elements that are repeated for each separate group. The Sales By State/ Province (Grouped) report is grouped by state and province, so there is a group header and group footer for each state and province. In Design view, the group header and group footer are labeled *StateOrProvince Header* and *StateOrProvince Footer,* because the report is grouped by the StateOrProvince field in the underlying query.

- **Expressions that calculate totals.** Depending on how you set up the report as you move through the pages of the wizard, Access 2000 inserts expressions that fulfill your requests.

  When an expression is placed in the group header or group footer, each calculation includes all the records for one particular group. In the group footer of this report, the Sum text box contains the =Sum([Amount]) expression, which calculates the total amount of sales for each state and province.

  When an expression is in a report footer or report header, calculations are made for all records included in the report. For example, the grand total in the report footer of this report calculates the total sales for all the states and provinces.

- **Expressions that calculate percentages.** The expression =Sum([Amount])/([Amount Grand Total Sum]) is placed in the Percent Of Amount text box, which is inserted to the right of the Percent label in the group footer. It calculates the percentage of the grand total that each state or province group represents.

- **Expressions that display date and page numbers.** The current date, page number, and total number of pages are displayed automatically in the page footer of this report.

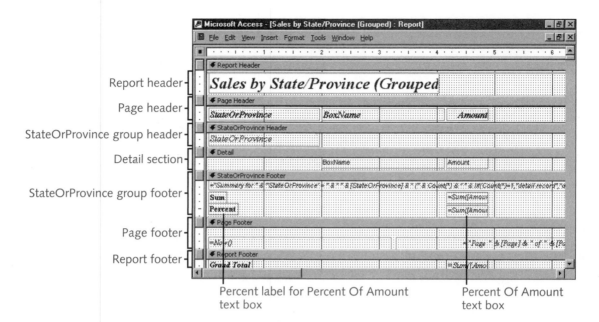

Report header — Page header — StateOrProvince group header — Detail section — StateOrProvince group footer — Page footer — Report footer

Percent label for Percent Of Amount text box

Percent Of Amount text box

It takes time to skim through the group report to determine which states and provinces have the highest percentage of sales. The executive staff asks you to place the percentage of total sales for each state or province next to the name of the state or province in the group header, where it can be seen at a glance. The name of the relevant state or province would also look better in bold text next to the percentage value of its sales total in the group footer.

With the customizing capabilities of Access 2000, it becomes a simple matter to showcase the critical information—the percentage of total sales made in each state or province—by modifying the StateOrProvince group header and footer.

Move a control from the group footer to the group header

In this exercise, you move the percentage expression from its default position in the group footer to a more visible position within the group header.

1 In the Database window, click Reports on the Objects bar, and then select Sales By State/Province (Grouped).

2 Click the Design button on the Database window toolbar.

The Sales By State/Province (Grouped) report opens in Design view.

The Percent label and Percent Of Amount text box must be clicked individually. Don't click and drag to select them both.

3 Hold down the Shift key, click the Percent label, and then the Percent Of Amount text box, which contains = Sum ([Amount])/ ([AmountGrandTotalSum]) which is directly to its right.

4 Drag the label and the text box from the StateOrProvince footer straight up to the StateOrProvince header and deselect by clicking elsewhere.

5 In the label, click slowly twice, change *Percent* to **Percent of Sales:** and press Enter.

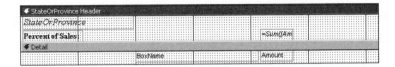

6 If necessary, resize the label by dragging a sizing handle.

View

7 On the Report Design toolbar, click the View button to switch to Print Preview view.

The Sales By State/Province (Grouped) report reappears in Print Preview view.

The sales percentage information is now located more prominently in the StateOrProvince group header.

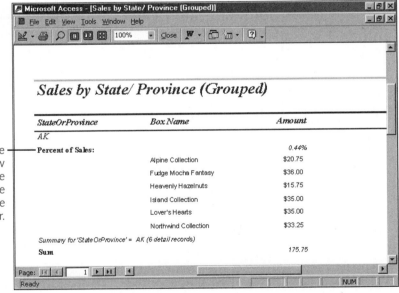

Add a text box to the group footer

In this exercise, you add the name of the relevant state or province next to the value of its sales total. You remove the current label and replace it with a text box containing an expression that automatically inserts the name of the state or province next to the value of its sales total.

View

Text Box

1 On the Print Preview toolbar, click the View button to switch to Design view.

The Sales By State/Province (Grouped) report opens in Design view.

2 In the toolbox, click the Text Box tool.

3 Click near the middle of the StateOrProvince group footer.

A label and text box appear where you clicked in the group footer at the 3 inch mark.

4 Click the new text box.

5 Type **="Sales for " & [StateOrProvince]** and press Enter.

important

All expressions must begin with an equal sign (=). Be sure that a space is included before the closing quotation mark to ensure proper spacing within the inserted text. For more information on expressions and how to use them, see Appendix C, "Using Expressions."

6 Click the Sum label in the group footer, and then press Delete to remove the label.

7 Click the label of the new text box in the group footer, and press Delete.

8 Click the edge of the Sales For text box in the group footer, and then drag the sizing handle to make the text box long enough to accommodate long province names, such as *Saskatchewan*.

9 Position the text box to the left of the Sum text box in the group footer.

The new Sales For text box
is added to the group footer.

10 Click the Sales For text box in the group footer.

Bold

11 On the Formatting toolbar, click the Bold button.

The text within the text box changes to bold.

12 Close the Sales By State/Province (Grouped) report, clicking Yes to save your changes.

Rearranging the Order of a Grouped Report

The executive staff likes the organization and clarity of the elements of the report, but they would like the ordering within each group, which is now simply an alphabetic list, to reflect sales information. The first box in each state or province should be the one that earned the most money; the last box should be the one that earned the least. You can change the sorting or grouping of a report with the Sorting And Grouping dialog box.

Sorting and Grouping		✕
Field/Expression	**Sort Order**	
⟨≣▶ StateOrProvince ▾	Ascending	
BoxName	Ascending	

Group Properties

Group Header	Yes	
Group Footer	Yes	Select a field or type an expression to sort or group on
Group On	Each Value	
Group Interval	1	
Keep Together	No	

Sorting and Grouping

The Sorting And Grouping dialog box is divided into three areas: Field/Expression, Sort Order, and Group Properties.

The Field/Expression column lists fields used for grouping and sorting, or for sorting only. The Grouping icon (identical to the Sorting And Grouping button on the Report Design toolbar), which appears in the bar to the left of the listed fields, indicates that this field is being used for grouping and sorting. The icon does not appear in fields used only for sorting.

The Sort Order column offers two choices for each field or expression selected in the Field/Expression column: ascending (A–Z) or descending (Z–A).

The Group Properties section, covering the bottom half of the Sorting And Grouping dialog box, allows you to define the grouping properties for each selected field in the Field/Expression column. The list changes when a new field is selected.

Grouped Data in a Report

12

In the Group Properties area, the following property options are available:

- **Group Header.** Displays a header for the selected group. Select Yes to have Access 2000 automatically insert the header.

- **Group Footer.** Displays a footer for the selected group. Select Yes to have Access 2000 automatically insert the footer.

- **Group On.** Allows the user to select the value or range of values that will start the new group. To group by each state and province, you would select Each Value.

- **Group Interval.** Allows the users to select an interval or number of characters to group with. The default value is 1; to group by more than one state or province at a time, you would increase this value.

- **Keep Together.** Keeps the group together on one page if possible, or with first the detail of the group. You would select Whole Group to have Access 2000 automatically ensure that the records for each group remain together on the same page whenever possible.

By using the Sorting And Grouping dialog box to reorganize the contents of your report, you can change the priority of your sort from Box Name to Amount (within each state and province). You can also change the sort order from ascending order to descending.

Change sort order using the Sorting And Grouping dialog box

In this exercise, you open the Sorting And Grouping dialog box and change the sorting from ascending order on the Box Name field to descending order on the Amount field.

1. In the Database window, click Reports on the Objects bar.
2. In the reports list, click Sales By State/Province (Grouped), and then click the Design button on the Database window toolbar.

    The Sales By State/Province (Grouped) report opens in Design view.

Sorting And Grouping

3. On the Report Design toolbar, click the Sorting And Grouping button.

    The Sorting And Grouping dialog box appears, displaying your original settings for the Sales By State/Province (Grouped) report.
4. In the Field/Expression column, click the BoxName field, click the drop-down arrow, and then select Amount.

    The Amount field replaces the BoxName field.

View

⑤ In the Sort Order column, click the cell to the right of the Amount field, click the drop-down arrow, and then select Descending.

⑥ Close the Sorting And Grouping dialog box.

⑦ On the Report Design toolbar, click the View drop-down arrow, and then select Layout Preview.

The Sales By State/Province (Grouped) report appears in Layout Preview view, showing the box sales amounts listed in descending order.

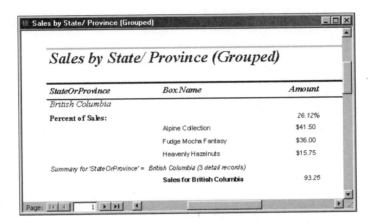

Keeping Related Groups Together

You notice that some of the groups are split across pages. You can use the Keep Together group property to make sure that the groups are not split between two pages unless the group itself is longer than one page. Several short groups of only a few lines each can appear together on one page.

Keep related groups on the same page

In this exercise, you use the Keep Together group property to keep the groups from being split between two pages when they are small enough to fit on a single page.

View

① On the Print Preview toolbar, click the View button to switch to Design view.

The Sales By State/Province (Grouped) report reappears in Design view.

② On the Report Design toolbar, click the Sorting And Grouping button.

The Sorting And Grouping dialog box appears.

③ Click the StateOrProvince field.

Sorting And Grouping

4 Click the Keep Together property box, click the drop-down arrow, and then select Whole Group.

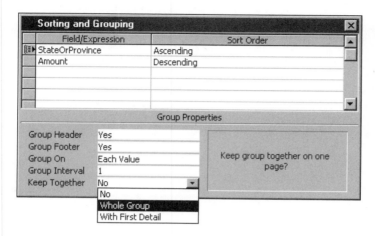

5 Close the Sorting And Grouping dialog box.

View

6 On the Report Design toolbar, click the View button to switch to Print Preview view.

The Sales By State/Province (Grouped) report opens in Print Preview view. No page breaks now interrupt a single group, unless the group itself is longer than a full page.

Customizing Page Numbers

When you created the Sales By State/Province (Grouped) report with the Report Wizard, a page numbering text box was automatically added to your report. This text box contains an expression that inserts a page number and the total number of pages. You can customize the page numbering of the report by using the Page Numbers dialog box.

Customize the report page numbers

In this exercise, you use the Page Numbers dialog box to adjust the page numbering style throughout the Sales By State/Province (Grouped) report and remove the page number from the first page.

View

1 On the Print Preview toolbar, click the View button to switch to Design view.

The Sales By State/Province (Grouped) report reappears in Design view.

   ② In the page footer, click the text box containing the page number expression ="Page " & [Page] & "of " & [Pages], and then press Delete.

   ③ On the Insert menu, click Page Numbers.

      The Page Numbers dialog box appears.

   ④ Under Format, select the Page *N* Of *M* option, and then, under Position, select the Bottom Of Page [Footer] option.

   ⑤ In the Alignment box, select Center.

   ⑥ Clear the Show Number On First Page check box, and click OK.

      The page numbering text box now appears centered in the page footer.

◆ Page Footer				
		=IIf([Page]>1,"Page " & [Page] & " of " & [Pages],"")		
=Now()				

   ⑦ Close the Sales By State/Province (Grouped) report, clicking Yes to save your changes.

One Step Further

Refining the Group Header

Having seen the clarity that grouped reports provide, the Sweet Lil's marketing department now wants a grouped report based on the Customers List query. The report is to be sorted by last name and grouped according to the letters of the alphabet: the first group will include all the last names that begin with *A*, and the last group will include all the last names that begin with *Z*.

You can set group properties and add an expression that will use only the initial letter of the LastName field of each group as a group header.

Set the group properties

To review how to create an AutoReport, see Lesson 11, "Presenting an Effective Report."

In this exercise, you create the Customer List grouped report and add an expression that places the first letter from each group as the group header.

   ❶ Open the Customer List query. On the Query Datasheet toolbar, click the New Object: AutoForm drop-down arrow and then select AutoReport.

   ❷ On the Print Preview toolbar, click the View button to switch to Design view.

      Report1 opens in Design view.

New Object: AutoForm

*Sorting And
Grouping*

3 On the Report Design toolbar, click the Sorting And Grouping button.

The Sorting And Grouping dialog box appears.

4 In the Field/Expression column, click the first empty cell. Click the drop-down arrow, and then select LastName.

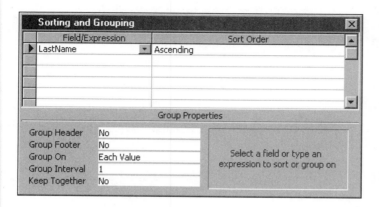

5 In the Sort Order column, verify that the Sort order is Ascending.

6 Under Group Properties, specify the following properties.

Group Header: **Yes**

Group Footer: **No**

Group On: **Prefix Characters**

Group Interval: **1**

Keep Together: **With First Detail**

Choosing Prefix Characters for the Group On property and 1 for the Group Interval property sets the sort order as the first letter of each group's last name. Selecting the With First Detail setting for the Keep Together property allows groups to continue on to another page while ensuring that the first detail record appears on the same page as the group header.

7 Close the Sorting And Grouping dialog box.

Use an expression in the group header

In this exercise, you create a text box in the Last Name group header and add an expression that displays only the initial letter under which the records are grouped.

Text Box

1 In the toolbox, click the Text Box tool, and add a text box and label to the Last Name group header.

A grid area appears in the group header area to encompass the new text box and its label.

Center

2 On the Formatting toolbar, click the Center button to center the text within the new text box.

3 Click the label to the left of the new text box, and then press Delete.

4 Click the new text box, type **=Left([LastName],1)** and press Enter.

The expression =Left([LastName],1) displays the first character of the LastName field, starting from the left.

View

5 On the Report Design toolbar, click the View button to switch to Print Preview view.

The Customer List report reappears in Print Preview view.

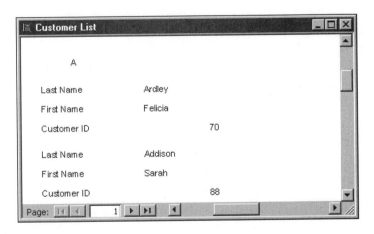

6 Close the report, saving it as Customer List (Grouped).

Finish the lesson

1 To continue to the next lesson, on the File menu, click Close.

2 If you're finished using Access 2000 for now, on the File menu, click Exit.

Lesson 12 Quick Reference

To	Do this	Button
Create a grouped report	In the Database window, click Reports on the Objects bar, and then click the New button on the Database window toolbar. Select Report Wizard, select a table or query, and follow the instructions.	
Move a control in a group	In Design view, click the control, move the mouse pointer until it changes to a hand, and then drag the control to the new location.	
Add a calculated control to a group	In Design view, click the Text Box tool in the toolbox, and then click where you want the control to appear. Click the new text box, and type the expression you want. Click the new label, and press Delete to remove it, or delete the placeholder text and type new text.	ab|
Change the sort order in a group	In Design view, click the Sorting And Grouping button on the Report Design toolbar. In the Field/Expression column, select the field you want to sort by. In the field's Sort Order cell, select Ascending or Descending.	[⣇⣇
Keep related groups together	In Design view, click the Sorting And Grouping button on the Report Design toolbar. Set the Keep Together group property to Whole Group.	
Customize page numbers	In Design view, click the page number control in the page footer, and press Delete. On the Insert menu, click Page Numbers and then select the options you want from the Page Numbers dialog box.	
Set group properties	In Design view, click the Sorting And Grouping button on the Report Design toolbar. In the Field/Expression column, click an empty cell, and then select the field you want. In the Sort Order column, select the sort you want. Under Group Properties, specify the grouping properties you want.	

PART

4

Review & Practice

**ESTIMATED
TIME
20 min.**

You will review and practice how to:

✔ *Add a label to a form.*

✔ *Add a picture to a form.*

✔ *Customize your forms.*

✔ *Use the Report Wizard to create a detail report.*

✔ *Create a grouped report.*

Before you move on to Part 5, which covers Internet-related Access features, you can practice the skills you learned in Part 4 by working through this Review & Practice section. In this section, you will briefly revisit related topics, including how to add labels and pictures to forms, how to give your forms a custom look and feel, and how to use the Report Wizard to create detail and grouped reports.

Scenario

The executive staff of Sweet Lil's marketing department agree that the new design of the forms adds a corporate cachet to the most basic tasks performed at Sweet Lil's, and they have high hopes that improved efficiency will cut costs at all levels. They are also happy with the report samples they've seen and very pleased with the simplicity of their construction. They ask that you conduct a short tutorial on creating and customizing forms and reports for several of the employees in the human resources department.

Step 1:   Add a Label to a Form

The first part of your tutorial covers the basic steps that must be taken in adding a label to a form. The Order Details form is a simple form containing only a few basic elements. You show the Sweet Lil's employees how to add a descriptive title to the Order Details form and to change the color of the form to the Sweet Lil's company colors.

❶ From the Access 2000 SBS Practice folder, open the Sweetlil.mdb database and then open the Order Details form in Design view.

❷ Expand the form Header Section about 1/2 inch. Use the Label tool in the toolbox to create a label in the form header section.

❸ Name the label Order Details.

Use the Font/Fore Color button to change the foreground colors to Sweet Lil's company color. (Hint: Refer to another form for color specifications.)

❹ Use the formatting tools on the Formatting toolbar to change the font size and type style.

For more information about	See
Adding a label to a form	Lesson 10
Using the Font/Fore Color button	Lesson 10

Step 2:   Give Forms a Common Look and Feel

All of the details in the Order Details form should match the details in the other Sweet Lil's forms, including font size, color, and positioning. You decide to include a review of the use of the Format Painter button, a helpful tool for maintaining consistency of design throughout the form.

❶ Create a new form based on Employees table.

❷ Select one table and change font color to chocolate brown.

❸ Use the Format Painter button to apply new formatting to all labels.

For more information about	See
Using the Format Painter button	Lesson 10

Step 3: Add a Picture to a Form

The manager of the human resources department wants to learn how to insert a picture. He tells you that he would like to eventually be able to add photographs of the Sweet Lil's employees to the database. As a demonstration of the illustrative capabilities of Access, you include steps that allow for insertion of graphic images into any form. In this case, you place the Sweet Lil's logo inside the Order Details form.

❶ Use the Image tool in the toolbox to create an image control in the form header of the form.

❷ Insert the Sweet Lil's Logo bitmap file (Sweetlil.bmp) from the Access 2000 SBS Practice folder.

❸ Preview the Employees form in Form view.

For more information about	See
Creating an image control	Lesson 10
Adding a picture to a form	Lesson 10

Step 4: Create a Detail Report

The human resources employees often have to create reports, including reports describing employees, potential employees, benefits packages, contact information, and referral information. The Access report-making capabilities you demonstrate enable them to quickly assemble the information they need in an easy-to-read format.

❶ Use the AutoReport:Tabular Wizard to create a tabular detail report based on the Employees table.

❷ Format the report with the AutoFormat button.

❸ Preview the report.

❹ Use the Sorting And Grouping button in Design view to sort by last name.

❺ Preview the report.

❻ Save the report as Employees (Last Name).

For more information about	See
Creating a detail report	Lesson 11

Step 5:   Create a Grouped Report

The human resources manager wants to create a salary increase and promotion algorithm in the near future. He expresses interest in the grouped report capabilities of Access and asks you to demonstrate how to list employees by department name and hire date—information relevant to his calculations.

❶   Using the Report Wizard, create a new grouped report using all the fields in the Employees table.

❷   Group the report by department name.

❸   Sort by hire date in descending order.

❹   Select the Stepped layout, Landscape orientation, and Corporate style for the report.

❺   Name the report Employees (Grouped).

❻   Edit the report labels in Design view.

❼   Close the report.

For more information about	See
Creating a grouped report	Lesson 12

Finish the Review & Practice

❶   To continue to the next lesson, on the File menu, click Close.

❷   If you're finished using Microsoft Access 2000 for now, on the File menu, click Exit.

PART 5

Taking Your Database to the World

13

Making Connections

In this lesson you will learn how to:

✔ *Add a hyperlink to a database.*

✔ *Publish a database object as a Web page.*

✔ *Create a data access page.*

✔ *Add an Office Web Component to a Web page.*

**ESTIMATED
TIME
40 min.**

One of the most important changes in computing is the growth of the Internet and, more specifically, the World Wide Web (the Web). The *Internet* is a complex system of interconnected networks that spans the globe. The *Web* is the collection of information available on the Internet that's connected by *hyperlinks*, which allow you to jump from one document to another or from place to place within a document. Many organizations share information with their suppliers, customers, and the general public by creating a permanent address on the Internet. Anyone interested in the company or its products can simply browse the company's Web site from anywhere in the world.

Ever-increasing integration of Web features into computer programs now makes it possible to send, store, and receive information in new ways. Microsoft Access 2000 allows database tables, forms, queries, and reports to be connected both locally and globally.

In this lesson, you use Web technology built into Microsoft Office 2000 to connect the Sweet Lil's database to other resources—those within the database itself as well as progressively more "distant" points, out to the global arena of the World Wide Web. You use hyperlinks to connect database objects to one another and to external files, publish a database object as a Web page, and create an interactive data access page.

Start Microsoft Access 2000 and reopen the database

● If Access 2000 isn't started yet, start it. Open the Sweet Lil's database. If the Microsoft Access window doesn't fill your screen, maximize the window.

If you need help opening the database, see Lesson 1, "Using Forms."

Understanding Hyperlinks, Hypertext, and HTML

To review linking to an external data source, see Lesson 6, "Working with External Data."

Connecting a database object such as a form or report to the World Wide Web is very similar to linking to an external data source. The only difference is the addressing scheme that you use to define the location of the data.

Traditional networks use the Universal Naming Convention (UNC) path to identify remote data. The UNC format provides the location of a file on an individual computer (for example, C:\Access 2000 SBS Practice\Sweetlil.mdb) or a local network (for example, \\MSPress\Catapult\Office 2000\Access 2000\Sweetlil.mdb). Its format is *server**share**path**filename*.

Instead of using traditional links, the Web uses hyperlinks. A *hyperlink* is just an address to which programs can "jump" when requested to do so. A hyperlink can lead from your database to data stored in another location. The other end of the hyperlink can be another object in the same database or another Office document, which can be on the same computer, on a networked computer, on an intranet, or on the Internet.

Hyperlinks use the Uniform Resource Locator (URL) path to identify remote data. The URL format provides both the location of the target data on the Internet or an intranet, and the set of rules or *protocol* used to access the data. Its format is *protocol://address/path/filename*. The standard protocol for the Web is the Hypertext Transfer Protocol, or *HTTP*. The address is an identifier, like a phone number, for the Web site. For example, the URL address *http://www.msn.com* is a connection to The Microsoft Network site.

Microsoft Office hyperlinks are able to use either UNC or URL addresses. Access 2000 recognizes a hyperlink as a data type that can be stored in a table or added to a form, making it easy to connect your database to other resources, including the Internet.

Web documents are a combination of plain text and commands, called *tags*, in a markup language called *Hypertext Markup Language* (HTML). The combination of text and HTML tags is called *hypertext*. The tags in a Web document are used to manage the active content (pictures, interactive scripts, media clips, and anything else other than text) and the hyperlinks to other Web documents. The most recent advance in HTML is dynamic HTML or DHTML. Microsoft Office uses DHTML to create Web documents containing much of the same functionality as Office documents.

Web documents are viewed using a *browser* (such as Microsoft Internet Explorer or the Web view in Windows Explorer) and can be created by programs that can save or export files in HTML format. Access 2000 and all of the other programs in the Microsoft Office suite can both read and write HTML, so any database object can be "published" as a Web document on the Internet by making the document available in HTML format on a computer with a permanent Internet connection, called a *server*.

Connecting Through Cyberspace

The technology that makes the World Wide Web possible has also changed the way many organizations operate internally. Corporate networks—individual computers wired together using expensive proprietary networking hardware and software—are now being replaced by intranets, in which the individual computers are interconnected, sometimes through the Internet, using inexpensive "open" (nonproprietary) networking systems.

An *intranet* is an internal communications system that uses the World Wide Web protocol to exchange information from desktop to desktop or across the world. Instead of being physically connected to one another, each computer connects to a communication "web" to pass information back and forth. Because an intranet uses the same protocol as the World Wide Web, it can be completely internal to the company, or it can choose to connect to the Web, allowing communication across the Internet.

Even though intranets were deregulated as a medium for conducting internal business, many organizations have begun allowing outsiders limited access to the organization's database through *firewalls*, which segregate data made available to the public from data available only to organization members.

One of the ways people connect on a traditional network, on a corporate intranet, or to the world at large is through the use of *hyperlinks*.

13

Making Connections

Adding Hyperlinks to Your Database

To review how to set field properties, see Lesson 5, "Keeping Database Information Reliable."

The simplest way to add a hyperlink to an Access 2000 database is to set the data type attribute of a designated field to Hyperlink. Any text typed into such a field is automatically converted to a hyperlink. The true power of hyperlinks is that they can be placed anywhere and link to almost anything. A hyperlink integrated into a form or report can be very effective.

In these exercises, you use hyperlinks to connect the Boxes form to three other resources: a report within the Sweet Lil's database, an external Office document, and an e-mail address.

Connect a form to a report

The Boxes form is already one of the most complex forms in the Sweet Lil's database. It currently displays information about each box of bonbons and its contents, with the option of viewing the daily sales figures for each box. Now the Sweet Lil's marketing department wants to add the ability to look up the information in the Sales By Customer report.

In the past, you would have had to write a "macro" program to display the Sales By Customer report and then create a command button to run that program. Now, however, you can use a hyperlink to connect the form directly to the report. In this exercise, you use a hyperlink to connect the Boxes form directly to the Sales By Customer report.

1 In the Database window, click Forms on the Objects bar.

2 In the forms list, select Boxes, and then click the Design button on the Database window toolbar.

The Boxes form opens in Design view. The Form Design toolbar replaces the Database toolbar, and the Formatting toolbar appears just below it.

3 On the Form Design toolbar, click the Insert Hyperlink button.

The Insert Hyperlink dialog box appears.

4 In the Insert Hyperlink dialog box, click Object In This Database on the Link To bar to display the database objects list.

Insert Hyperlink

Text To Display text box

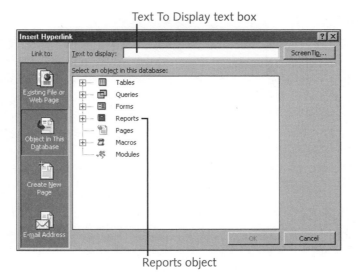

Reports object

❺ In the database objects list, click the plus sign (+) to the left of the Reports icon.

The list expands to display all reports.

❻ In the database objects list, select the Sales By Customer report, and click OK.

Sales By Customer appears in the Text To Display box when you select the report, and the Insert Hyperlink dialog box closes when you click OK. The Boxes form reappears in Design view, with the Sales By Customer hyperlink in the upper-left corner of the detail section of the Boxes form.

❼ Point to the Sales By Customer hyperlink, and when the mouse pointer changes to a hand, drag the hyperlink to a point midway between the BoxName controls and the BoxID controls.

Verify the report hyperlink

View

❶ On the Form Design toolbar, click the View button to switch to Form view.

The Boxes form reappears in Form view. The Form View toolbar replaces the Form Design toolbar, and the Formatting toolbar disappears.

❷ On the Boxes form, click the Sales By Customer hyperlink to test it.

The Sales By Customer report opens. A Web toolbar appears below the Formatting toolbar.

❸ Close the Sales By Customer report.

The Boxes Form reappears.

❹ Close the Boxes form, clicking Yes to save your changes.

13

Making Connections

Connect a form to an Office document

The operations department at Sweet Lil's wants to be able to call up the payroll information for each Sweet Lil's employee from within the Employees form. The payroll information is updated quarterly by an outside accounting firm and delivered to Sweet Lil's as a Microsoft Excel spreadsheet. The operations department has already imported the current payroll spreadsheet into the database, where it can view the employee and payroll data side-by-side, but it would like to view the original Microsoft Excel spreadsheet as well. In this exercise, you use a hyperlink to connect the Employees form in Access 2000 to the original Payroll.xls spreadsheet file in Excel.

❶ In the Database window, verify that Forms is selected on the Objects bar.

❷ In the forms list, select Employees, and then click the Design button on the Database window toolbar.

The Employees form opens in Design view.

Insert Hyperlink

❸ On the Form Design toolbar, click the Insert Hyperlink button.

The Insert Hyperlink dialog box appears.

❹ On the Link To bar, click Existing File Or Web Page.

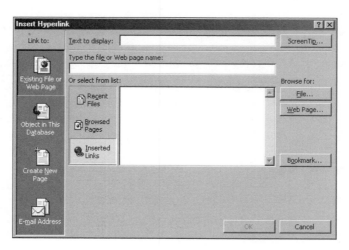

❺ Under Browse For, click File.

The Link To File dialog box appears.

❻ In the Look In drop-down list, select your hard disk.

7 Double-click Access 2000 SBS Practice.

The Sweet Lil's database file and the Payroll spreadsheet file, Payroll.xls, appear in the file list.

8 Select Payroll.xls, and click OK.

The Link To File dialog box closes, and Payroll.xls appears in the Text To Display box and the Type The File Or Web Page Name box.

9 In the Text To Display box, select Payroll.xls and type **Payroll Sheet**

10 Click OK.

The Insert Hyperlink dialog box closes, and the Payroll Sheet hyperlink appears in the upper-left corner of the Details section in the Employees form.

11 Point to the hyperlink. When the mouse pointer changes to a hand, drag the hyperlink to the right until it's on the far side of the Employee ID text box.

Verify the Office spreadsheet hyperlink

View

1 On the Form Design toolbar, click the View button to switch to Form view.

2 On the Employees form, click the Payroll Sheet hyperlink to test it.

Microsoft Excel opens, displaying the Payroll spreadsheet.

3 Quit Microsoft Excel.

4 On the Taskbar, click the Employees button

5 Close the Employees form, clicking Yes to save your changes.

Connect a form to an e-mail address

Sweet Lil's has started a customer help desk to answer questions and resolve issues regarding orders. To ensure that all of these questions and issues are recorded, tracked, and resolved in a timely manner, all communication with the help desk will be conducted through e-mail. In this exercise, you add a hyperlink to send an e-mail message from the Orders form to the Sweet Lil's help desk, with a subject line identifying the message as a request for help about the Orders form.

1 In the Database window, verify that Forms is selected on the Objects bar.

2 In the forms list, select Orders, and then click the Design button on the Database window toolbar.

The Orders form opens in Design view.

*Insert
Hyperlink*

3 On the Form Design toolbar, click the Insert Hyperlink button.

The Insert Hyperlink dialog box appears.

4 On the Link To bar, click E-mail Address to display the E-mail Address box.

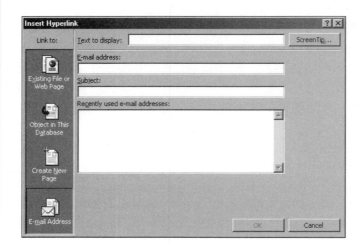

5 In the E-mail Address box, type **helpdesk@sweetlil.com**

As you begin typing, *mailto:* is inserted in front of the address in the E-mail Address box, and the same text appears in the Text To Display box at the top of the dialog box.

6 In the Text To Display box, select mailto:helpdesk@sweetlil.com and type **E-mail Help Desk**

7 In the Subject box, type **Orders Form Help Request** and click OK.

The Insert Hyperlink dialog box closes, and the E-mail Help Desk hyperlink appears in the upper-left corner of the Orders form.

8 Point to the hyperlink. When the mouse pointer changes to a hand, drag the hyperlink to the right and down until it's immediately below the Gift check box.

Verify the e-mail address hyperlink

View

Skip steps 2 and 3 if you do not have Microsoft Outlook installed.

1 On the Form Design toolbar, click the View button to switch to Form view.

2 On the Orders form, click the E-mail Help Desk hyperlink to test it.

Microsoft Outlook opens, displaying a new message with the subject Orders Form Help Request, addressed to helpdesk@sweetlil.com.

3 Close the message.

4 Close the Orders form, clicking Yes to save your changes.

Publishing a Database Object as a Web Page

A document is *published* when it's saved in HTML format and saved or copied to a Web server, where it's available to Web browsers. Because Access 2000 supports the HTML format, any database object (table, form, query, or report) can be imported from and exported to Web documents just as easily as files in any other data format. Exporting an object in HTML format produces usable Web pages, but the object is converted directly into hypertext with minimal formatting and without user input. This "raw" data can be refined using a Web publishing tool like Microsoft FrontPage, but the cleanup process can be long and tedious. To reduce the time and effort of turning a database object into a functional Web document, Access 2000 works in concert with Microsoft Word and Excel to produce a more refined version of your database object and publish it directly to the Web.

For a demonstration of how to publish a database object as a Web page, in the Multimedia folder on the Microsoft Access 2000 Step by Step CD-ROM, double-click WebPage.

You want to add a Web page to the Sweet Lil's Web site to describe each bonbon collection. All of the necessary information is contained in the Boxes table, but it's not in the HTML format required for publication as a Web page, and there's some data in the table that should *not* be published. You publish the Boxes table as a Web page with just the data you want.

In these exercises, you convert the Boxes table to Rich Text Format (RTF). Rich Text Format is a Word format that preserves text formatting by converting formats to instructions that other programs can interpret. You can use Word 2000 to make the necessary changes to the Boxes table and publish it by saving it to a Web folder in HTML format.

View an Access 2000 table as a Web page

1 On the Object bar, select Tables.

2 Select the Boxes table.

3 On the Tools menu, point to Office Links, and then click Publish It With MS Word.

Microsoft Word opens, displaying the Boxes table in Rich Text Format (Boxes.rtf). The data is arrayed neatly in a Word table. Some of the text appears truncated within the text boxes, but the data is still there, out of view.

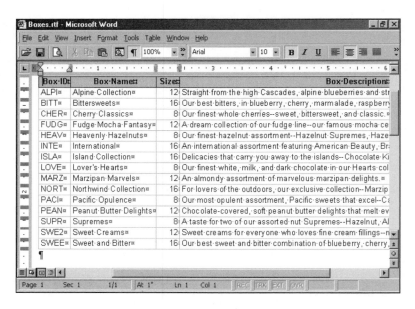

⑤ On the File menu of Microsoft Word, click Web Page Preview.

Your Web browser opens, displaying the Boxes table as a Web page. All of the data is now clearly visible within the text boxes.

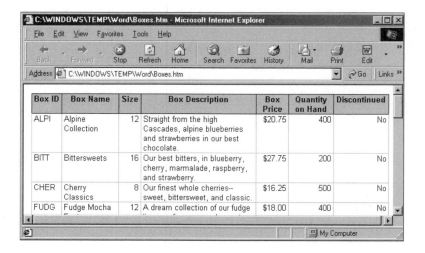

⑥ Close your Web browser.

The Boxes.rtf document reappears as a Rich Text Format table in Word.

Modify an Access 2000 table for Web publication

1 In the Word document, position the mouse pointer at the upper edge of the Box ID column. When the pointer changes to a downward-pointing arrow, click the Box ID column.

The entire column is selected.

Cut

2 On the Standard toolbar in Word, click the Cut button.

The Box ID column is deleted, and all remaining table columns slide to the left.

3 Select the Box Description column. On the Tables menu, select Autofit:Autofit to Window.

4 Select the Discontinued column and delete it. If necessary, scroll to the right to bring the column into view.

Center

5 Select the Size column. On the Formatting toolbar in Word, click the Center button.

The text in the Size column is centered.

6 Select the Box Price and Quantity On Hand columns, and center the text.

Verify formatting changes

1 On the File menu of Microsoft Word, click Web Page Preview.

Your Web browser opens, displaying the Boxes table as a Web page. The Box ID and Discontinued columns have been removed, and the text in the Size, Box Price, and Quantity On Hand columns is centered.

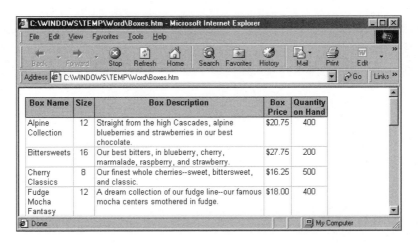

2 Close your Web browser.

The Boxes.rtf document reappears as a Rich Text Format table in Word.

To learn more about Web Folders, see "About Web Folders" in Microsoft Access 2000 Online Help.

Web Folders

If your computer has a network connection to a Web server, you can manage files and folders on that server through the Web Folders shortcut on the Places bar. A Web server connection is required for direct publication to the Web from Microsoft Office. The Web Folders shortcut appears on the Places bar even if you don't have a Web server connection. If you click Web Folders when there is no server connection, you start the Add A Web Folder Wizard.

If your computer is NOT connected to a Web server

If your computer isn't connected to a Web server, you can't use the Web Folders feature. You must save your Web files on your computer or local area network until they can be published to your Web server using a separate Web publishing or Internet file transfer program.

To simulate publishing a Web file, select drive C (instead of Web Folders) on the Places bar, and then double-click Access 2000 SBS Practice (instead of the Web folder you'd otherwise use).

To simulate opening a Web file, click the down arrow in the Save In box, and then select drive C, and then double-click Access 2000 SBS Practice.

Publish an Access 2000 table as a Web page

In Windows NT, the Personal list is displayed in place of the My Documents list.

1 In Microsoft Word, click Save As Web Page on the File menu.

The Save As dialog box appears with the My Documents list displayed.

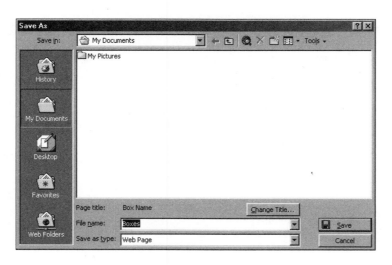

If you're simulating publishing, after selecting the Access 2000 SBS Practice folder, click Save and skip to step 5.

② Click Web Folders on the Places bar.

The Web Folders list replaces the My Documents list.

③ In the Web Folders list, double-click the Web folder to which you want to publish the Boxes table, and then double-click Boxes.htm.

④ In the Web Folders list, select the Web folder to which you want to publish the Boxes table, and then click Save.

A message appears, warning you that Web browsers don't support some features of the document and that the At Least row height setting will be used instead of the Absolute row height setting.

⑤ Click Continue.

The Save As dialog box closes. The Boxes table appears in HTML format (Boxes.htm).

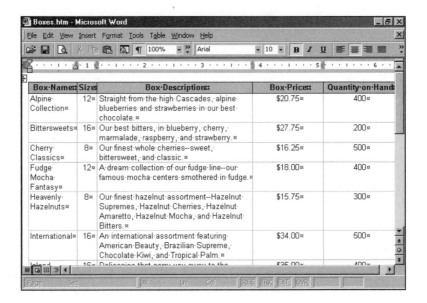

⑥ Quit Microsoft Word.

The Boxes table from the Sweet Lil's database has been published as the Boxes.htm Web page.

Making Connections 13

Understanding Data Access Pages

While it's easy to publish your database to the Web, the result is a "static" Web page. If the information changes, you must either publish an updated version of the entire database by hand or republish the source table or query. To create a "dynamic" or interactive Web page, in which the information published to the Web is updated along with the source, you need a table or query that runs as a program or script within a Web browser. Access 2000 lets you create such tables and queries as data access pages.

A *data access page* is essentially an HTML page with the ability to maintain a live link to a data source. You create the data access page in Access 2000 and interact with the resulting page through Microsoft Internet Explorer 5 or another browser. In addition to putting Access 2000 forms and reports on the Web, data access pages also support VBScript and JavaScript, so you can program in the language of your choice using the familiar Access 2000 design environment.

You can create a data access page from scratch, just as you would a form or report. But it's easier to create one by using the Page Wizard, or by using any existing Web page. You can then modify it using the data access page designer.

The *data access page designer* uses the Internet Explorer 5 browser as a design window, to which it brings all the familiar Access design tools: the toolbox, the field list, the property sheet, and the tool wizards. Working with a data access page is very similar to working in Design view within Access 2000. The controls that you place on data access pages are ActiveX and HTML controls that are similar in form and function to the controls that you place on Access 2000 forms.

Creating a Data Access Page with a Wizard

You can also edit with a Web publishing program like Microsoft FrontPage.

As with forms and reports, the easiest way to get started with data access pages is to use the Page Wizard to create a working data access page. Later you can refine the page using the data access page designer.

important

To view the active content of data access pages, the user must be using Internet Explorer 5 as the Web browser and have Office 2000 or an Office 2000 license installed on the same computer as the browser.

Create a data access page with the Page Wizard

You want to add another Web page to the Sweet Lil's Web site that would allow customers to browse the descriptions, ingredients, and current prices of all available bonbons, updated automatically whenever the underlying data changes. The Bonbons table contains all the necessary information. You create a data access page based on the Bonbons table.

① In the Database window, click Pages on the Objects bar to display the pages list.

② In the pages list, double-click Create Data Access Page By Using Wizard.

The first page of the Page Wizard appears.

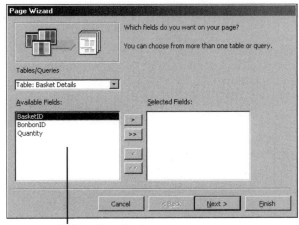

Tables/Queries box

③ In the Table/Queries drop-down list, select Table: Boxes. In the Available Fields list, double-click all of the fields except BonbonID, and then click Next.

To review grouped data and grouping levels, see Lesson 12, "Presenting Grouped Data in a Report."

All the field names in the Available Fields list except BoxesID move to the Selected Fields list. The second Page Wizard page appears, asking whether you want to add any grouping levels.

④ Click Next.

The third Page Wizard page appears, asking what sort order you want for detail records. You will not be sorting records.

Adding grouping levels results in a read-only data access page.

⑤ Click Next.

The last Page Wizard page appears, with Boxes already selected in the What Title Do You Want For Your Page? box.

6 Be sure the Modify The Page's Design option is selected, select the Do You Want To Apply A Theme To Your Page? check box, and then click Finish.

The Page Wizard closes, and the Theme dialog box appears.

7 In the Choose A Theme list, select Romanesque. Be sure the Active Graphics and Background Image check boxes are selected, and click OK.

The Theme dialog box closes, and the Boxes data access page opens in Design view. All the fields from the Boxes table are now available interactively on a Web page.

Close the field list if it appears.

8 Click the title text and type **Sweet Lil's Bonbons**

9 Click the body text and type **Select a bonbon box and see what mouth-watering wonders await you!**

View

10 On the Page Design toolbar, click the View button to switch to Page view.

The Bonbons page displays the revised title and body text, Bonbon Name field, field expander button, and navigation bar.

Box Name field

Title text

Body text

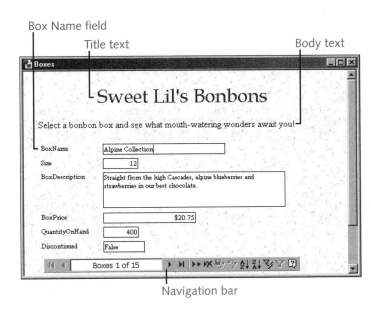

Navigation bar

11 Close the Boxes data access page, name it Boxes, and then click Yes to save your changes.

One Step Further | Adding a Microsoft Office Web Component

New!
2000

Microsoft Office 2000 extends Web page functionality even further with a set of Office Web Components that brings the analytical power of three of the most popular Office online analytical processing (OLAP) tools to your Web page. Using the Office Chart Component, the Office PivotTable Component, and the Office Spreadsheet Component, you can deliver features such as Excel functions and formulas, recalculation, dynamic data analysis, and automatic chart updates through your Web pages.

- The *Office Chart Component* creates interactive graphical displays of the data in your tables and provides automatic updates as the underlying data changes.

- The *Office PivotTable Component* is very similar to PivotTable views in Microsoft Excel, allowing users to browse, sort, filter, group, total, and summarize reports.

- The *Office Spreadsheet Component* allows users to enter text or numbers, create formulas, recalculate, sort, filter, and apply conditional formatting.

important

To view and work with Office Web Components on a Web page, the user of the Web page must be using Internet Explorer 5 as the Web browser and have Office 2000 or a licensed set of stand-alone Office Web Components installed on the same computer as the browser.

One of the simplest yet most effective ways to interpret data is in a chart, which turns otherwise bewildering tabular data into a more meaningful picture. The Office Chart Component allows you to add colorful interactive charts to your Web page.

These exercises require that you complete the exercise in "Publishing a Database Object as a Web Page," earlier in this lesson.

In these exercises, you add a chart to the Boxes Web page, showing the available quantities of all nine types of Sweet Lil's bonbon boxes. In the process, you convert the Boxes page from a static Web page to a data access page.

important

Before you create a chart for the Web, you must ensure that the data on which the chart will be based is available for use. When your chart is based on a Spreadsheet Component or a PivotTable Component, your source data must exist on the same Web page where you want to put your chart.

Create a data access page from an existing Web page

1 In the Database window, click Pages on the Objects bar.

2 In the pages list, double-click Edit Web Page That Already Exists.

The Locate Web Page dialog box appears, with the My Documents list displayed.

3 Select Boxes.htm, and click Open.

The data access page designer opens, displaying the Boxes Web page as a data access page. The Page Design toolbar replaces the Database toolbar, and the Formatting toolbar appears just below it.

When you open an HTML document as a page object, it is converted to DHTML and becomes a data access page.

Toolbox

Add a chart to a data access page

1 If the toolbox isn't already open, on the Page Design toolbar, click the Toolbox button.

The Page Design toolbox contains all the tools that are available in the Form Design toolbox, plus several Web-specific tools.

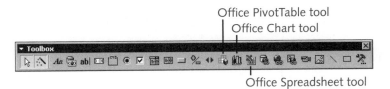

Office PivotTable tool
Office Chart tool

Office Spreadsheet tool

Office Chart

2 On the Boxes data access page, scroll down to the bottom of the page.

3 In the toolbox, click the Office Chart tool. Move the pointer onto the page, and when the mouse pointer changes to a chart, click anywhere beneath the Navigation bar.

The first Chart Wizard page appears, displaying the Clustered Column chart.

4 In the Chart Type list, select Pie, and then click Next.

The second Chart Wizard page appears.

5 In the Available Database Tables list, select Boxes, and then click Next.

The third Chart Wizard page appears.

6 Select the Entries For The Legend Are In Multiple Columns option, and then click Next.

The last Chart Wizard Page appears, with all the boxes inactive.

7 Click Add.

The Preview, Series Name, Values, and Category (X) Axis Labels boxes become active, with Series selected in the Series list and the Series Names box.

Preview box

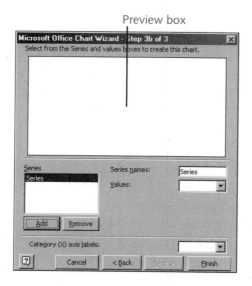

8 In the Values box, select QuantityOnHand.

A multicolored pie chart appears in the Preview box, with nine numbered color boxes aligned vertically to the right of it.

9 In the Category (X) Axis Labels box, select BoxName.

The numbers on the color boxes reappear as the names of the boxes.

10 Click Finish.

The wizard closes, and the pie chart appears on the Boxes data access page.

11 Close the Boxes data access page, clicking Yes to save your changes.

Finish the lesson

● If you're finished using Access 2000 for now, on the File menu, click Exit.

Lesson 13 Quick Reference

To	Do this	Button
Add a hyperlink to a table	In Design view, select the field and change the data type to Hyperlink.	
Add a hyperlink to a form or report	In Design view, click the Insert Hyperlink button on the toolbar. Select the type of hyperlink in the Link To bar, and enter the information needed to make the connection.	
Publish a table or report as a Web page	On the Tools menu, point to Office Links, and then click Database toolbar, and select Publish It With MS Word. Edit the table or report as necessary. On the File menu, click Save As Web Page, and quit Word.	
Create a data access page	In the Database window, click Pages on the Objects bar, double-click Create Data Access Page By Using Wizard, and follow the directions.	

5

Review & Practice

You will review and practice how to:

✔ *Add a hyperlink to your database.*

✔ *Publish a database object as a Web page.*

✔ *Create a data access page.*

ESTIMATED TIME 20 min.

You can practice the skills you learned in Part 5 by working through this Review & Practice section.

Scenario

The Web browser technology integrated into Microsoft Windows, Microsoft Office 2000, and Microsoft Access 2000 allows database tables, forms, queries, and reports to be connected to other resources, both locally and globally. You'll use the Web technology built into Office 2000 to connect the Sweet Lil's database to these other resources, from the desktop to the World Wide Web.

Step 1:

You created the Payroll table in Lesson 6 by importing a Microsoft Excel spreadsheet.

Use a Hyperlink to Connect a Form to a Table

Hans Orlon would like to have a hyperlink to the Payroll table in Access 2000 as well. You insert a hyperlink onto the Employees form connecting it to the Payroll table.

① If Access 2000 isn't started yet, start it.

② Click Forms on the Objects bar. Open the Employees form in Design view.

③ Insert a hyperlink to the Payroll table, using the objects in this database.

④ Name the new hyperlink Payroll Table.

⑤ Position the new hyperlink directly beside the existing Payroll Sheet hyperlink.

For more information about	See
Using a hyperlink to your database	Lesson 13

Step 2:   Publish a Table as a Web Page

Donna Petri wants to add a Web page to the Sweet Lil's Web site describing all of the bonbons now being sold. You publish the Bonbons table to the Web, with appropriate revisions, using Microsoft Word 2000.

1 Select the Bonbons table, and use Office Links to publish it with Microsoft Word.

2 Using Microsoft Word, delete the BonbonID and Picture columns, and center the text in the BonbonCost column.

3 Use Web Page Preview to view the revised table in Microsoft Internet Explorer. Exit the browser.

4 Use Save As Web Page to publish the revised table to the appropriate Web Folders network connection (if available) or to the Access 2000 SBS Practice folder (if a Web Folders network connection is not available). Exit Word.

For more information about	See
Publishing a database object as a Web page	Lesson 13

Step 3:   Create a Data Access Page

Mary Culvert wants to publish the Boxes table as a dynamic, rather than static, Web page. You use the Page Wizard to create a data access page based on the Boxes table.

1 Start the Page Wizard.

2 Select all of the fields from the Boxes table except BoxID and Discontinued.

3 Group the page by BoxName and apply the Romanesque theme.

4 Title the page Sweet Lil's Chocolates with Select a box and see what we have in store for you! as the body text.

For more information about	See
Creating a data access page	Lesson 13

Finish the Review & Practice

● If you're finished using Access 2000 for now, on the File menu, click Exit.

Index

Get a **Free**
*e-mail newsletter, updates,
special offers, links to related books,
and more when you*
register on line!

Register your Microsoft Press® title on our Web site and you'll get a FREE subscription to our e-mail newsletter, *Microsoft Press Book Connections.* You'll find out about newly released and upcoming books and learning tools, online events, software downloads, special offers and coupons for Microsoft Press customers, and information about major Microsoft® product releases. You can also read useful additional information about all the titles we publish, such as detailed book descriptions, tables of contents and indexes, sample chapters, links to related books and book series, author biographies, and reviews by other customers.

Registration is easy. Just visit this Web page and fill in your information:
http://www.microsoft.com/mspress/register

Microsoft®

- -

Proof of Purchase

Use this page as proof of purchase if participating in a promotion or rebate offer on this title. Proof of purchase must be used in conjunction with other proof(s) of payment such as your dated sales receipt—see offer details.

Microsoft® Access 2000 Step by Step
1-57231-976-3

CUSTOMER NAME

Microsoft Press, PO Box 97017, Redmond, WA 98073-9830

Catapult, Inc. & Microsoft Press

Microsoft Access 2000 Step by Step has been created by the professional trainers and writers at Catapult, Inc., to the exacting standards you've come to expect from Microsoft Press. Together, we are pleased to present this self-paced training guide, which you can use individually or as part of a class.

Catapult, Inc., is a software training company with years of experience. Catapult's exclusive Performance-Based Training system is available in Catapult training centers across North America and at customer sites. Based on the principles of adult learning, Performance-Based Training ensures that students leave the classroom with confidence and the ability to apply skills to real-world scenarios. *Microsoft Access 2000 Step by Step* incorporates Catapult's training expertise to ensure that you'll receive the maximum return on your training time. You'll focus on the skills that can increase your productivity the most while working at your own pace and convenience.

Microsoft Press is the book publishing division of Microsoft Corporation. The leading publisher of information about Microsoft products and services, Microsoft Press is dedicated to providing the highest quality computer books and multi-media training and reference tools that make using Microsoft software easier, more enjoyable, and more productive.

The
Access 2000
Step by Step CD-ROM
Microsoft®

The enclosed CD-ROM contains time saving, ready-to-use practice files that complement the lessons in this book. To use the CD, you'll need either the Windows 95, Windows 98, or Windows NT operating system. You will also need to be running Microsoft Access 2000.

Before you begin the Step by Step lessons, read the "Using the Microsoft Access 2000 Step by Step CD-ROM" section of this book. There you'll find detailed information about the contents of the CD and easy instructions telling you how to install the files on your computer's hard disk.

Please take a few moments to read the License Agreement on the previous pages before using the enclosed CD.